MW00608904

THE ECONOMIC DIPLOMACY OF *OSTPOLITIK*
ORIGINS OF NATO's ENERGY DILEMMA

Werner D. Lippert

Berghahn Books
New York • Oxford

First published in 2011 by

Berghahn Books

www.berghahnbooks.com

©2011 Werner D. Lippert

All rights reserved. Except for the quotation of short passages
for the purposes of criticism and review, no part of this book
may be reproduced in any form or by any means, electronic or
mechanical, including photocopying, recording, or any information
storage and retrieval system now known or to be invented,
without written permission of the publisher.

Library of Congress Cataloging-in-Publication Data

Lippert, Werner D., 1972–
The economic diplomacy of Ostpolitik : origins of NATO's energy dilemma /
Werner D. Lippert.
     p. cm.
   Includes bibliographical references and index.
   ISBN 978-1-84545-750-1 (alk. paper)
  1. Germany (West)—Foreign economic relations—Soviet Union. 2. Soviet
Union—Foreign economic relations—Germany (West) 3. Cold War—
Economic aspects. 4. Diplomacy—Economic aspects. I. Title.
   HF1546.15.S63L57 2010
   337.4304709′047—dc22

                                                                  2010023972

British Library Cataloguing in Publication Data

A catalogue record for this book is available from the British Library

Printed in the United States on acid-free paper.

ISBN: 978-1-84545-750-1 Hardback

To my beloved wife, Carola, for her infinite support and encourgement
and my two wonderful children, Katharina and Victoria

 # Contents

 # FIGURES

Figures

Table

◈ ACKNOWLEDGEMENTS

This book is the result of the support from many individuals and institutions. In particular, though, I am indebted to Prof. Thomas A. Schwartz, without whom this book would never have happened. As teacher, mentor, and friend he supported me with his wisdom and encouragement at every stage of composition.

I would also express my gratitude to the faculty of the Vanderbilt History Department as they guided me through the early stages of this project. In particular, Dr. Helmut Smith, Dr. Matthias Schulz, and Dr. Michael Bess have afforded me extensive professional guidance and influenced my thinking significantly. Similarly, my gratitude extends to the faculty of the History Department at Indiana University of Pennsylvania for welcoming me into my new academic home, where I was able to write and grow intellectually.

In addition, the following people have provided me with inspiration and assistance that I cherished and benefited from during my research: Dr. Norbert Frei for guiding me during my research in Germany, Dr. Christian Ostermann and Mircea Munteanu at the Cold War International History Project, and Dr. James Goldgeier, Dr. Hope Harrison, Dr. Oliver Bange, Dr. Gottfried Niedhart, and David Geyer for many inspiring conversations and ideas.

I would also like to mention the archivists who proved invaluable in aiding my research: Heinz Hoffmann and Kurt Braband at the Bundesarchiv Koblenz, Knud Piening at the Politisches Archiv des Auswärtigen Amts, Harry Scholz at the Willy Brandt Archiv, Dr. Ulrich Soenius at the Stiftung Rheinisch-Westfälisches Wirtschaftsarchiv, Dr. Horst Wessel at the Mannesmann Archiv, and Patricia Anderson and Michael Hussey at the National Archives and Records Administration.

Lastly, special thanks go to Vanderbilt University, Indiana University of Pennsylvania, the Deutscher Akademischer Austauschdienst (DAAD), and the Society of Historians for American Foreign Relations, for supporting my research endeavors financially.

 # ABBREVIATIONS

AAPD	Akten zur Auswaertigen Politik der Bundesrepublik Deutschland
BAK	Bundesarchiv Koblenz
BAL-SAMPO	Bundesarchiv Lichterfelde, Stiftung Archiv Massenorganisationen
CPL	Jimmy Carter Presidential Library
CWIHP	Cold War International History Project Virtual Archive
DEB	Depositorium Egon Bahr
FPL	Gerald L. Ford Presidential Library
FRUS	Foreign Relations of the United States
MA	Mannesmann Archiv
NA	National Archives
NSArch	National Security Archives
PAAA	Politisches Archiv des Auswärtigen Amtes
RAC	Remote Archives Capture Project
RWWA	Rhein Westfälisches Wirtschaftsarchiv, Köln
WBA	Willy Brandt Archiv, Bonn

CDU	Christian Democratic Party
FRG	Federal Republic of Germany
GDR	German Democratic Republic
SPD	Social Democratic Party
U.S.	United States

❦ Prelude

On the first day of February 1970, at the Kaiserhof Hotel in Essen, Soviet Trade Minister Nikolai S. Patolichev and West German Economics Minister Karl Schiller signed a triangular trade deal agreement of hitherto unheard-of proportions. Three separate treaties between the Soviet Union, the German steel industry, and a German bank consortium constituted the first natural gas pipeline deal. In the speeches following its signing, Schiller described this deal as a significant milestone in Soviet-German economic relations that should give rise to the resumption of a lively East-West trade relationship—a trade relationship, he pointed out, that went back to the first shipment of German-manufactured steel pipes delivered to Russia in 1867. Yet the resounding significance of this agreement far exceeded the mere resumption of a traditional trade relationship between two long-time trading partners. A significant deal in its own right, its ties to Willy Brandt's *Ostpolitik* propelled it to a turning point in East-West relations for the remainder of the Cold War and beyond.

For the Soviet Union, this agreement constituted a quantum leap forward in terms of technological advancement and a crucial component in Brezhnev's plan to reinvigorate a sluggish Soviet economy. Lackluster attempts at East-West trade with the French and Italians during the past decade had run up against a negative trade balance and the inability to effectively cooperate with Western companies. This gas pipeline deal represented a showcase project that seemingly solved both problems. For one, it featured a low-interest long-term Western credit to create an energy industrial infrastructure within the Soviet Union that allowed for repayment in kind rather than in scarce hard currency. For another, it would allow the influx of high-quality steel pipes and Western know-how to develop previously inaccessible natural gas resources. Unlike President Kennedy's U.S. grain deals in 1963, which had to be paid back with hard currency, the gas pipeline deal offered the Soviets an inexpensive way to access and distribute a highly marketable commodity: natural gas. For the Soviets, lifting their moratorium on West German–Soviet trade in the aftermath of the 1962 pipeline embargo was well worth it: West German industrialists and politicians bent over backward to ensure very generous conditions for the Soviet side in order to facilitate a swift resumption of East-West trade.

For the West German government under the leadership of Willy Brandt, this trade deal represented more than the resumption of their traditional *Osthandel*: it meant another chance for *Ostpolitik*.[1] Following a low in bilateral relations owed to the perception of West German agency in the Czechoslovakian uprising of 1968, then Foreign Minister Willy Brandt utilized economic incentives to reestablish a high-level dialogue between West Germany and the Soviet Union. As it had already done in 1925 and 1939, East-West trade would satisfy the Soviet desire for material tokens of goodwill and thus open the door for the political cooperation. In short, *Osthandel* would open Soviet doors to a new *Ostpolitik*.

Such a deal, along with its successors in 1972 and 1975, raises significant questions of economic diplomacy and alliance cohesion beyond possible economic gains. In a sense, advances in East-West trade mirror the heavily debated questions over the political rapprochement of the 1970s. How far should allies be allowed to pursue their national interests, even if they run counter to alliance cohesion? What long-range consequences do such policies have? Did strong ties with the East undermine loyalty within NATO, or did they hasten the demise of the Soviet Union?

In order to examine these questions, there is no better case than West Germany, as the formerly faithful ally with the greatest agency in European détente of the 1970s, and its relationship with the United States during the *Ostpolitik* and *Osthandel* of the 1970s. Within this field, much attention is given to the two statesmen that shaped their countries' respective détente policies like no other: Richard Nixon and Willy Brandt. The intense controversy that surrounds Richard Nixon's presidency and the passionate feelings evoked by Willy Brandt's *Ostpolitik*—particularly strong in the former East Germany—make it especially challenging to write an objective and interpretative analysis of the policies in question. However, these difficulties do not lessen the importance of the task. Indeed, such an analysis would be especially timely, given that recently declassified documents have allowed a more comprehensive picture of the nature of the relations between the East and West.

Before these documents materialized, the "new" *Ostpolitik* of Chancellor Willy Brandt was widely categorized as a German, and perhaps more effective, version of American détente. Even in Brandt's most recent biography, Gregor Schöllgen speaks of *Ostpolitik* and American détente as being "virtually identical," while Raymond Garthoff's classic work on this time period, *Détente and Confrontation*, sees Nixon as scrambling to catch up to Brandt's policies.[2] M. E. Sarotte contends that the Nixon-Kissinger team was "thinking along lines similar to those of Egon Bahr and Willy Brandt," and Peter Bender parallels *Ostpolitik* and détente to such an extent that he suggests Kissinger was in fact jealous of Brandt's successes in formalizing a détente with the East.[3] Even Jeremi Suri's recent book does not shake this assertion, as he sees both Brandt's and Nixon's diplomacy as "steps toward a conservative world order after the global disruption of 1968 … in the puzzle of détente."[4] Most recently, differences between Nixon and Brandt have been explored in the political realm, allowing historians Carole Fink and Bernd Schaefer to conclude that "Ostpolitik paralleled but also diverged from the course of U.S.-Soviet détente."[5]

In short, analyses comparing Nixon and Brandt are numerous in approaches and conclusions. The recent releases of Nixon's Oval Office tape recordings and Kissinger's telephone transcripts have added a new dimension of name-calling to the already complex plethora of analyses on the U.S.–West German relationship. Whether the relationship between Nixon and Brandt was forged by personal dislike, jealousy, or ideological divides, the transatlantic cooperation during the formative years of détente, 1970–1972, exhibits many achievements. The German-American summit of 1970, the coupling of the Eastern Treaties with a Four Power Agreement on Berlin, Brandt's political endorsement of Nixon, and the ever present back-channel diplomacy all speak to the intense cooperation that existed between the Nixon White House and the Brandt government. The opposing viewpoint concentrates on personal dislikes, West Germany's unilateral strengthening of its relations with the East, and superpower détente. As a result, it seems quite reasonable to find the overall picture of the 1970s-era transatlantic alliance blurred by many inconsistencies.

Even more byzantine is the prospect of making a possible value judgment on the efficacy of respective détente policies in ending the Cold War. With the fall of the Soviet Union a relatively recent phenomenon, ideology seems to inspire a multitude of teleological assessments of Cold War events. Liberal interpretations hold *Ostpolitik* to be decisive in infusing Eastern European and Soviet societies with Western ideas, forcing the East to commit to human rights, and affording democratic opposition groups the necessary standing and leverage to bring down the communist regimes.[6] On the other hand, conservative interpretations see détente policies as prolonging the lifespan of communist regimes through Western economic aid. From this point of view, it was Reagan's hard-line approach that forced the Soviets to compete with the U.S. in a military arms race that ruined the Soviet economy, ultimately leading to the fall of the Soviet Union.[7] The question of agency in ending the Cold War, though still unclear, is essential to understanding and evaluating the decades of the 1970s and 1980s.

An example of the difficulty of agency is clearly evident in historian John Gaddis's recent work on the Cold War. Implicit here is an evaluation of the two irreconcilable interpretations on the efficacy of détente and their role in bringing down the Soviet regime. On one hand, Gaddis sees détente as a "legal and moral trap" set for the Soviet Union, upon which the anti-communist resistance could base their claims. On the other hand, he labels Reagan as "one of the sharpest grand strategists ever" because he recognized that "only killing détente could end the Cold War."[8]

This book seeks to resolve some of the existing conflicting interpretations by introducing a perspective that has received little attention in the historiography so far: economic diplomacy. Just as the signing of the first gas pipeline deal received scant attention in 1970, so too have the economic interests on both sides of the Iron Curtain barely figured into the discourse on Cold War history. Angela Stent has done pioneering work in regard to West German–Soviet relations, and a few studies have been conducted regarding U.S. economic policy during the Cold War.[9] Yet none have explored *Ostpolitik* and *Osthandel* within the context of U.S. and Soviet economic policy. The one coming closest, Angela Stent, did not have the benefit of recent insights into Soviet interests, which place their need for Western technology at a premium. Consequently, her view of economic policy is that of a catalyst—"a fat communist may be much easier to deal with than a thin one"—but misses the agency economic needs created within the Soviet Union.[10] Equally important are the recent insights into U.S. economic policy and the mercantilist view Nixon developed on East-West trade after 1971. Here again, economic interest *created* policy, triggering an interplay between politics and economics that far exceeds the traditional interpretation of economics being subservient to politics. If we accept the premise that, in one way or another, economic factors played a crucial role in ending the Cold War, then the impact of economic diplomacy deserves to be analyzed more thoroughly.

This, then—the complex interweaving of political and economic strategies in the pursuit of détente on both sides of the Iron Curtain, and the lasting dilemma that the Western alliance inherited in the energy sector as a result of this—is the overarching theme explored in this book. Driven by my personal conviction that policy is shaped more by perception than reality, this will be largely a qualitative rather than a quantitative analysis. In other words, my aim was not to write an economic history of détente in which I add up the individual trade deals in monetary terms and conclude with a net gain/loss figure for each participant. Apart from the fact that such a feat would be a near impossibility for political concessions such as the dithering status of the city of West Berlin, for example, it is mostly the perception of economic opportunity and gain that intersects with the creation of public policy, not the net monetary result, which is only apparent in hindsight.

Exploring the interface between business interests and policy raises another issue altogether. When exploring the agency of West German business in the context of international diplomacy, the case can be made that business transactions in free market economies are concluded on the basis of monetary gains, not political agendas: business deals are apolitical, so to say. Adding the diverse and often contradictory agendas of various elements of "German industry," it is impossible to speak of a monolithic agenda of German industry.[11] Consequently, it is not the agenda of individual businesses or industrialists that this book focuses on but the economic environment in general: the public's perception (and manipulation thereof) of a country's economic potential, the creation of a conducive framework for trade (or its prevention), financial enticements and loan guarantees, and personal pressure on individual industrialists.

In short, all the factors that allow politics to guide and direct economic development constitute economic diplomacy. When analyzing economic diplomacy in a planned economy such as the Soviet Union, it becomes even more apparent how political Western business dealings really were. By placing economic diplomacy and trade interests alongside politics, then, this book provides new and unique insights into the following topics.

- *Osthandel* and *Ostpolitik* went hand in hand. Brandt, seeking to carve out a more flexible diplomatic position between the two blocs, utilized the West German industrial potential and know-how to spark Soviet interest in Western technology and markets. Establishing East-West trade deals offered an opportunity to engage the Soviet leadership and introduce new political initiatives. Thus, in a way, the gas pipeline deal constituted the first significant milestone for *Ostpolitik*.
- Seen through the lens of economic diplomacy, Brandt's *Ostpolitik* differs significantly from Nixon's concept of détente. Far more suspicious of the long-term goals of the communist bloc, the White House conceptualized détente as a process of give and take from which the West had to benefit. Brandt, on the other hand, freely offered tokens of goodwill in the hopes that they would jump-start East-West cooperation

and eventually lead to a European security system and a unified Germany.[12] Brandt initiated and actively fostered a political process and an economic diplomacy that stood to benefit the Soviets and far exceeded the scope and intensity with which the White House was comfortable.

• The topic of economic diplomacy also nicely highlights the question of ideology within Nixon-Kissinger foreign policy and discriminates between Nixon's and Kissinger's respective foreign policy visions. Because the Nixon presidency remains such a controversial topic, few scholars have seen fit to give Nixon any credit for his administration's achievements. This is mostly due to the fact that Kissinger portrays himself as the key foreign policy maker in his extensive, albeit somewhat misleading, memoirs. As a result Nixon's foreign policy profile is rather disjointed, and it is my contention that Nixon's ideology and "gut feelings" proved remarkably accurate in pinpointing Soviet economic interests.

• As neither Nixon nor Brandt—and by extension neither the U.S. nor the Western NATO allies—were willing to modify their mutually exclusive détente designs, the differing visions of détente created contradictory structural dynamics within the alliance. Long-term Western European trade and energy dependencies with the Soviet Union precipitated a moderating and reconciliatory tone in international diplomacy, whereas the United States, for whom such ties were of little political consequence, remained reserved and more prone to escalate a conflict with the Soviet Union.

• With regard to agency in ending the Cold War, it would be presumptuous to offer a definitive answer based on a study of economic diplomacy alone. Other factors, such as human rights activism or the intricacies of the military buildup and arms negotiations, to name only a couple, can only be touched on briefly. However, this study demonstrates that the Soviet Union reaped significant economic advantages and political leverage in West Germany from *Osthandel* and the inter-alliance controversy over détente. On the other hand, the very trade that bolstered the Brezhnev regime shifted Eastern-bloc thinking from ideological cohesion to a competition for Western markets and products. Trade, like few other areas in international relations, strikingly demonstrates the difficulty of alliance cohesion when divergent interests are at stake. This study will argue for a more differentiated interpretation in which both the efficacy of *Ostpolitik* and the economic effects of the arms race of the 1980s receive their due.

• Lastly, this study illustrates the long-term effects of Nixon's and Brandt's détente policies on the Western alliance. It was their policies that laid the groundwork for NATO's energy dilemma: the inability to formulate effective and unified Western policies vis-à-vis the Soviet Union during the late 1970s and early 1980s as the alliance suffered from a clash of economic interests that pitted Western European NATO partners against the U.S. This dilemma resurfaced soon after the end of the Cold War with Putin's nationalization of the Russian energy sector, leading some authors to pronounce a new Cold War, fought with economic weaponry.[13] However imminent such concerns may be, NATO's energy dilemma is real, and this book traces its origins squarely to the policies of Nixon and Brandt.

In structuring my analysis, I have divided the materials into five chapters. I explore the underpinnings of *Ostpolitik* and U.S. détente in chapter 1 and parallel the alliance partners' interest in détente with their respective trade policy. Just as *Ostpolitik* developed under a different paradigm from U.S. détente, so East-West trade during the 1960s in the U.S. was treated as a political tool, while European allies looked more to the economic gains of such trade. I outline the inability of successive U.S. administrations to develop a coherent and consistent trade policy toward the Eastern bloc and the frustrations this constant wavering inflicted on alliance cohesion. The busted German-Soviet pipeline deal of 1962/63 is discussed here as the obvious example. Again, paralleling European frustrations with U.S. leadership over security, diplomacy, and trade alike, chapter one illustrates the onset of a reorientation in Western European diplomacy and trade practices during the late 1960s and, with it, the emerging clashes over economic diplomacy within NATO.

Chapter 2 covers the implementation of respective détente policies, exemplified by President Richard Nixon and Chancellor Willy Brandt. It discusses Nixon's attempts to have his Western European allies assume more geopolitical responsibilities and Brandt's usage of East-West trade, *Osthandel*, to reach out to the Soviets during his initial hundred days in office. Key aspects include the first gas pipeline deal and the inter-German summit meeting at Erfurt.

Chapter 3 analyzes economic relations, their structure, and necessity as it relates to the Western as well as the Eastern Alliance. The particular focus of this chapter rests not so much on the already thoroughly debated Eastern Treaties as on the intensification of trade and the accompanying geopolitical shifts. This chapter also emphasizes the contrasting economic diplomacy between the Brandt and Nixon administrations and delineates the successes attained by *Ostpolitik* and *Osthandel* while U.S. policy lagged behind.

Chapter 4 addresses the Soviet shift toward superpower détente and its ultimate failure. Internal factors, a lingering fear of Germany, and the attractive alternative of a superpower détente brought the differences between *Ostpolitik* and Soviet or American détente to the forefront. The Yom Kippur War is portrayed as a turning point that finally undermined U.S. leadership in Western détente efforts, leaving a permanent rift in the Western alliance.

Chapter 5 takes this rift in NATO and illustrates the results of these clashing economic diplomatic initiatives within the Western alliance. Analyzing the Ford, Carter, and Reagan presidencies and their triangular relationship with Schmidt and Brezhnev, respectively, illustrates the fundamental shift in strategic interests that the détente policies of the early 1970s had precipitated.

The conclusion reconsiders the argument and draws inferences about current-day events and NATO's difficulties in dealing with resurgent Russian energy diplomacy.

1

Détente, Trade, and the Alliance

Pro-American *Ostpolitik*: Nothing But East-West Trade

The ambiguous and malleable term "détente" would not be coined for another few years, yet the initial sentiment could be attributed to U.S. Secretary of State John Foster Dulles when he suggested that West German Chancellor Konrad Adenauer be more amenable to the East.[1] The previously inconceivable concept of a rapprochement with the East had become a political possibility. America, gripped by fear of global nuclear war, sought to deescalate potential conflicts wherever possible. Even when Vice President Richard Nixon and Soviet General Secretary Nikita Khrushchev argued over the durability of the home appliances produced in their respective countries, it seemed that a transposition of the struggle between two superpowers from the military realm to an economic and cultural one had begun.

From a Western European perspective, the launch of Sputnik and the then-apparent Soviet ability to deliver nuclear warheads to the continental U.S. undermined the projection of American strength and influence. As America's nuclear umbrella became brittle, the Berlin Wall was being built, and the U.S. sought more and more financial contributions from its European allies, Western European politics began to shift eastward. This reorientation, rooted in the perceived geopolitical shift between the superpowers, resulted in Western European policies of détente and increased East-West trade. With these two elements mutually reinforcing and strengthening one another, it strained the alliance and created more independent European contacts with the Soviet Union.

In no country was this truer than in West Germany. Chancellor Adenauer heeded Dulles's advice and tried to establish ties with the Soviet Union throughout the late 1950s. Almost immediately after the U.S. military had relinquished authority of West German export controls to the new West German government, Adenauer and his Economics Minister Ludwig Erhard dangled East-West trade in front of the Soviets in the hope of garnering Soviet political concessions. Despite few concrete later become part of his *New Ostpolitik*. While trying to bring about an Allied Four Power Conference on Berlin, he worked not through unilateral initiatives or by contacting the Soviets, but by prodding the Western allies to begin such negotiations. He criticized his own party members' suggestions to establish nonpolitical contacts, in order to alleviate the division between the two Germanys and possibly establish political contacts in the long run. He even eschewed his later visionary model of a confederation between the two German states, as negotiations leading up to such a solution could hinder allied dialogue or hurt the position of the West.[8] Subordinating Germany to the tutelage of the United States in the areas of inter-German dialogue, reunification, and nuclear armament, he implicitly rejected *Osthandel* as a tool for establishing direct communications with the Soviets.

Vice President Richard Nixon could not have been happier with the "Socialist" mayor of Berlin. As vice president under President Dwight Eisenhower, and with his hard-core anti-communist reputation, he must have appreciated Brandt's staunch position. Despite the traditional affinity of U.S. Democrats and German Social Democrats, during the U.S. presidential election of 1960 Brandt expressed confidence in both presidential candidates, Richard M. Nixon and John F. Kennedy, for supporting "allied responsibility in the Berlin and German questions."[9]

With West Berlin under constant threat of Soviet invasion or interference, it seems reasonable that Brandt's interest in American strength led him to gravitate toward the presidential candidate who had already been vice president in the previous administration and, if anything, stood for the greater show of military strength and political involvement over Berlin.[10] Practical considerations such as these must have prevailed over any ideological similarities that might have existed between Brandt and Senator John F. Kennedy (D-MA). On 11 November 1960 Brandt publicly criticized President-elect Kennedy over his friendly overture with Soviet Premier Khrushchev.[11] In 1960, Mayor Brandt sought Western strength, not dialogue with the East. Nixon would most likely have delivered this strength, as he criticized Kennedy for not having a "firmer and tougher United States policy toward the Soviet Union."[12] Despite having supported Nixon, Brandt's pro-American stance made him the candidate of choice for President John F. Kennedy during the 1961 German elections.[13]

Yet regardless of Brandt or Adenauer, in the early 1960s both large parties, the CDU and the SPD, supported American leadership sufficiently to maintain strong cohesion within the transatlantic alliance. NATO was the pillar of West German foreign policy, and political contacts with the East were limited and subordinated to American tutelage.

Economic interactions with the East were well contained through the U.S.-dominated coordinating committee COCOM. Were a picture to be painted of an ideal U.S. ally, it would be the FRG in the early 1960s.

The Berlin Wall as the Turning Point

The building of the Berlin Wall ushered in sweeping change. Domestic and international opinion mimicked Brandt's facial expression at the construction site: sheer disbelief and helplessness. Yet despite the public outcry, Western military presence was conspicuously absent. It took twenty hours for the first American military patrols to arrive at the construction site, leading Brandt to comment angrily: "These shitheads are at least finally sending some patrols to the sector borders so that the Berliners won't think they are totally alone."[14]

Even then, NATO support was not apparent. Two days elapsed before the Soviet commander of East Berlin received a protest note, and only after three days did the three Western allies register their protests with Moscow.[15] Rumors that the allies had been informed in advance or that John J. McCloy might have actually suggested this "solution to the Berlin Crisis" to Khrushchev further underscored that the West was not willing to risk the status quo over German reunification.[16] If Brandt had any doubts about the U.S. position on the Berlin Wall, they would have been laid to rest upon receipt of Kennedy's response to Brandt's letter. Brandt, outraged about the lack of allied action, had written directly to Kennedy to seek American support. In his response, Kennedy, rather than promising to support, implied that this was not a threatening crisis and twice suggested that further communications should remain within the proper channels. He explained to Brandt that the United States was not willing to challenge the status quo as long as West Berlin was not threatened.[17]

Kennedy's aloof attitude toward one of West Berlin's gravest crises was underscored by Vice President Johnson's interest in Brandt's slippers. Rather than being allowed to study Kennedy's letter, which Johnson had carried to Berlin, Brandt had to arrange for a West Berlin department store to reopen so that the American dignitary could purchase the same slippers that Brandt was wearing while receiving Johnson.[18] Brandt recalls losing "certain illusions" about the Western alliance when the East "had been allowed to take a swipe at the Western superpower, and the United States merely winced with annoyance." As Brandt recalled, "it was against this background that my so-called *Ostpolitik*—the beginning of détente—took shape."[19] For Brandt, this crisis destroyed the paradigm that had bolstered German-American postwar relations, namely America's role as the advocate for West German military and political interests in international diplomacy, in return for the FRG being a loyal ally of the United States.[20]

Brandt's outrage was not limited to the Western side, however. His anger at the Soviet Union was also evident in his speech of 13 August 1961, in which he criticized the German Democratic Republic (GDR) as well as the supporting communist-bloc nations by protesting against the "illegal and inhumane acts of the peoples dividing Germany, oppressing East Berlin and threatening West Berlin."[21] That he mostly targeted the Soviet Union can be seen in his speech before the German parliament the following week. In it he outlined the need for a concerted response to this new development since "the Soviet Union may not believe that it can slap us in the face and we smile in response. ... The government of the Soviet Union must be reminded how dangerous it is to insist on breaking the Four-Power-Agreements."[22] Yet herein lay the problem: West Germany and West Berlin, while secure, were unable to respond in any way. What Brandt had supported before now became untenable: West Germany's sole reliance on its Western allies to advance its foreign policy interests. Meanwhile, all it had with the East was economics.

Kennedy's Use of East-West Trade as a Political Tool

Incidentally, fostering East-West trade coincided with President Kennedy's approach to East-West relations. Kennedy's new approach to foreign policy included a more direct utilization of East-West trade, i.e., establishing connections with the East for the sake of propagating Western values. In a sense, he sought to continue the Cold War with economic and political rather than military means. In his 1961 State of the Union Address, Kennedy had asked Congress "for increased discretion to use economic tools" in reestablishing ties with "the Eastern European peoples." Kennedy, thus, saw trade as helpful in enhancing relations with the people of Eastern Europe and useful for propagating Western ideals, while not supporting or legitimizing their communist governments.

Yet with this vision Kennedy inherited the dilemma of his predecessors. Since the Second World War each president had been confronted with strong opposition in the U.S. Congress to the liberalization of trade with communist nations. Using the discretionary powers of the presidency, presidents sought to overcome this rigidity and liberalize East-

West trade, albeit without a "cumulative ... political effect."[23] Gaining Congressional approval became the linchpin.

Even after excluding the Soviet Union as a potential beneficiary of East-West trade, Kennedy's proposed trade legislation was a political tightrope act. On 18 September 1961 Secretary of Commerce Hodges, listing several Congressional actions, concluded that there existed "the very strong sentiment in Congress—and the country—against trade with Soviet bloc countries."[24] Even within the administration, opinions were divided on the benefits of East-West trade. These opinions can be divided into three different camps that remained remarkably consistent throughout the remainder of the Cold War.[25] The first camp viewed trade as a beneficial, stabilizing, and peace-fostering element in international affairs. Usually representing the State Department, proponents of this view pushed for liberalization of the Export Control List of embargoed items in the Coordinating Committee of all Western Allies (COCOM). The second position saw East-West trade as a tool employed by the enemy that did little to facilitate stability but rather served to bleed away U.S. economic advantages. The Defense Department traditionally advanced this argument and pushed Kennedy to levy additional embargoes on items not included in the COCOM lists. Views in the middle typically saw the COCOM system as functional and the Eastern demand for consumer items as legitimate. With each department pursuing its own vision of what guiding principles East-West trade should follow, Kennedy was forced to set the tone for the administration in January 1962. Leaning toward the first position, he decreed that the administration would take a liberal stance when deciding the fate of individual trade deals.[26]

Certainly, Kennedy's most notable decision on East-West trade was his agreement to allow grain exports to the Soviet Union. Especially after the Cuban Missile Crisis, Kennedy would view economic interaction as a vital tool to convey Western prosperity and beliefs. As he pointed out in a speech given at the University of Berlin, it was through personal contacts between people and trade that the Cold War would be won by the West.

> It is important that the people on the quiet streets in the East be kept in touch with Western society. Through all the contacts and communication that can be established, through all the trade that Western security permits, above all whether they see much or little of the West, what they see must be so bright as to contradict the daily drum beat of distortion from the East.[27]

Nonetheless, because of Congressional opposition and the politicization of trade, Kennedy did not establish clear, predictable guidelines on trade, opting instead to decide sensitive exports on a case-by-case basis. Questions on what export article constituted a militarily useful commodity, what was destined for civilian use, and what technology would improve the civilian sector of the Soviet economy would plague this administration and its successor administrations for the next thirty years.

Judgment calls on "dealing with the enemy" not only created internal disagreement within the Kennedy administration but caused much conflict within the Western alliance. Embracing the adage "trade is trade and politics is politics," most Western European countries were eager to develop trade with the Soviet Union and were all too willing to cut the COCOM lists down to bare essentials. Expanding or limiting COCOM lists thus remained a hotly debated issue.[28] Just two months into his tenure in the White House, Kennedy faced a British request for increased consultations on the COCOM lists, as the actual fourteen-member council meetings resulted in heated discussions.[29] These discussions centered on the British delivery of Viscount airplanes to the People's Republic of China and copper wire to the Soviet Union. The politicization of East-West trade and the "dual-use" nature of, say, copper wire, in military as well as civilian applications often pitted the American administration against the Western European ones. Ultimately, the Kennedy administration could only prevent American suppliers from delivering spare parts for Viscount airplanes to Great Britain, and the British went ahead with their East-West trade regardless of American concerns.[30]

After the Cuban Missile Crisis the need for a coherent trade policy with the East had become even more apparent as Kennedy had stopped granting any new export licenses to the Soviet bloc. A coordinated Western approach to East-West trade was called for, especially in regard to financing. As the Soviet surplus gold reserves were being eaten up by grain imports, Western European countries started a bidding war for credit terms and interest rates, hoping to attract Soviet orders to their respective economies. Therefore, the State Department felt that the United States should take "a more vigorous approach to our Allies for a more effective ... multilateral economic defense program."[31] This new approach, Kennedy hoped, would be an overarching policy that would ensure proper—political—compensation for East-West trade as well as align it with the White House's larger Cold War policies.[32] In May 1963 he ordered an inter-agency study to explore such new policies, with the resulting insight that American trade restrictions only made sense when conducted on "a broad front" alongside Western European allies.[33]

Afraid of being left behind on East-West trade due to "evidence of greater trade by our allies with the Soviet and Eastern Bloc," Kennedy announced in a news conference on 9 October 1963 that the U.S. would not prohibit the sale of surplus wheat to the Soviet Union.[34] Simultaneously, the Department of State announced that it was seeking to harmonize East-West trade with other Western powers. This meant that the White House would seek an understanding at the NATO council meeting in December 1963 on financing and credit terms in East-West trade. To drive home the need for cooperation, Undersecretary George Ball was sent to West Germany and Britain to argue that long-term credits would allow Moscow to pursue its development of civilian and military goods at the same time.[35]

The Soviets, depending on competition between the different Western powers to drive down the price, pulled their own "economic" punches. In mid September, Nikita Khrushchev had proposed billions of dollars' worth of orders of industrial goods, mostly from the then depressed British wharves. Khrushchev's only precondition for such orders from the Soviet Union, which was notoriously poor in hard currency, was the extension of large, long-term credits by Great Britain.[36] Money spoke louder than words, and the British refused to heed Undersecretary Ball's calls for a united economic front vis-à-vis the Soviet Union. Instead, in February 1964 they granted a five-year credit to finance the British construction of a chemical plant in the Soviet Union. Despite a CIA finding that Khrushchev needed all his resources for military expenditures and sought to remedy a slump in Soviet agricultural production with the help of East-West trade, the U.S. could not convince its allies to abstain. Meanwhile, outside of Britain, France had already heavily engaged in trade with the Soviet Union. French Economics Minister Giscard d'Estaing returned from his trip to Moscow glowing with the prospect of sizable trade opportunities.[37] There was no doubt that President Johnson had inherited a growing transatlantic schism on East-West trade.

The Busted Pipeline Deal of 1962

While a general assessment sees Kennedy's attempt to develop a coherent East-West trade policy for NATO as a failure, he was "successful" in garnering loyalty among the newly elected Christian Democratic Union (CDU) government, led by Ludwig Erhard. Fairly soon after the Adenauer government opened the gates to *Osthandel,* the Soviets began purchasing large-diameter steel pipes to be used in their natural gas pipelines. After increasing orders of steel pipes in 1959 and 1960, the Soviets found that their grain purchases in the U.S. had left them with little currency to spend on the West German steel pipes. In February 1962 the Soviets offered to provide the steel themselves and have the three leading West German steel producers, Mannesmann, Phoenix-Rheinrohr, and Hoesch, turn it into high-quality large-diameter pipes for the construction of natural gas pipelines. As pipe-manufacturing plants in West Germany were struggling to survive in the economically weak years of the early 1960s, the West German firms readily agreed to the deal. Hopes for a continuously flourishing East-West trade and a positive impact on West German–Soviet relations, however, were soon crushed. The Kennedy administration, citing serious concerns over energy trade with the Soviet Union, managed to pass a resolution in the NATO council making large-diameter steel pipes a strategic export good.

The Western European allies were not happy about this curtailment of East-West trade at a time when the U.S. itself was selling vast quantities of grains to the Soviet Union. Europeans were especially wary of jeopardizing trade relations with the Soviet Union after rumors surfaced that the American advance on steel pipes had little to do with military necessity but much more with American oil companies' fears about an influx of Soviet crude oil.[38]

Italy and Britain, having just reestablished promising trade ties with the Soviet Union, continued to supply steel pipes until their contractual obligations had been fulfilled. In West Germany, however, the pipeline issue became a tug-of-war game between the U.S. administration on one hand, and the Soviet Union, flanked by the powerful West German steel industry, on the other. An overzealous Erhard government quickly followed up on the nonbinding NATO resolution, issuing an administrative order on 14 December 1962 to immediately require export licenses for large-diameter steel pipes—only to turn around and deny these licenses for pipe exports to the Soviet Union.

To up the ante on East-West trade, the Soviets touted the possibility of a Soviet order for the construction of an oil refinery and processing plant by a consortium of Western European firms. To avoid "possible American protests against these deliveries, this consortium should have the largest possible diversification among European countries." Largely German licenses, as well as some French and some Italian ones, should be used in this undertaking, but none from the U.S.[39] By January 1964 a consortium had been formed under the leadership of Salzgitter Corp., eager to reinvigorate the floundering West German steel industry with a large-scale Soviet order.

It was Chancellor Erhard's unwavering commitment to the trans-atlantic alliance that doomed Soviet efforts to drive a wedge between Western European and American economic interests, wholesale-style. Pointing to a "noticeable alienation between Great Britain and the United States," Erhard was not willing to jeopardize ties with the United States, no matter what other European nations were doing.[40] He instructed his Economics Minister Schmücker to give the Salzgitter consortium "no further hope" of closing the deal.[41]

Nonetheless, *Osthandel* had already gained a life of its own in West Germany. Rather than conveying Erhard's clear "no-go," Schmücker encouraged the Salzgitter consortium to pursue financing without governmental support and promised to continue to advocate their case.[42] It would take another two years and some cunning to get Erhard to agree to grant export licenses as well as Hermes federal loan guarantees. In June 1964 Schmücker passed Erhard a note during a meeting, stating

> Yesterday, I explained to Mr Berg, Wolff von Amerongen and Weiss that there is no hope for federal loan guarantees or any other help for the German-French project [of constructing a oil refinery in the Soviet Union]. I presume that, in accordance with your views, they will try to get German banks to finance the deal without loan guarantees. In such a case we should agree.[43]

Schmücker took Erhard's nod as an instruction to fundamentally alter German trade policy, even though the note expressed assent to granting export licenses as an afterthought on this handwritten note. Whether Erhard was tricked into granting the necessary export licenses is unclear, but he remained steadfast in refusing federal loan guarantees.[44] His approach still closely followed American concepts of a restrictive trade policy, used for political leverage.[45]

The Soviet Union countered by playing various Western countries against each other. A Salzgitter delegation in Moscow in January 1965 was told that German five-year loans were not competitive compared with those offered by other nations (twelve years by Great Britain, even fifteen years by Japan). Only with long-term loans and federal Hermes guarantees would a deal be feasible.[46] With strong lobbying, the Salzgitter consortium was able to bring some movement into the German government's position. Still taking small, reluctant strides, the German government, for the month of February and first half of March, tried in vain to level the playing field by getting the other Western nations to agree to uniform export subsidies and credit arrangements. Finally, on 18 March 1965 the German government decided to implement a temporary regulation that allowed Hermes loan guarantees for the Eastern bloc and an extension of the five-year loan limit, matching the conditions offered by their competitors.[47]

But even with Hermes, god of commerce and market, finally holding sway over the prospective deal, the Soviets brought up the failed pipeline deal of 1962/63. They demanded a reparation payment of 8 million marks as well as the federal government's assurance that it would not interfere with binding agreements in the future.[48] As one of the consortium members put it: "He [Ambassador Smirnow] told us in no uncertain terms that there was not enough trust, with regards to the pipeline embargo, to complete such a large project, which is a key project in the Russian petrochemical industry."[49] For West Germany, the message was clear. It would continue to suffer for its close adherence to U.S. wishes. The Soviets had chosen to punish West German firms for breaking existing contractual obligations and embracing the U.S. steel pipe embargo of 1963.

Johnson's Ambivalence toward East-West Trade

Its commitment to American leadership, however, did not gain West Germany much in the way of benefits under the new Johnson administration, mainly because of a lack of a consistent American stance toward following up on the issue. Bickering over East-West trade quickly arose over eight beet harvesters that the Soviets sought for a more effective harvesting of their crops. The Export Control Review Board, set up by Kennedy in 1961, was divided on the issue. The State Department wanted to grant the export, as it viewed beet harvesters as "nonstrategic" items. The Department of Agriculture felt that these harvesters would make the Soviet Union more competitive in the Cold War, while the Defense Department and Commerce Department feared the copying of these harvesters for manufacture by Soviet industry. Betraying a lack of presidential direction on the issue, the board squabbled over how President Kennedy would have dealt with the sale of these harvesters.[50] Special Assistant for National Security Affairs Bundy, summed up the problem within the Kennedy administration succinctly: "no one short of the President has had authority to make clear-cut decisions" and, lacking general guidelines, "it became necessary to appeal individual cases over and over again to President Kennedy."[51]

President Johnson, although generally supportive of liberalizing East-West trade, did not establish clear guidelines for his administration either. Torn between industry pressures to liberalize trade and a

Congress that was unwilling to commit to the necessary import/export reforms, he chose not to settle as divisive an issue as East-West trade before the 1964 election.[52] Consequently, he did not decide on the immediate case before him, the beet harvesters, but postponed this decision.[53] The result, however, was that the Soviets withdrew their offer to purchase beet harvesters altogether.[54]

The absence of a consistent trade policy further befuddled the administration and the alliance, sparking clashes over numerous issues. One such example was the Commerce Department inhibiting the global resale of chemical products made from American petroleum. Bundy frustratingly commented that this "appears to be an excellent way of increasing the business of Japanese and German exporters of competing plants."[55] Yet even Western Europeans sought a wholesale liberalization of East-West economic policy. During a visit to the Johnson White House, then Mayor Willy Brandt urged the development of a common policy between the U.S. and the European countries to foster East-West trade.[56]

President Johnson did announce the exploration of new ways to boost East-West trade in his State of the Union Address in 1965, only to back away from the issue afterward. No consistent guidelines were set forth, and East-West trade remained in limbo. Indeed, while the lost sale of beet harvesters can only be described as a minor setback, the potential sale of television equipment to all of Europe was also botched by interdepartmental conflict. As the Europeans met in Vienna to establish a continent-wide system television standard, RCA approached the Johnson administration in August 1964 for permission to export American televisions and recording equipment to Europe. The Europeans were poised to determine a uniform system for all of Europe, and RCA stood to profit immensely if it could win against the French system SECAM. Rather than supporting RCA in the way the French government did SECAM, the Commerce Department reminded RCA of its policy of "denying strategic materials to the Soviet Bloc" regardless of "commercial considerations."[57] This half-hearted support for RCA exports was then followed by a nine-month stint of inactivity, during which the Commerce Department tried to resolve interdepartmental conflict on the issue. The frustrated RCA chairman, David Sarnoff, frantically wrote directly to the president on 5 March 1965, asking him to grant the licenses as a decision by the Europeans would be taken soon.[58]

As it turned out, the holdup had been caused by the CIA over concerns that the sale of video recorders could improve Soviet "intercept capabilities," "analysis and advanced radar development," and "missile and space telemetry data recording and analysis."[59] By the time

Johnson intervened in favor of a sale on 15 March, the decision-making process in Vienna had already ended. On 22 March, France and the Soviet Union announced that they had agreed to combine their technical knowledge and work together for the European adoption of the French SECAM color television system. Bureaucratic inactivity had just made the Atlantic a little bit bigger.

Cultural or even economic implications of East-West trade, though, were hardly on the presidential radar screen—for Johnson or for his successors. East-West trade lacked the scale to be meaningful in economic terms, and cultural implications were not measurable. To placate the American business community, which was outraged over losing lucrative Eastern contracts to Western European competitors, Johnson established a joint commission of government officials and civilians in July 1965 with the express purpose of seeking to increase East-West trade with the Soviet Union.[60] The commission's findings, the Miller Report, confirmed the American ambivalence toward East-West trade. On one hand, it reaffirmed the primacy of politics as "trade with the Communists is a matter of international politics and not profit" but on the other urged the White House to "drive hard, realistic political bargains with European Communist countries—bargains which would clearly be in the United States' interest."[61] In concrete terms, regardless of the export control policy, the Miller Report recommended the granting of Most Favored Nation (MFN) status to communist countries. If Johnson favored such a policy he did not afford it high priority, refusing to send a trade bill with an MFN provision to the Senate because he did not wish to add "to the current legislative load."[62] When Johnson finally, after much internal back-and-forth, did forward a draft to Congress a year later, it stalled in Congress because, as House Leader Hale Boggs (D-LA) explained, it was "difficult to sell East-West trade legislation as long as we were fighting in Viet Nam."[63] The political sensitivity of East-West trade in the United States would prevent Congress from passing legislation on East-West trade for the remainder of Johnson's term.

The lack of U.S. enthusiasm for East-West trade also translated into incoherent leadership within NATO. This holds truest of all for West Germany, where the Erhard government still awaited its reward for steadfastly touting the American line. Instead the pro-American Erhard government was undermined in the area where it hurt the most: the German question. By June 1965 it had become public knowledge that the State Department had allowed two American firms, Standard Oil and Latwin Engineering Co., OH, to construct a chemical plant for 55 million marks to produce textiles in the German Democratic Republic. Not only had West German officials not been notified of this, as strengthening the East German economy clearly ran counter to West German interests, but to add insult to injury, the chemical compound to be produced was Orlon, a material developed by a German scientist during the Second World War, seized by American forces after the war, and then marketed by DuPont in the United States.[64]

Such blunders demonstrated to the West Germans and the rest of Europe that staunch adherence to Washington's leadership in the alliance constituted an ill-advised policy. When a disillusioned Erhard government lifted the steel pipe embargo in 1965, the embargo had yielded no significant effect on the completion of the Soviet "Friendship" pipeline. Rather, as this pipeline was to supply Eastern Europe, it had strengthened the Eastern alliance and forced the Soviet Union to become more self-sufficient in the creation of its energy infrastructure.[65] In retrospect, America's foreign policy seemed less than sound and certainly not beneficial to its adherents. West Germany's ambivalence about alliance with the U.S. is expressed in an opinion poll (Figure 1.1) in which West Germans felt that the U.S. gained more from German-American cooperation than did West Germany.

Brandt's *Ostpolitik* Takes Shape

The glaring disadvantages of close allegiance to the U.S. had ripple effects throughout West Germany's political culture. After all, détente entailed a legitimizing of contacts with the Soviet bloc as well as the opportunity to criticize Western diplomacy. While Erhard would remain pro-American to a fault (one could argue that his political career ended because he was too subservient to American leadership), other German politicians articulated dissatisfaction with the status quo. West Berlin Mayor Willy Brandt was one of those willing to criticize Western dip-

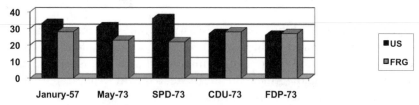

Figure 1.1 Opinion Poll of West Germans: "Who has the greater interest and benefit from German-American cooperation?" taken from Elisabeth Noelle-Neumann, ed. *Jahrbuch der öffentlichen Meinung: 1968–1973*. Allensbach: Verlag für Demoskopie, 1974, "Das Bündnis," 558.

lomatic efforts to which he previously had yielded. Frustrated by the lack of movement, he observed that "during the past years the political practice of the West has frequently suffered from insufficient ability to conduct realistic negotiations."[66]

More than that, he saw the framework of détente as an opportunity to enact more independent policies, himself. During the early 1960s he had reached out to the GDR, succeeding in the highly publicized *Passagierscheinabkommen* and other humanitarian gestures to make the effects of the Wall more bearable for Berliners.[67] Stepping out of the shadow of the U.S., be it political or economic, Brandt rhetorically widened the self-assigned limits of German *Ostpolitik* from humanitarian issues to include economic and cultural contacts. Frustrated with Johnson's neglect of his European allies in the shadow of Vietnam, Brandt embraced a pan-European peace concept and anchored his *Westpolitik* less and less with the United States and more with the European Economic Community. This also entailed throwing the shackles off German diplomacy once he came into office.

If détente was an admission of Western limits in economic terms, it was even more so militarily. During the mid 1960s it became increasingly clear that the nuclear protection upon which West German security was based was not as strong as it had been before the launch of Sputnik in 1958. The nuclear parity reached between the two superpowers in the mid 1960s increased tensions in the Western camp. The United States seemed increasingly reluctant to engage in a nuclear war that was "unwinnable." This reduced the credibility of nuclear deterrence for the European allies, as it was questionable whether the United States would be willing to engage in a nuclear war for Western Europe if this implied self-destruction.[68] Changes in NATO strategy, which set the benchmark for nuclear escalation increasingly higher, and a strong emphasis on conventional (European) military reinforced this fear. Maintaining a nuclear deterrent, though, was the name of the game in the mid 1960s, and West Germany's reliance on a now apparently reluctant United States placed it in an awkward position. Since Germany had renounced building its own nuclear weapons, the creation of the Multi Lateral Force (MLF), a nuclear force manned with troops from various nations under the auspices of NATO, was the preferred method for the FRG to gain nuclear credibility. Thus, more than ever, Brandt had to continue to rely on NATO and the U.S. backing of the MLF proposition.[69]

Brandt also pushed for nuclear sharing during his visit to the Johnson White House in April 1965. After reiterating to Vice President Humphrey that Germany had no interest in becoming a nuclear power, he drove home the point that it "was legitimate for Germans to participate in a strategy involving nuclear arms."[70] Prevention of future conflicts over the inter-German border was one of Brandt's primary concerns; a German nuclear deterrent would lend credence to West Germany's interest in this regard.[71] It may not have been Johnson's fault that the FRG ultimately had to resign itself to trading nuclear weapons–sharing for a paper tiger, the Nuclear Planning Group. Germany's European allies had little interest in seeing the German military in charge of nuclear weapons. Most likely, MLF was already dead by the time Brandt brought it up with Johnson.[72] Sweet-talking the Germans into supporting this dubious trade and the Nuclear Non-Proliferation Treaty (NPT), which historian Thomas Schwartz views as a successful maneuver by Johnson in that Germany could make a virtue out of its non-nuclear status, might have saved face for the FRG (if not necessarily for Chancellor Ludwig Erhard). With Brandt, however, Johnson's détente policies, among which the NPT certainly was crucial, backfired.

For Brandt, disillusionment over nuclear weapons–sharing increased his emphasis on Europe, not the Atlantic, as the central stage for his foreign policy. Again, this was more a structural necessity of détente in general than Johnson's doing. In a sense, the military might of the U.S. became less significant to the same degree that détente implied military deescalation in Europe. Johnson telling the Germans that MLF did not matter was tantamount to belittling one's own strength. Johnson's strategy was probably quite successful with the German conservatives in government, as they were thoroughly immobile in their outdated position of Western strength and Johnson wanted to jolt them in order to move ahead with détente. This would explain the "cooperative and harmonious" German-American relationship in 1968.[73] However, to Brandt, who was already disillusioned by the lack of American support in the Berlin crisis of 1961, the failure of the U.S. to meet German interests—not just in political and economic, but now even in military terms—was a warrant to flesh out his *Ostpolitik.*

Brandt's initiatives focused on using the nuclear stalemate between the superpowers to Germany's advantage. While Brandt, as an Atlanticist, clashed with de Gaulle's vision of a French-led Europe in many ways, he admired the French president for "using the political room that was created by the nuclear stalemate in his own way."[74] In a speech before an American audience on the topic of German self-confidence, he outlined the need for "healthy self-confidence and real power of the FRG."[75] A strong European Community was of utmost importance for the exercise of this newly claimed authority, and a pan–European détente the prerequisite for Germany's reunification.[76] With this linkage,

Germany was elevated to a key player in the emerging détente policies with the East. Such a key player did not "always have to wait for American, French, or British suggestions."[77]

Unlike de Gaulle, who pursued a nationalistic policy of strengthening France, Brandt did not wish for his Europe to become a third superpower.[78] Rather, he wished to use de Gaulle's internationally accepted attempts at independent diplomacy with the East to pursue his axiom of "preserve[ing] the status-quo militarily so it can be overcome politically." In anchoring his diplomacy within Western Europe, one could say he supplemented this axiom "through an alliance with the United States militarily and European unity politically." This distinction between military policy on one hand and cultural and economic issues on the other allowed him to pursue a strategy separate from that of the U.S.

When *Ostpolitik* is contextualized within alliance politics, historians frequently point to the embedding of West Germany in the Western alliance as a necessary prerequisite.[79] *Ostpolitik* could only succeed with American support, as Kissinger would try to convince Nixon in the early 1970s.[80] By implication, then, *Ostpolitik* had to stay contained within the alliance, since an independent *Ostpolitik* would necessitate a weakening of the German position. Such arguments, however, view Brandt's Eastern policies as linear and singular in nature. Distinguishing various aspects of international relations allowed a much wider range of actions. Assuming the military situation to remain constant, no matter what developed in cultural or economic areas, allowed for the execution of policies that ran counter to the interests of NATO or the U.S. Herein lay the heart of Brandt's ability to pursue an independent *Ostpolitik*: the conviction that the United States would not withdraw its troops from Germany and that West Germany would be part of a united Europe.[81]

When Willy Brandt came into office as foreign minister in 1967 (as part of a grand coalition with the CDU) it appeared as though Johnson had abandoned Germany's interests in favor of superpower détente. Nuclear sharing had finally been discarded, largely on the basis of opposition by Western allies but also due to heavy opposition from the Soviet Union. That year, the doctrine of "flexible response" would become official doctrine, making a global nuclear escalation as improbable as possible—thereby arguably exposing the FRG to the threat of invasion, which was winnable by Soviet conventional forces. To save face, Germany had been admitted as a permanent member of the Nuclear Planning Group, which granted it an increased level of nuclear consultation without any effective military gains. This policy was in line with American foreign policy. For Johnson, as for the Soviets, détente primarily meant an understanding between the two superpowers in military affairs. Détente was therefore considered a bilateral issue between the Soviet Union and the United States, not a dialogue between all parties involved. Since Germany was utterly dependent on the backing of the United States, Soviet-American talks led to extreme tensions and doubts within the alliance, and especially in the German-American relationship.[82]

Despite grave concerns over this superpower détente, Brandt indicated to Bahr that he was unwilling to push for a revamping of West German policy under the grand coalition between the SPD and CDU, as he did not wish to "strain the new [coalition] government to the limit." He had "the realization that the issues, [which] he thought needed to get done, would not get done with this coalition."[83] Thus limited by the constraints of the coalition partner, the CDU, Brandt was able to pursue only a watered-down version of *Ostpolitik*. The common denominator between the two parties with regard to foreign policy was the goal of creating a collective security system that would overcome the division of Europe as well as any military aggression.[84]

The military situation in Europe had become highly volatile. On one hand, the military security that the United States provided for the FRG was increasingly drawn into question. One public opinion poll after another (Figure 1.2) indicated the deterioration of German confidence in the U.S. as an ally.

Throughout the 1960s, the desirability of the U.S. as a partner on the international scene had dropped roughly twenty points while that of the Soviet Union had risen by that same amount. The Soviet invasion of Czechoslovakia would alter this trend temporarily, shattering short-term hopes of rapprochement with the Soviet Union and renewing fears of military conflict. West Germans wanted a stronger NATO but also sought better relations with the Soviet Union only one year after the invasion.[85]

As Figure 1.3 illustrates, by 1969 the German perception of threat from the Soviet Union had resumed its sharp pre-1968 decline. Given the lack of credible nuclear retaliatory capabilities and the perceived Soviet threat to invade West Germany, public opinion polls seemed to support the tightrope walk of Brandt's new *Ostpolitik*. U.S. military presence and NATO, therefore, remained crucial elements in Brandt's policies despite his outreach to the East.[86] Yet this military protection had shifted from being the crucial pillar holding up West Germany's security to a necessary geopolitical element in the pursuit of other diplomatic goals with much greater flexibility.

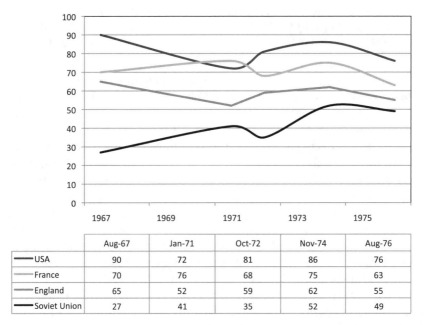

	Aug-67	Jan-71	Oct-72	Nov-74	Aug-76
USA	90	72	81	86	76
France	70	76	68	75	63
England	65	52	59	62	55
Soviet Union	27	41	35	52	49

Figure 1.2 Opinion Poll of West Germans: "Which countries should we work most closely with?" taken from Elisabeth Noelle-Neumann, ed. *Jahrbuch der öffentlichen Meinung: 1968–1973*. Allensbach: Verlag für Demoskopie, 1974, "Zusammenarbeit," 533.

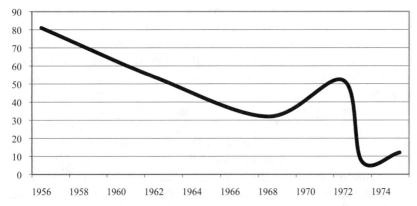

Figure 1.3 Opinion Poll of West Germans on their threat perception emanating from the Soviet Union, taken from Elisabeth Noelle-Neumann, ed. *Jahrbuch der öffentlichen Meinung: 1968–1973*. Allensbach: Verlag für Demoskopie, 1974, "Sowjetunion," 575.

> Our security interests and the necessity of the Atlantic partnership cannot be pursued against the United States but only through an independent policy vis-à-vis the United States, and wherever possible in conjunction with it.[87]

Brandt was not the only one pursuing such an independent stance. Most Western European countries embraced an East-West dialogue as the way to overcome perceived American weakness. A striking example of this was the restructuring of NATO in 1967/68. Here Brandt not only welcomed but actively fostered the shift in NATO doctrine away from a strong emphasis on nuclear deterrent toward an increased emphasis on diplomacy.[88] In the resulting Harmel Report, NATO saw military security and détente as two sides of the same coin, "not contradicting but complementing each other." The report further called for involving NATO, along with the United States and the Soviet Union, in a policy of détente for the sake of peace and stability in Europe. Lastly, it stipulated that "a final and stable agreement on Europe is not possible without a solution of the Germany question, which constitutes the core of the current tensions in Europe."[89] This last goal would be reached with a European security conference.[90] To this end, a peaceful Europe, based on cooperation and relaxation of tensions, became of prime importance for Brandt.[91]

The existing European Community played a crucial role in this. It demonstrated a possible role model as a community that was economically integrated enough to be attractive to Eastern European countries and politically powerful enough to transcend the limitations of German foreign policy. As Brandt stated in a speech before the Council of Europe, "the close Franco-German cooperation, which holds a decisive role for the future or Europe, has been revived."[92]

The purpose of *Ostpolitik*, then, was to lure the Eastern European countries into a close cooperation with the West—and East-West trade would play a crucial role in this endeavor. Brandt strove for European cooperation through "the economic, technical, scientific, cultural, and—wherever possible—political contacts with the peoples and states of Eastern Europe."[93] Brandt, then, aggressively tried to normalize relations with the states of Eastern Europe as well as to enhance the relationship with the Soviet Union. Much to his credit, the FRG established numerous trade agreements with Eastern European states, such as Czechoslovakia, Yugoslavia, and even diplomatic ties with Romania. Détente with the Soviet Union would play a crucial role in this process. Brandt had already mentioned the possibility of a non-aggression pact with the Soviet Union in a conversation with de Gaulle in December 1966, and as Sarotte argues, the invasion of Czechoslovakia gave Brandt a new conviction that his diplomatic initiatives ultimately had to go through Moscow.[94]

By the end of President Johnson's term, West Germany and Western Europe as a whole had moved further away from alliance cohesion. Johnson's disregard of allied interests in favor of national interests had diminished Western European willingness to follow American leadership.[95] Nowhere was this more apparent than in the FRG. The political culture in West Germany underwent a drastic transformation throughout the 1960s. The formerly loyal ally took big strides toward détente, with the national interest seen as furthered more through close cooperation between European states and good contacts with the Soviet Union than through strict loyalty to the United States. This growing importance of the Soviet Union was mirrored by other Western European states in the area of trade. Britain and France, for example, became bolder in confronting the U.S. over high-tech exports to the Soviet Union. Britain and France exported computers and tape-handling equipment to the Soviet Union over strong American reservations.

Yet the most significant and influential departure from the alliance cohesion of the 1950s and early 1960s lay undoubtedly with Willy Brandt. While at first he held a decidedly pro-Western stance in every respect, the more American military and political strength waned, the more independent his diplomatic and economic initiatives became. As mayor of Berlin and later West German foreign minister, Brandt gradually moved out from underneath the blanket of American diplomatic tutelage to advocate new diplomatic initiatives based on a vision of a European framework of cooperation and security. Meanwhile, trade policy in the 1960s mirrored the military and political vacillations of NATO and its leadership. Case-by-case decisions in the White House, a general Congressional mistrust of East-West trade, and numerous clashing concepts of what strategic commodities COCOM should regulate left trade policy without a sense of direction and angered European allies.

2

OF HONEYMOONS AND IDEALISM (1968–1970)

Richard M. Nixon, returning in 1967 from a five-year hiatus from politics, recognized the unhappiness over the state of the transatlantic alliance in Western Europe, albeit as a temporary, not as a structural, development. Focused on the "ABJ" (Anything But Johnson) vote, Nixon's main criticism of the Johnson administration focused on the conduct of the Vietnam War but also condemned Johnson's ignorance of the needs of the Western European allies. Nixon advocated his own style of détente with three main components: an honorable exit from Vietnam, a strengthening of the Western alliance, and a curtailment of the Soviet expansion of communism.

During his address to the Bohemian Club in San Francisco on 29 July 1967, he articulated the need for an American foreign policy that would undo President Johnson's détente policy and bring Western Europe back in lockstep with the United States. Nixon recognized not only that "Western Europe is strong economically" but also that "economic independence has inevitably led to more political independence."[1] Nixon also pointed to the reason for this independence: "The winds of détente have blown so strongly from East to West that, except for Germany, most Europeans no longer fear the threat from the East."[2] To Nixon, trusting the Soviets was the great fallacy of Western European détente. The Soviet Union remained a threat because Soviet détente was "of the head and not the heart—of necessity, not choice."[3] Ironically, such a characterization could equally be ascribed to Nixon's "era of negotiations."

Having learned from his defeat against Kennedy, "the new Nixon" of 1968 tried to shed his hawkish reputation from his days as vice president by moving toward the center. During a news conference in Miami Beach on 6 August 1968, he sported a dovish window dressing, suggesting that the "era of confrontation with the Communist world has ended, ushering [in] a new era of negotiations with the Soviet Union."[4] Despite such rhetoric, Nixon's view had not substantially changed, and when the Soviet Union invaded Czechoslovakia the Nixon camp saw it as "a net plus for the candidacy of Nixon" since people would see him "as realistic, tough-minded, skeptical ... and able to negotiate from strength."[5] For politics this was quite convenient, as Nixon could either hold up the new wine, the era of negotiations, or the old wineskins, a tough anti-Communist stance. For policy, it was quite another matter.

Viewing Soviet détente as implicitly aggressive had implications for U.S. policies in the military, economic, and diplomatic areas. In regard to the military aspects, Nixon continued to struggle for military superiority despite détente. Whereas Brandt's vision was of a military de-escalation, Nixon felt that because "the primary Soviet goal is still victory rather than peace, we must never let the day come in a confrontation like Cuba and the Mid-East where they, rather than we, have military superiority."[6]

In an even more striking contrast to Western European practices, Nixon had a very clear concept of East-West trade in that "to them [the Soviets] trade is a political weapon."[7] While both Kennedy and Johnson had wavered on this issue, Nixon bluntly demanded that "there should be no extension of long term credits or trade in strategic items with any nation, including the Soviet Union, which aids the enemy in North Vietnam."[8]

Even on the level of diplomacy, the underlying premise for diplomatic discourse differed from that of the Western Europeans and led to differing judgment calls on what constituted sensible diplomatic relations.

> Diplomatically we should have discussions with the Soviet leaders at all levels to reduce the possibility of miscalculation and to explore the areas where bilateral agreements would reduce tensions. But we must always remember in such negotiations that our goal is different from theirs: We seek peace as an end in itself. They seek victory with peace being at this time a means toward an end.[9]

Ultimately, Nixon's conviction rested on just that premise, namely that the Soviet Union remained an aggressive power and a realistic threat to the world. Détente was just a means to make the conflict of systems less dangerous. This kind of détente was a far cry from the East-West cooperation that Brandt sought through his *Ostpolitik*. Ever suspicious of the Soviets resuming global expansion, Nixon's views were more reminiscent of peaceful coexistence than détente policies and were sure to clash with European views on détente.

Nixon's Vision of a Responsible Europe

Despite—or because of—a cooperative Western European policy toward the Soviet Union, Nixon intended to strengthen NATO ties soon upon his inauguration as president of the United States on 20 January 1969. Like most presidential candidates, he sought to set himself apart from his predecessor's policies. Nixon's election slogan "We have to fix the transatlantic alliance" had resonated strongly with the American electorate, and he did not wait long to deliver on this promise.

Only two weeks after his inauguration, on 6 February 1969, he announced that he would take a trip to Europe to "revitalize" the transatlantic alliance.[10] The underlying hope, as Ronald Powaski points out, was to move the European allies away from their European-focused foreign policy toward assuming more responsibility for global Cold War politics. The carrot for such a move was an American promise of more intense consultations.[11] Being only the first of many envisioned trips, the top political priority this time around was undoubtedly to get French president Charles de Gaulle back into the fold of the Western allies. Germany, however, held its own personal challenges for Nixon. He did not fear the relatively easy visit with Chancellor Kiesinger in Bonn but rather the obligatory visit to West Berlin. As has been illustrated by Ambrose, Nixon's resentment of the East Coast liberals led to a strong aversion to anything reminiscent of President John F. Kennedy's policies.[12] Not wanting to stand in the shadow of Kennedy's famous visit, Nixon was deeply troubled by the possibility that his reception would be compared unfavorably to the cheering crowds of Berliners still remembered vividly in the minds of Germans and Americans alike. Nixon need not have worried, for the Berliners came through for him. Under chants of "He-He-He—Nixon ist ok," on 27 February 1969 the American president committed himself to "defending the rightful status of West Berlin" and offered to "view the situation in Berlin as an invocation, a call to end the tension of the past here and everywhere."[13]

In a foreshadowing of future difficulties with France and Germany, though, certain government representatives were not as easily convinced. A striking clue to Nixon's ideological underpinnings is that he had great admiration for the conservative French President Charles de Gaulle and almost revered him as an idol, despite de Gaulle's staunch anti–American policies.[14] De Gaulle, however, held no such inherent respect for Nixon. He boldly told Nixon that Europe must determine its own destiny, not follow Washington or Moscow. Of course, more amicable relations between the United States and the Soviet Union would help in this matter, and thus Nixon was able to leave Europe with a sense of a common transatlantic interest in détente.[15] Nonetheless, he discovered a harbinger of problems to come, namely "a new trust on the part of the Europeans in themselves, growing out of the fact that they have had a remarkable recovery economically and politically."[16]

Nixon's assessment of this new European self-confidence was certainly correct as far as Germany was concerned. As outlined earlier, West Germans viewed themselves as contributing as much to the transatlantic alliance as the Americans, making it understandable that by the 1960s they felt they deserved the right to influence U.S. policy.[17] This new quality of West German self-confidence became even more apparent with Willy Brandt's ascension to power. Brandt not only reiterated the trite, but true, call for more U.S. consultation with West Germans on foreign policy, but elevated the FRG to the role of a pioneer in Western foreign policy. During Nixon's visit to Bonn, Foreign Minister Brandt boldly suggested that "some real progress toward a stable settlement on Berlin would be highly desirable."[18] The implication was clear: Nixon's vision of détente was not enough to bring about the changes Brandt wanted.

The overall excitement and success of Nixon's trip to Europe, however, pushed such criticism to the background. Nixon had managed to articulate a new vision for the transatlantic partnership. Undoubtedly, notions of America's respect for its European allies and their interests as well as the desire for increased consultation were sincere—in theory. As Kissinger wrote to Nixon, with notable enthusiasm,

> I am convinced that your trip drove the key message home: we are sensitive to the critical problems; we respect and value the opinions of our Allies, we will approach talks with the Soviets with great prudence and only in full consultation with our friends; and we do not intend to try to dictate solutions to international problems anywhere at any time.[19]

Only a little while later Kissinger admitted to Secretary of State William P. Rogers, however, that when it came to consulting the European allies, "The Pres[ident] is not so much for consultation in practice as in theory."[20] Heavily relying on his foreign policy experiences during his tenure as vice president under Eisenhower, Nixon offered Western European security and relative autonomy within a framework that retained a strong element of U.S. tutelage. In short, Nixon was willing to strengthen the alliance as long as it did not interfere with his vision of détente.

Such détente, then, constituted a cautious coexistence with the communist bloc, derived through tough negotiations, more in line with the conservative views of then Chancellor Kiesinger than with Brandt's vision of full-fledged cooperation between Germany and Eastern Europe. In Kissinger's reflections on Nixon's only presidential trip to Germany, he asserts that "Kiesinger's views were closer to Nixon's: [and] Brandt's were more comparable with the convictions of our State Department."[21]

The fact that Nixon would sympathize with a former Nazi officer who looked toward a strong Franco-German understanding within a new Europe already gives an indication of the qualitative differences between Brandt's and Nixon's détente policies. In practical terms, though, the key difference between these two visions was that Nixon only needed a Soviet acceptance of the status quo, i.e., a peaceful military coexistence that did not undermine the economic and ideological competition between the two superpowers and their allies. Brandt, on the other hand, saw a true cooperation between Western and Eastern Europe as the only way to achieve the ultimate purpose of West German diplomacy: reunification. To achieve this goal, close political and economic ties were necessary, requiring intensive diplomacy and sacrifices on part of West Germany.

Unfortunately for Nixon, transatlantic relations had changed considerably since his tenure as vice president. Back then, U.S. economic support and military protection against Soviet aggression had assured Western European compliance with U.S. foreign policy. As previously outlined, various international developments during the 1960s eroded this willingness to comply with American wishes. The same week that Nixon returned home, German politics began its watershed transition from a conservative to a socialist/liberal government. As evidenced by the addresses of the newly elected German president, Gustav Heinemann, Brandt's visions of reconciliation with the East had become popular rhetoric on the left. Upon election to the German presidency, Heinemann unleashed the 1969 parliamentary election campaign rhetoric by declaring his election the beginning of the "changing of the guard."[22] He suggested that membership in NATO could not be "the terminal station of German policy" and that West Germany should work with other states to "get out of this creation of blocs again."[23] Heinemann not only asserted German national interests that were contradictory to American ones, but in doing so also rejected U.S. moral leadership.

Exploring *Osthandel* in 1968/69

Long before President Heinemann articulated the desire for a German position beyond NATO, Brandt had already initiated attempts to reach out to the Soviet Union. If the Soviet invasion of Czechoslovakia in August 1968 had demonstrated one thing to Brandt, it was the failure of Western policy to pry Soviet satellite states away from the Soviet Union through trade. To Brandt, political change without the Soviet Union was impossible.[24] Trade with the Soviet Union represented the key avenue to cooperation between Eastern and Western Europe. Consequently, *Osthandel* has often been interpreted as complementary to *Ostpolitik*. In truth, *Osthandel* was much more than simply a by-product of détente policies: it was a prerequisite to *Ostpolitik,* and Brandt was the driving force behind it.[25] Brandt had already recognized this after his disappointing visit with President Johnson in 1965, when he called for increased Western trade with the Soviet Union. He stated this even more explicitly in his 1969 book, outlining a peace policy for Europe: "The interest of the East European states in cooperation with us rests to a large extent on a desire to make economic progress and to participate in Western technology. Economics, therefore, remains for the foreseeable future an especially important element of our policy in Eastern Europe."[26]

The search for "new fields of economic opportunity" in the East began without Chancellor Kiesinger's tutelage, namely in a conversation between the two SPD-led ministries, Schiller's Economics Ministry and Brandt's Foreign Office, in 1968.[27] Egon Bahr, Brandt's right hand in the Foreign Office, initiated a "search for a new connection to Soviet politicians." His team picked up on a conversation between the Economics Ministry undersecretary von Dohnanyi and the Soviet trade representative Volkovich over the possibility of inviting Soviet Trade Minister Patolichev to Germany. The novelty of Bahr's *Osthandel* proposal becomes apparent when one considers the administrative resistance in the Economics Ministry, even though it was led by a fellow Social Democrat, Klaus Schiller.

Ministerial Director Harkort, part of von Dohnanyi's team, approached the Economics Ministry director Steidle to float the suggestion of inviting Soviet Foreign Trade Minister Patolichev to the Hanover trade fair in April 1968. The Economics Ministry stalled on the proposition and even insinuated that Brandt, clearly identified as its source, could not properly assess the implications of such an invitation as "Foreign Minister Brandt has not been to Moscow."[28] Upon Harkort's insistence, Economics Minister Klaus Schiller became directly involved, finally acquiescing to the conveyance of such an invitation—though only unofficially, so as to avoid loss of face.[29] Patolichev, toying with the Germans, claimed he needed an official invitation so he could seek approval from the Soviet Council of Ministers. When Harkort went back to Schiller for an official invitation, Schiller was only willing to express his regrets that Patolichev could not attend.[30] At the Foreign Office, however, Bahr modified Schiller's message, causing German Ambassador Sante to extend an official invitation to Patolichev, which the latter promptly declined.[31] Clearly, in April 1968 the Soviet Union was not interest in intensifying its East-West trade with West Germany, despite the unusual effort and embarrassing situations that the Foreign Office underwent in extending the invitation. Had Brezhnev wished to strengthen the more liberal part of the grand coalition in West Germany, simply accepting the trade fair invitation could have done so. As it was, the Foreign Office saw itself confronted with the same lack of high-level contacts as before.

The New Year brought another attempt by Brandt to establish closer German-Soviet ties. He convened a brainstorming session between the German embassy in Moscow and von Dohnanyi on 15 January 1969 with the same purpose: to create more high-level contacts between the Soviet Union and the Federal Republic of Germany.[32] Lacking any political leverage to bring such contacts about, the group reverted to East-West trade as the best avenue and decided, again, to invite Soviet Trade Minister Nikolai Patolichev to the 1969 Hanover trade fair.[33] Brandt reiterated his interest to Soviet Ambassador Semen K. Zarapkin, dangling the possibility of greater economic relations with the FRG before him. Brandt pulled out all the stops, offering close cooperation on cultural, economic, and technical exchange, suggesting nuclear physics, molecular biology, and cybernetics as possible fields.[34]

But despite Brandt's overtures, the Soviet side demonstrated little interest in pursuing economic ties with the FRG. After the 1963 pipeline embargo had strained German-Soviet relations, it was widely understood in German government circles that the Soviet Union was deliberately trying to freeze Soviet-German trade. The Soviets' aversion to trade with West Germany went so far that in 1967 they were willing to import German-made steel pipes only through the Austrian Voest AG as a middleman. Voest could provide only one-third of the steel for the order and had no capabilities of producing the actual pipes.[35] Still, the Soviets preferred to deal with the Austrians, turning a blind eye to the steel pipes' country of origin.

Thus, when Brandt raised the issue of East-West trade during a luncheon on 11 February 1969, Zarapkin only rehashed the old line that oil import quotas would need to be increased before German companies could be considered for any sizable trade.[36] This issue of heating oil import quotas, however, was a dead end. The Western European market was saturated in this, the only area of significant Soviet energy overproduction. Even though the West German demand in 1969 had risen 29 percent over the previous year, the market was so saturated that the current price in winter was still below that of the previous summer.[37] Since the West German market had already reached saturation, continued exports of the only marketable and plentiful Soviet commodity could not be a basis for future Soviet-German trade. Ambassador Zarapkin's comments, thus, indicated that the Soviet Union would only be willing to expand existing trade in a one-sided manner, with no interest in large-scale projects or anything that would require a fundamental reorganization of the Soviet economy. Despite Soviet inflexibility in exploring mutually beneficial trade options, *Osthandel* remained the only, albeit dim, hope for pursuing a rapprochement with the Soviets.

Certainly Brandt could not hope for U.S. support in his endeavors. In a conversation of 10 March 1969, Brandt and French Foreign Minister Michel Debre agreed that President Nixon had shown little concern for European interests and that Germany and France would need to pursue their economic and political ties with the Soviet Union independently of the United States. Détente with other Eastern European countries should also continue in parallel rather than in unison with the United States, if for no other reason than to "keep the states of Eastern Europe on the right course of a development toward Europe."[38] After Brandt showed a certain anxiety over the American reaction toward European détente initiatives, Debre assured him that de Gaulle had stated the French intention of a continued dialogue with the Soviet Union and that Nixon "considered this normal."[39] This misrepresentation of Nixon's attitude toward trade with Eastern Europe foreshadowed the many times the Europeans would skillfully claim an inability to coordinate export controls with the United States with reference to EC trade guidelines.

At the time, Brandt's conversation with Debre seemed academic, as the Soviets were clearly not willing to engage West Germany in East-West trade.[40] This would change, however, in a complete turnabout within a week of Brandt's conversation.[41] During the Warsaw Pact Conference in Budapest on 17 March, Soviet leaders renewed calls for a European Security conference and opened the door for more economic cooperation between communist countries and Western Europe. This was done for various reasons. Certainly, the intensification of the Sino-Soviet conflict that occurred in March 1969 would have served as a catalyst to facilitate Soviet interests in cementing the status quo in Europe. In view of this, Angela Stent speculates that the Soviets might have sought to undo the negative effects of the Czechoslovakian invasion and hoped that positive relations might lead the West German government to sign the Non-Proliferation Treaty.[42] Politically, the Soviets would benefit from East-West trade. Additionally, as historian Andrey Edemskiy points out, the resurfacing of the extremely nationalistic rhetoric of the Nationaldemokratische Partei Deutschlands [NPD] and its electoral victories in 1968 might have been an additional factor contributing to the embrace of West Germany.[43]

Aside from the political factors, Soviet need of East-West trade for economic reasons is often overlooked. By 1969 the Soviet Union was experiencing the first signs of economic weakening, particularly in the agricultural and industrial sectors. As Brezhnev, still unsure in his position as leader of the Soviet Union, explained, "the central problem is the general increase in grain production. ... Not enough vegetables and fruits are produced. Apparently the people's need for meat is not met by far."[44] The Soviet Union had enjoyed benefits of East-West trade to stimulate Soviet productivity, but it was in March 1969 that Brezhnev managed to focus the Politburo on making the influx of Western technology the linchpin of a reinvigoration of the Soviet economy.[45] This move elevated East-West trade from an economic benefit to a primary policy objective—an objective by which Brezhnev's political success and prestige could be measured.

This need is not always reflected in the secondary literature on the history of the Soviet economy. Drawing heavily on CIA data from this period, economic historian Philip Hanson, for example, views Brezhnev's policies on agriculture in the 1960s as successful and does not perceive a downturn in the Soviet economy until, somewhat arbitrarily, the year 1973.[46] While this would support Hanson's ultimate argument that the Soviet economy functioned best under an authoritarian leadership style, it also suggests that the Soviet agricultural sector was poised to catch up with the United States in terms of efficiency and productivity.[47] Yet this assessment—based on the evaluation of five-year plans— glosses over the fact that it was the mid 1960s, not the late 1960s, that saw strong agricultural growth. In addition, the strength of the years 1970–1973 was facilitated by the influx of Western trade, paid for with extensive Western credits. In 1972, for example, the Soviet Union imported nearly as much grain as it would following the two disastrous harvests of 1978 and 1979. But to Brezhnev in 1969, the situation in the agricultural sector looked bleak. After making it a priority in politics and economic allocations, the agricultural output remained unsatisfactory. Infusion of Western technologies was supposed to change this.

However, intensification of East-West trade was fraught with difficulties. The primary partner for such trade had traditionally been France. Yet, according to an assessment of the German Economics Ministry, Franco-Soviet trade was plagued by what would remain a problematic issue for the planned economies throughout the remainder of the 1970s and 1980s: a negative trade balance. Ultimately, the Soviet unwillingness to allow for more sophisticated commercial interactions through joint business ventures and foreign investment left the Soviet

Union unable to balance its trade deficit and made Western expansion into the Soviet market less attractive.[48]

Thus, in negotiations over a new Franco-Soviet trade agreement in March 1969, the French pushed for a new approach. During de Gaulle's last few days in office, his government tried to reshape the nature of Franco-Soviet trade. France, no longer willing to extend eight-year loans, would instead cut back to the commonly accepted five-year loans. Furthermore, the French refused to have Finance Minister Francois-Xavier Ortoli lead the negotiations or initial the agreement, thus giving the previously much publicized Franco-Soviet trade relationship a significantly lower profile. But most importantly, the French changed the nature of the new five-year trade deals, calling for expanded trade deals in which "economic exchange would only represent one element among broad exchanges of thought, experience, and services."[49] This, however, flew in the face of existing Soviet business practices. The extension of deals beyond strict economic interchanges to prospective interchanges of "thought" and "services" ran counter to Soviet expectations in dealing with the West. The Soviets considered anything other than an exchange of goods and currency an infringement in domestic affairs.

The other hope for increased hard-currency inflows appeared stalled, as well. The previously planned Soviet natural gas pipeline through Austria and Italy into France was suddenly of questionable benefit to the French, in addition to being in limbo due to stalled Soviet-Italian transit negotiations. Nor was there a sizable demand for natural gas in either Italy or France for long-term expansion. Both countries had enough domestic natural gas resources to supply their countries until at least 1975, and without the Italian section the pipeline into France was dead anyway.[50] With a lack of hard currency and no Franco-Soviet energy trade in sight, it seemed only logical to explore other possibilities.

While Budapest's call for a European Security Conference was nothing new in and of itself, Brandt, desperate for an opening move by the Soviet Union, jumped on the occasion. As the first major Western statesman to comment on the declaration, he fully embraced the idea.[51] Brandt's quick and categorically positive response to the Budapest appeal reveals how far he was ultimately willing to go in order to create goodwill with the Soviet Union. The Soviets had repeatedly made it clear that they did not consider the United States or Canada party to talks on European cooperation, and Brandt's positive response would suggest a willingness to conduct *Ostpolitik* without *Westpolitik*. In contrast, the firm stance of the CDU party whip Rainer Barzel, "that without the United States there is nothing to discuss between East and Western

European governments on issues of peace and security," was certainly more in line with American interests.[52]

The Nixon administration, for its part, did not consider the Budapest appeal a proposal worthy of a response.[53] Even after Soviet ambassador Dobrynin indicated several days later that the United States would not be barred from participating in such a security conference, Nixon's speech at the Commemorative Session of the North Atlantic Council on 10 April demonstrated his conservative views on détente as he warned the delegates never to lose sight "of our great common purposes. Living in the real world of today means understanding old concepts of East versus West" and being wary of permitting "either stereotyped reacting or wishful thinking to lay waste our powers."[54] Assuming the mantle of the moral leader of the Western world, he warned the allies to take a realistic look at the East and refrain from weakening the alliance through selective détente. His warnings, however, fell on deaf ears.

German public opinion had already shifted in the direction of a more reconciliatory approach with the East. Despite the Brezhnev Doctrine and its implicit threat to invade the Federal Republic of Germany in the aftermath of the Czechoslovakian uprising of 1968, the threat perception of the Soviet Union dropped from 52 points in November 1968 to its all-time low of 7 points in September 1969.[55]

Furthermore, during the spring of 1969 the majority of West Germans began to see the Soviet Union as *the* superpower on the rise, economically as well as militarily (Figure 2.1).

This change in the public perception of the Soviet Union coincided with Brandt's opposition to the Americans' claim to moral leadership.[56] In fact, Brandt had already unilaterally followed up on the economic part of the Budapest declaration. Bureaucratic inertia in the Econom-

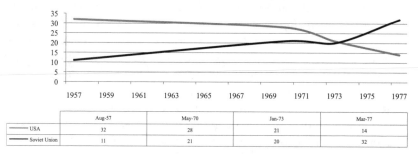

	Aug-57	May-70	Jan-73	Mar-77
USA	32	28	21	14
Soviet Union	11	21	20	32

Figure 2.1 Opinion Poll of West Germans: "Which country will be more powerful in 50 years?" taken from Elisabeth Noelle-Neumann, ed. *Jahrbuch der öffentlichen Meinung: 1968–1973*. Allensbach: Verlag für Demoskopie, 1974, "In fünfzig Jahren," 545.

ics Ministry had bogged down the discussion over the possible second invitation of Soviet Trade Minister Patolichev to the Hanover trade fair. Brandt's ally in the Economics Ministry, von Dohnanyi, reinvigorated the idea on 25 March 1969, and Schiller finally acceded to issuing an invitation.[57] To insure its smooth delivery, Brandt took it upon himself to personally convey Economics Minister Schiller's invitation to an only moderately interested Ambassador Zarapkin the next day.[58]

The reserved Soviet stance toward the FRG changed with Patolichev's acceptance of the invitation on 23 April 1969.[59] During the subsequent meeting between Patolichev and Schiller in Hanover, Patolichev pushed Soviet energy exports. He bluntly explained that the Soviet oil sector, as the main Soviet export commodity, had only limited potential. As already indicated, the Soviets had unsuccessfully sought to boost their export of the one type of oil they had plenty of: heating oil. Of the other two types, the Soviet Union had little: virtually no reserves of crude oil, and only minor export capacities in gasoline.[60] Consequently, the German proposals for cooperation led to the development of another hard-currency export commodity: natural gas. Patolichev demonstrated no willingness to make political concessions and mentioned negotiations on the long-expired trade agreement only "in a very casual way."[61] It was clear that the Soviet Union was interested in one thing only: the initiation of Soviet gas delivery negotiations to the FRG.

Brandt, having just reoriented his party to a new, conciliatory foreign policy toward Eastern Europe, jumped at the chance. Concerns of becoming overly dependent on Soviet energy exports were pushed aside with the rationalization that the volume of the potential trade deal would not be large enough to present a serious threat. The wisdom of supplying a communist country that had recently threatened to invade the FRG with a significant inflow of hard currency was never even questioned.[62] The most striking display of a desire to create, at any cost, good relations with the Soviet Union was that the Soviet gas was not even of significant commercial interest to the FRG. The German Economics Ministry assessed a potential gas pipeline as feasible only if it were to connect Italy, France, Austria, Southern Germany, and even Czechoslovakia. Northern Germany was well supplied with Dutch and Norwegian gas for the foreseeable future. Southern Germany was also well supplied, although here, starting in 1975, the market had the potential to possibly absorb 2–3 billion cubic meters. Even this relatively small quantity would require the creation of strong market incentives to lure consumers from oil to natural gas and at heavily discounted prices.[63] In essence, the FRG had no compelling need for what the Soviet Union was offering.

Whether it was because of the Soviet realization of how desperately the FRG wanted to free itself from the Soviet-imposed economic isolation, or of how important a role the Soviet Union was to play in Brandt's political vision, or simply the fact that Soviet negotiators were well informed of German negotiation positions through their intelligence services, the roles of beggar and chooser were oddly reversed in these interchanges.[64] German Ambassador Helmut Allardt assured a very reserved Soviet minister on 26 May 1969 that the German Economics Ministry would try to assist the Soviets in selling their natural gas in Germany under the conditions the Soviets had envisioned. To further the dialogue, the German ambassador also suggested an industrial-technological exchange between the two countries.[65] Other German incentives proved to be more concrete. In connection with Undersecretary von Dohnanyi's trip to Moscow, the Economics Ministry raised, per Soviet request and without any reciprocal gesture, the import quota on heating oil, which resulted in a virtual doubling of heating oil imports from the Soviet Union in an already saturated market.[66]

But not everyone in the German government was happy with the manner in which this trade deal was being negotiated. Dr. Herbst, a deputy undersecretary of trade policy in the German Foreign Ministry, observed that in the negotiations with the Russians on the proposed pipeline deal West Germany had not obtained adequate Soviet concessions. The reason, it seemed to Herbst, was the dependence of large German firms such as Daimler Benz, Siemens, and Mannesmann/Thyssen on the proposed agreement for Russian natural gas deliveries to West Germany.[67] But this assumption that German firms depended on the trade with the East was flawed. While Mannesmann stood to profit from the proposed natural gas pipeline deal, and in 1975 even built a new plant specifically for the steel pipe orders from these deals, Steel production plants in 1968/69 were already at full employment and production capacity without any Soviet orders.[68] Meanwhile, Diamler Benz AG came to the conclusion that the proposed construction of a truck manufacturing plant on the Kama River held no commercial interest for the German side. In June 1970 a Daimler assessment concluded that the entire project "is commercially without interest. It would be a matter of prestige and not a penetration of the Soviet market by the German automobile industry."[69]

In addition, the Soviets had not firmly earmarked any of these projects to the German firms mentioned above. In fact, the "Daimler" truck manufacturing plant was first offered to Ford Motor Co., which turned it down over political concerns. In short, these economic benefits for the German economy were not nearly as tangible as the pro-*Osthandel* faction would have liked them to be. Yet this Soviet strategy of dangling industrial projects of unheard-of proportions before Western European countries, sometimes without the means or understanding of how to complete them, worked well in pressuring Western European governments and companies.[70]

It certainly worked in this case. By June 1969, the Economics Ministry had in principle already condoned Russian natural gas deliveries as long as they were limited to "reasonable amounts" and "entire industrial regions would not become dependent on Soviet deliveries."[71] This eliminated the greatest potential leverage the Economics Ministry had held in gaining Soviet concessions from the deal. The Soviet position was further improved through another fortunate circumstance: the proposed pipeline, with its promises of cheap heating, stood to benefit the state of Bavaria and thus gained the support of the already latently anti-American Christliche Soziale Union [CSU], one of the parties forming the great coalition in West Germany. The CSU's presence as part of the governing coalition assured that the gas pipeline negotiations would not become politicized, as they would undoubtedly be in the United States.[72]

Domestic and International Dissent over a New *Osthandel*

Despite the absence of serious public debate on the issue, parts of the German government bureaucracy remained concerned. The Economics Ministry official Herbst pointed to the majority in-house opinion that the West German government should seek to use this deal for political leverage. Since the annual Soviet revenues from the natural gas deliveries would allow the Soviet Union to finance one-fifth of its total imports from West Germany, Herbst felt that the federal government could wrestle the long sought-after comprehensive trade agreement from the Soviets.[73] This trade agreement, which had last been discussed in October 1966, had failed because of the Soviet refusal to include West Berlin in the agreement. Herbst and the foreign trade section of the Foreign Ministry, therefore, argued for tougher negotiations with the Soviet delegation on the natural gas pipeline deal. Foreign Ministry Undersecretary Harkort concurred with Herbst on the need for Soviet concessions and further considered the 20 percent Soviet natural gas import quota proposed by the Economics Ministry to be surprisingly high.[74]

Apparently concerned over the criticism of the proposed deal, Brandt intervened personally with Economics Minister Schiller. He outlined the great significance of such a pipeline deal for commercial and political reasons and thus "wouldn't have any concerns about a considerably large quantity of Soviet natural gas deliveries." Furthermore, he reminded Schiller that an increase in East-West trade "requires an increase of export capabilities by the Soviet Union." Like Herbst, Brandt still sought to use this deal to get a trade agreement that would also include West Berlin and advised that the commercial aspects of this deal be settled speedily and in such a manner that they could be used as a basis for a trade agreement. Lastly, he proposed the formation of a working group between the Foreign and Economics Ministries to further coordinate their efforts.[75]

Schiller agreed with Brandt in general on the desirability of a trade agreement but did not show the same readiness to sacrifice commercial interests on the altar of political goodwill. With a vague reference to interministerial coordination, Schiller blocked Brandt's interference from the Foreign Office and bluntly referred him to his staff, should Brandt have further questions.[76] Evidently, East-West trade was still viewed with caution and reservation. Even SPD ministers like Schiller did not share Brandt's enthusiasm for Soviet trade deals. It is thus not surprising that Brandt, once he became chancellor, had to rely on Bahr and von Dohnanyi to bring negotiations to fruition, something that a reluctant government bureaucracy was unable to do.

The importance of economic cooperation with the Soviet Union, if not the Soviet gas pipeline deal directly, led to a rift within the grand coalition between the SPD and CDU. West German Chancellor Kiesinger did not place the same value on trade East-West trade as did Brandt. He assured U.S. Ambassador Kenneth Rush that he "held no illusions in regard to the Soviet stance on the German question. The Soviets are perhaps more interested in certain economic issues than in previous years, but this does not change their political attitudes."[77] While he planned to continue a friendly dialogue, he did not have "high hopes" and reassured Rush that relations with the United States were "the most important aspect of German foreign policy."[78] This rift within the grand coalition was not one of simple preference in negotiation strategy. At its core lay the debate over the perception of the Soviet Union and its foreign policy ambitions. If the Soviet Union had once been the unquestioned villain, by 1969 the image of the Soviet Union as a dangerous enemy had begun to shift to that of a potential partner promising economic stability and a chance for a European peace order.

For Brandt, political visions, not security concerns, were the driving element in German-Soviet relations, leading to a sometimes wishful interpretation of Soviet actions. Between 13 and 21 July 1969, the director of Thyssen A.G., Ernst Wolf Mommsen, held high-level talks on trade issues in Moscow and concluded "that the Soviets were interested in improving the climate in economic respects and intensifying interchanges."[79] Brandt's assistant, Bahr, after talking to Mommsen, elevated the significance of these negotiations to a political level, calling them a "political test for the Soviet Union."[80] To Brandt, close economic ties in the energy sector could be a precursor to broader European cooperation. His vision was based on the belief that growing economic interdependence would create the basis for a peaceful order. Ultimately, he sought to replicate the success story of Western European integration in East-West relations under the auspices of the United Nations Economic Commission for Europe and cooperation between the European Economic Community and the Soviet-led Council for Mutual Economic Assistance (CEMA).[81]

Despite Brandt's optimism, Moscow's negotiation style would prove less helpful than Brandt or Bahr had hoped. Arkady N. Shevchenko, former Soviet ambassador to the United Nations, provides an insightful reflection on Soviet negotiation strategy that makes it readily apparent why most German businessmen considered their negotiation with Soviet representatives hard and tedious.

> All Soviet negotiators are agents of limited authority who may not express opinions differing from the Politburo's position. … A Soviet's first instinct is to be suspicious of goodwill and to doubt his counterpart's objectivity. Part of this intractable attitude can be blamed upon instructions. In order to make them tougher bargainers, Kremlin leaders usually do not include in their representative's directives any fallback position, thus leaving them singing one stubborn note at the bargaining table until a compromise is worked out back in Moscow.[82]

Thus, with the Kiesinger administration torn between the need for Soviet goodwill and concessions and Soviet negotiators' inability to make major concessions, it is not surprising that by September negotiations had progressed no further than a general understanding regarding the annual delivery of three billion cubic meters of natural gas for five to six years, starting in 1972. By September Herbst, thus, reported that the German industry had little interest in expanding into the Soviet market due to "Soviet administrative hurdles."[83] Once again, *Osthandel* had been stymied.

Nixon's Concepts of East-West Trade

Most of these negotiations occurred below the radar of the Nixon administration, which in any case had turned a blind eye to East-West trade.

Much like his predecessors, Nixon soon had been confronted with the question of East-West trade. His initial response, like that of his predecessors, was noncommittal: commissioning a study on how to expand trade. Unlike his predecessors, though, Nixon enjoyed a more forthcoming approach from Congress on East-West trade. Driven by a vision of East-West trade that would bring jobs and new markets, and ultimately afford U.S. industry's expansion into Eastern Europe, Congress passed the Export Administration Act of 1969. This act struck a balance between the hard-line "economic warfare" stance and the one advancing a liberalized East-West trade. It limited export controls to militarily significant goods.[84] As such, this was a significant step forward from the Export Control Act of 1949, which had prohibited not just military goods but any goods that could lend economic potential to the Soviet Union or Eastern Europe. For the first time since the Second World War, Congress had vested the president with the authority to vastly expand US-Soviet nonmilitary trade. The legislation both Kennedy and Johnson had sought was received by Nixon as a welcome gift.

Yet Nixon did not seize the opportunity Congress had handed him, and the year 1970 saw no advances in US-Soviet trade, save for the commissioning of another study to look into the matter more closely. This is not to say that he was opposed to the general idea of East-West trade. Quite to the contrary, he viewed the boycott policy of the 1950s as anachronistic because "Communist states were too important to ignore."[85] In preparation for Secretary of Agriculture Clifford Hardin's Eastern Europe trip, Nixon had even instructed him to explore economic ties with these communist countries.[86] Yet Nixon neither established clear directives toward liberalizing trade nor displayed much interest in foreign economic issues at all.[87] In fact, during the first two years of Nixon's tenure East-West trade had real importance for the White House only as a political tool amidst an ideological struggle. To that end, it did not matter whether this meant restricting or liberalizing export quotas.[88] Even as a political tool, though, it seemed a rather weak one. When in May 1969 the National Security Council presented a study on the benefits of East-West trade, it concluded that such trade amounted to only $200 million annually and that lifting trade restrictions would increase trade volume with the East only insignificantly. This was due in part to a lack of Soviet currency reserves and also rooted in the problem that the Soviet market was not as readily suited for American goods as it was for Western European ones.[89]

The lack of profits, therefore, placed the issue of liberalizing trade restrictions in the political rather than the economic sphere, and Nixon's subsequent rejections of trade exemptions in the Coordination Committee (COCOM) must be attributed to his mistrust of communist regimes, as "they will never act out of altruism, but only out of self-interest."[90] A summary by C. Fred Bergstein expressed Nixon's views unequivocally. Regarding trade policies with the Soviet Union, he wrote to Kissinger that "I fully recognize that he [Nixon] wishes to avoid giving the Soviets anything at this time."[91] For those parts of the Nixon administration not categorically opposed to trade with the Soviet Union, the absence of firm economic data paired with the political difficulties of liberalizing trade elevated export controls to "an instrument of negotiation."[92] This approach to trade, which linked political conditions to trade concessions, fell in line with Kissinger's geopolitical linkage strategy and Nixon's election slogan of détente as "an era of negotiation."[93]

The political "linkage" of export controls is especially significant with respect to Vietnam, the issue that permeated American foreign policy above all else. Here, the Nixon administration used trade incentives to seek political concessions. In particular, Kissinger and Nixon were hoping that limiting exports to the Eastern bloc "would put pressure on them to help in Vietnam and would signal that we are prepared to deal with them after the war."[94] In his own words, Nixon decided that the U.S. "should be prepared to move generously to liberalize our trade policy toward the Soviet Union and the other Eastern European countries whenever there is sufficient improvement in our overall relations with them."[95] Or, as Kissinger put it, "expanding trade without a political quid pro quo was a gift; there was little the Soviets could do for us economically."[96]

Brandt's policy of economic liberalization in return for nothing but Soviet goodwill, therefore, heavily clashed with Nixon's policy. In essence, Brandt stole Nixon's thunder. In fact, European business deals with Eastern Europe were observed with a sense of helpless frustration in the U.S. "Our policy of denial denies very little and simply forces the satellite nations to obtain comparable products from Britain, France, West Germany, Italy and other European nations, and Japan at the expense of American business and industry."[97]

Ultimately, though, it was not clashing opinions that dominated the White House East-West trade policy in the year of the pipeline deal but neglect. In early March 1970, Nixon sent a memorandum to Kissinger arguing that it was necessary to "farm out" issues of lower priority. "Trade policy is a case in point. This is something where it just isn't going to make a lot of difference whether we move one way or another on the glass tariff. Oil import is also a case in point. While it has some political consequences it is not something I should become deeply involved in."[98] The Nixon White House, then, continued its predecessors' erratic policy on East-West trade, albeit not for lack of conviction on the topic but simply because neither Nixon nor Kissinger viewed it as important enough to bother with.

This, however, was a clear miscalculation, for the Soviets placed paramount importance on trade. As Robert M. Spaulding points out, the Soviets insisted "on material progress in the form of trade and economic cooperation before agreeing to any major new political agreement."[99] East-West trade had opened the door for Brandt to pursue his *Ostpolitik*. Disregarding trade policy to the extent the Nixon administration did, then, created a power vacuum that Western European nations would fill. Beyond trade, though, Brandt's rhetoric in the 1969 West German election campaign offered some interesting possibilities that stood to benefit Nixon's foreign policy.

Initial *Ostpolitik*: Brandt's Honeymoon Period

By the late 1960s, both superpowers hoped to resolve tensions in Europe in order to focus on more pressing matters in the Asian theater: the Soviet Union had to deal with an increasingly hostile China, while the United States was increasingly hampered by the Vietnam War. As such, resolution of the deadlock over Germany was the key element for an understanding and for possibly reducing troop levels and military expenditures in Europe. Chancellor Kiesinger's stubborn refusal to revise Germany's foreign policy and participate in American détente policies became a major source of contention between the FRG and its Western allies in several respects.

The first problem arose from Germany's continued application of the Hallstein Doctrine, which claimed that the FRG was the sole representative of the German people and made it policy not to recognize the GDR until a peace treaty between the allies in the Second World War had been negotiated successfully and the East Germans were able to freely express their political will. Furthermore, no government that recognized the illegitimate government of the GDR could enjoy diplomatic relations with the FRG. While it proved a rather divisive doctrine at times, it nevertheless succeeded in keeping the German question at the forefront of international diplomacy and forced third world countries to side overwhelmingly with the economically stronger West Germany, even as they played the two Germanys against each other for economic aid.[100] Yet the Hallstein Doctrine also effectively blocked the path to diplomatic relations with Eastern European countries, which had naturally recognized the communist GDR over the democratic

FRG. This confrontational policy was seen as anachronistic by Nixon, as communist states were too important to ignore.[101] This issue became a hot topic in the West German election campaign when Cambodia recognized East German statehood on 8 May 1969. The SPD faction of the government under Brandt's leadership was opposed to breaking relations with Cambodia over this recognition, and it was Chancellor Kiesinger who cast the decisive vote in a party-line split on the issue. Even though Brandt remained in the grand coalition for the time being, it became increasingly clear that the internationally divisive Hallstein Doctrine would be discarded should Brandt become chancellor.[102]

The second hurdle that West Germany presented to superpower détente was the issue of the Nuclear Non-Proliferation Treaty. NPT was a key ingredient in the relaxation of tensions between East and West. The United States, concerned about Chinese nuclear weapons tests in 1964, initiated a push for an NPT.[103] The Soviet Union, for its part, was gravely concerned about the possibility of the FRG obtaining nuclear weapons, whether by acquiring them independently or via allied nuclear sharing.[104] For Germans, though, a nuclear strike capability was seen as the only way to make the threat of a nuclear counterstrike credible, should the Soviets single West Germany out for an attack. As German Foreign Minister Gerhard Schröder noted, Soviet interest in a nuclear-free Germany and German interest in reunification needed to remain connected.[105] This stance isolated West Germany from all Eastern-bloc countries as well as most of its Western allies, since no one wanted to see Germany acquire nuclear weapons, even on a sharing basis.[106] Not even the United States was interested in allowing Germany to have nuclear weapons.[107] Brandt had pushed for a quick West German signature to the NPT and was stopped only by Kiesinger's insistence on postponing the decision until after the 28 September elections.[108]

Furthermore, the recognition of the Oder-Neisse line as the final border between Poland and Germany was deemed essential to relaxation of tensions between Germany and its Eastern European neighbors. As long as the FRG did not recognize the Oder-Neisse line, fear of German revanchism remained strong. The powerful political lobby of refugee organizations, however, made it a difficult task to formally surrender territories that were already under Soviet control. While this was true in the case of the SPD, it was even more so for the CDU. With most refugee organizations sympathetic to the more conservative CDU, it would have been political suicide for a CDU politician to recognize the Oder-Neisse line as Germany's eastern border in the 1960s. Insisting on these antiquated positions not only hindered FRG diplomacy but also upset U.S.-Soviet negotiations on détente. Brandt, in contrast, was clearly willing to accept the Oder-Neisse line. On 19 May 1969 Brandt indicated he was ready to talk with Poland over such an acceptance, despite Polish skepticism regarding the fruitfulness of such an endeavor.[109]

Lastly, Brandt appeared to be more flexible than Chancellor Kiesinger on issues of international monetary policy. The strength of the German mark had been a source of contention throughout the Kiesinger administration. On the European side, the French demanded tight monetary control, wishing to stem the flow of currency into West Germany. U.S. interests, stemming from financial overextension in Vietnam, demanded a revaluation of the mark so as to relieve the dollar. With fixed exchange rates as the cornerstone of the international monetary system (known as the Breton-Woods system), any alteration of the exchange rate would be a political act rather than an automatic economic mechanism. When the Breton-Woods system experienced two explosive runs on the mark in May and September 1969, Germans' fear of inflation and sense of frustration vis-à-vis the loosely handled monetary policy of the other Western countries brought the issue of international monetary policy to the forefront of the German election campaign. Brandt, again on the side of Atlantic interests, advocated a revaluation, whereas Kiesinger refused to do so out of a need to cater to his constituency: farmers and conservatives. The first group stood to lose export opportunities while the second retained a general fear of currency manipulation akin to the experience of the Weimar Republic.[110]

In an odd twist of fate, then, the Nixon administration saw Brandt as the potential West German leader with whom U.S. foreign policy could be advanced most effectively. Even so, Nixon had little interest in Germany during the hot phase of the German election campaign. For the Nixon White House, undoubtedly preoccupied with Vietnam, the German election campaign was of secondary significance. Beginning with the student protests at Harvard over the leakage of information regarding the secret bombing raids in Cambodia at the beginning of May, and followed by the fiasco of Hamburger Hill in late May and the publication of photos of recently killed U.S. soldiers in Vietnam in *Life* magazine on 27 June 1969, a highly media-conscious Nixon must have remembered the old adage that all foreign politics is domestic politics.

The American public certainly agreed that Vietnam held primacy over other issues. When asked in January 1969 about the most important problem the United States faced, Vietnam by far topped the list at 40 percent, the highest it would ever be, leaving other international problems at an insignificant 2 percent. The largest anti-war demonstrations in U.S. history, during October and November 1969, certainly underscored that message to the president (Figure 2.2).

results and often unhelpful Soviet demands, West German negotiators continued to push for a general trade agreement. When negotiations for the Long-Term Agreement on Trade and Payments, the Agreement on General Questions of Trade and Navigation, the Protocol on Commodity Trade for 1958, and the Consular Treaty were finally concluded in 1958, they contained many notable concessions on the part of the West Germans.[2]

Adenauer, thus, had carried out Dulles's suggestion for a shift in West German relations with the Soviet Union in the only way possible: through economic means. While Francophile Adenauer would later lean toward a more independent and European-led foreign policy under Charles de Gaulle, his independent attempts to secure a political understanding with the Soviet Union through East-West trade failed.[3] The most notable attempt to push politics as a precondition for trade was Adenauer's attempt to include West Berlin in a Soviet–West German trade agreement, which would have implicitly attested to West German sovereignty in Berlin. Soviet Deputy Trade Minister Borissov simply left, thus sending a clear message to the West Germans about mixing trade and politics.[4] The Soviets did not need *Osthandel* and therefore resisted any attempt to marry political topics to economic incentives.

In the pivotal year of 1959, when Dulles advised CDU Party Chairman and Chancellor Adenauer to reach out to the Soviets, Willy Brandt, then mayor of Berlin and one of the leading figures in the SPD, became a true Atlanticist. In 1959 at the party congress in Bad Godesberg, the SPD rejected its Marxist philosophy, condemned the oppression of the communist dictatorships in Eastern Europe, supported democratic principles with free elections, and embraced a market economy with social responsibilities. This transition from a worker's party to a people's party also altered SPD foreign policy goals. At Bad Godesberg Brandt's support for NATO and the United States' hegemonic role within it was complete. He rejected political considerations that would limit the role of NATO or involve German troops in more Europe-focused defense initiatives.[5] Brandt even went so far as to indicate during his election campaign in 1960 that, as chancellor, he might override party policy and allow tactical, albeit not strategic, nuclear weapons for the German army.[6] In a 1959 speech he advocated "not to veer away from the Western community" but instead seek only those foreign policy goals "which do not weaken the overall position of the West."[7]

This absolute concern for the cohesion of Western unity, unthinkable just a decade later, even led Brandt to oppose Khrushchev's overtures to establish a back channel in March 1959. Clearly signaling his pro-American stance, in 1961 he rejected numerous strategies that would

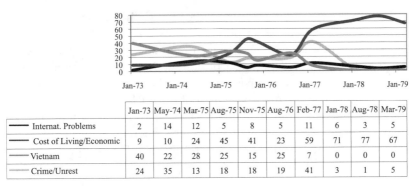

	Jan-73	May-74	Mar-75	Aug-75	Nov-75	Aug-76	Feb-77	Jan-78	Aug-78	Mar-79
—— Internat. Problems	2	14	12	5	8	5	11	6	3	5
—— Cost of Living/Economic	9	10	24	45	41	23	59	71	77	67
—— Vietnam	40	22	28	25	15	25	7	0	0	0
—— Crime/Unrest	24	35	13	18	18	19	41	3	1	5

Figure 2.2 Gallup Poll of Americans: "What are the most important problems facing the US today?" (1969–1975). Gallup Organization, *The Gallup Poll* [CD-ROM] (Wilmington, DE: Scholarly Resources, 1997), 2252, 18 June 1970; Gallup, 2292, 18 March 1971; Gallup, 2338, 19 December 1971; Gallup, 48, 6 August 1972; Gallup, 230, 31 January 1974; Gallup, 353, 12 September 1974; Gallup, 443, 3 April 1975.

Another reason for the relative American silence on the German election might have been an American presumption that Kiesinger would win again. When Nixon asked Kiesinger about the election during their meeting on 7 August, Kiesinger exuded confidence, boasting that "most Social Democrats were resigned to losing and most Christian Democrats convinced of winning."[111]

When the election results came in on the night of 28 September, Kiesinger's CDU remained the largest party, albeit with only a narrow majority in its coalition government with the Free Democratic Party. Nixon's quick telephone call to congratulate Kiesinger may indicate he was pleased by a continued conservative German government, but certainly bespeaks of how little the Nixon White House understood the German political situation close to a year after being in office.[112] Within the next couple of weeks Brandt convinced the FDP to join the SPD, giving him a razor-thin majority in the Bundestag and making Brandt the new chancellor-elect of Germany.

The American response to Brandt's sudden rise to power was divided. Nixon, maintaining a cold war warrior ideology, was opposed to Brandt in principle for being a Socialist and in particular for the thrust of his Eastern policy. As Hillenbrand recalled, Nixon viewed Brandt as "ideologically suspect" and his attempts at selective détente as "downright treasonable."[113] Kissinger, in his own words, approached Brandt's election with more flexibility as he "recognized the inevitable" and was "determined to spare no effort to mute the latent incompatibility between Germany's national aims and its Atlantic and European ties."[114]

Looking beyond the uncanny dedication to the European allies undergirding Kissinger's description of his own actions, Kissinger's support of Brandt certainly had more pragmatic reasons. One was the previously mentioned prospect of eliminating West Germany's resistance to American rapprochement with the Soviet Union: *Ostpolitik* would necessitate Germany's signing of the NPT and the acceptance of the Oder-Neisse border. The other reason for lending support to Germany's new foreign policy was Kissinger's inherent suspicion of Soviet intentions. Brandt needed Nixon, for only with U.S. support would it be possible to induce the Soviet Union to compromise vis-à-vis West Germany.[115]

Barring Nixon's ideological concerns, the White House had every reason to support Brandt in the same fashion it had supported Kiesinger. Kissinger viewed the FRG's attempt at unification legitimate and unalterable. Any American attempt to block a policy leading to unification would force the FRG to abandon the Western alliance. *Ostpolitik* therefore was a "must." This was, however, not very troubling to Kissinger since he assessed Brandt as severely limited in his "attempt to be much more flexible toward the East."[116] In short, Kissinger concurred with the large segment of the American public who did not think much would come of *Ostpolitik*.

Kissinger, thus underestimating the threat of Brandt's *Ostpolitik*, was pleased when Kiesinger's outdated foreign policy came to an end. Kissinger quickly agreed to see Germany as "a partner, not a client" when notified by Egon Bahr, Brandt's emissary, that under SPD leadership Germany would pursue a more independent policy toward Eastern Europe.[117] While the language Bahr employed seemed rather direct coming from a previously submissive FRG, Kissinger seemed to appreciate Germany's more independent approach toward alliance politics. He is said to have responded "Thank God" when Bahr elaborated the fact that Germany would not seek constant reassurances of friendship from the United States.[118] Kissinger even remembered from the meeting that "to him [Brandt], America was a weight to be added to West Germany's scale in the right way at the right time, but his priority was to restore relations between the two Germanys above all."[119] Kissinger's assessment of Bahr is less flattering than that of Brandt, considering him "a German nationalist who wanted to exploit Germany's central position to bargain with both sides" and "was obviously not as unquestioningly dedicated to Western unity as the people we had known in the previous government."[120]

Regardless of the harsh tone and the exploitative policy, Kissinger promised Bahr that the U.S. would deal with Germany as "a partner, not a client," and the two statesmen agreed on establishing a back chan-nel that bypassed the State Department in order to facilitate closer co-operation.[121] This pleased Kissinger for two reasons. First, it enhanced his position within the Nixon administration, and second, it allowed him to conduct foreign diplomacy the way he liked: through unoffi-cial back-channel dialogues. For Kissinger, the establishment of back channels, which had also been initiated with numerous other countries, allowed him to consolidate decision-making for U.S. foreign policies in the White House, i.e., under President Nixon and himself. Nixon clearly approved of this policy and had initiated back channels for Kissinger with governments of other countries, such as France and the Soviet Union. Back channels also reflected the way in which Kissinger thought foreign policy should be conducted: as agreements between gentlemen, away from the scrutiny of the public eye.

On the official level, Brandt's inaugural address to the German par-liament on 28 October 1969 was even more promising. He elaborated on all the policies that the United States could have wanted from a German rapprochement with the East, even mentioning that "NATO continues to guarantee our safety in the future. Its firm cohesion is the basis for the common effort to reach a détente in Europe."[122] He emphasized that "the German people need peace in the full sense of the word, also with the peoples of the Soviet Union and all the peoples of Eastern Europe," and went on to commit his presidency to formal negotiations with the Soviet Union and Poland, and the approval of the Non-Proliferation Treaty.[123] Furthermore, Brandt abandoned the Hallstein Doctrine alto-gether and accepted the GDR as a political entity with which one could negotiate.[124]

One harbinger of the coming tensions between the U.S. and Germany was also included in Brandt's speech. He criticized Nixon where it hurt most: Vietnam. As Kissinger's advisor, Helmut Sonnenfeld, summa-rized, Brandt's public view of the U.S. role in Vietnam was extremely critical.[125] He cited the key passage in Brandt's inaugural address on the new relationship with the United States as a possible reason for the West German outspokenness on Vietnam. Brandt self-confidently assumed a more independent role for West Germany within the trans-atlantic partnership: "Our common interests require neither additional assurances nor recurrent declarations. They are capable of support-ing a more independent policy and a more active partnership on the part of Germany." In other words, the Brandt administration realized that it did not need to defer to American interests because the United States was so committed to Europe that it could not afford to withdraw, barring a direct political affront to the United States. In an ominous comment, Kissinger noted on the memo that "we will come to regret German 'flexibility.'"[126]

Despite this small blemish, on a political level the White House had good reason to be pleased with Brandt and to support his policies. The Non-Proliferation Treaty was signed on 18 November 1969, and German talks with the Soviet Union and Poland began in December 1969 and February 1970, respectively. Accepting Bahr's anti-American intentions was a small price to pay, especially since Kissinger considered Brandt to be solidly in the Western camp.[127] American public opinion, while cautious, was also convinced of Brandt's loyalty to the West. *New York Times* correspondent Roger Berthoud outlined Brandt's *Ostpolitik* in detail and concluded that "as former mayor of Berlin Herr Brandt is fully aware of the value of solidarity and has none of the illusions about communism which his political opponents love to attribute to him."[128]

In his memoirs Kissinger remembered the initial White House approach to Brandt's *Ostpolitik* as very supportive. Driven by the realization that without the support of its allies the FRG had a very weak bargaining position vis-à-vis the Soviet Union, the White House stood ready to support Brandt's initiatives toward the East without reservation.[129] Whether this support of *Ostpolitik* extended to Nixon is not clear, but it is unlikely. Kissinger recalls that in January 1970, roughly three months after Brandt came to power, Nixon's "suspicion of Brandt had not abated."[130] Nixon also was concerned that selective détente would act as a Soviet means of dividing the West. In a statement at the NATO ministerial conference in April 1969 he warned against Soviet tactics of isolating individual NATO partners. "Since we approach a time of negotiations, it is important that we do not agree to a 'selective' form of rapprochement that Moscow determined."[131] In essence, Nixon was reminding NATO to choose Alliance—not Détente.

Nixon's relative quietness on Brandt's *Ostpolitik* in the winter of 1969 must be viewed in light of Nixon's other priorities, specifically Vietnam. His failure to stall the American anti-war movement until an "honorable" withdrawal from Vietnam could be achieved, in conjunction with the North Vietnamese refusal to give way in diplomatic negotiations, left Nixon with a conflict that had a more immediate impact on his popularity.[132] His announcement of troop withdrawals from Vietnam in September 1969 and the subsequent talks in Paris with the North Vietnamese held much greater political risk for Nixon than did Brandt's *Ostpolitik*. In addition, negotiations with the Soviet Union, the Strategic Arms Limitation Talks (SALT), began in Helsinki in November and stood to affect the United States more directly than did West Germany's foreign policy. Once Germany had taken all the steps the Nixon administration considered crucial in "adjusting" German foreign policy to clear the way for a superpower détente, Brandt and his *Ostpolitik* held less interest for President Nixon. Through the removal of the "German problem," the United States was now able to consolidate its position in Europe, reserving its strength for dealing with Vietnam and the Soviet Union. Americans viewed Brandt and his *Ostpolitik* with the benevolence of a grandfather toward an impulsive child who, when confronted with the realities of life, will soon come to understand the limits of his idealism. With regard to German-U.S. relations, Brandt was in his "honeymoon" period. For the first hundred days, he stayed within the acceptable political framework of what Kissinger had predicted: a limited rapprochement with the East that did not upset the status quo.

The First Gas-Pipeline Deal

Kissinger and Nixon's preoccupation with political issues blinded them to the economic and cultural implications of East-West trade, developments that stood to profoundly affect Germany's foreign policy orientation. Unlike the Nixon administration, the Soviets valued trade highly. While they—most likely—did not seek to buy Lenin's proverbial rope with which to hang the Western capitalists, they did see an opportunity to gain influence in West Germany and improve their hard-currency position.

Soon after it became clear that Brandt would be chancellor, Soviet Premier Kosygin sent his son-in-law, Professor Belonov, to Bonn on 20 November 1969 in order to reiterate the strong Soviet interest in forming a commission on industrial-technological cooperation. The Economics Ministry's assessment of the Belonov visit was ecstatic:

> There are many indications that the Soviet Union is ending its policy aimed at conducting trade agreements with other Western industrialized nations while isolating the Federal Republic. It appears that they will now also suggest to the [German] Federal Government a closer cooperation in economic matters and its institutionalization on a governmental level.[133]

Brandt pulled out all the stops. Under Bahr's auspices, the German government coaxed talks along between the Soviets and representatives of the German steel industry. In an unprecedented move, Brandt directly encouraged Ruhrgas AG to sign on to the deal, which boiled down to aiding a future competitor to gain a foothold in the German natural gas market.[134] After much political pressure, the long-negotiated pipeline deal was to be finalized by January 1970.

Opposition to the deal quickly formed within the German government, since West Germany had not managed to use the negotiations to gain from the Soviets "a basic set of rules, regulating trade deals between Western countries and the Soviet Union."[135] Deputy Undersecretary Herbst thought such concessions quite feasible, considering the unprecedented nature of the loans that West German banks had extended to the Soviet Union, expanding the customary five-year limit to eight and ten years. The West German government also secured the loan with a Hermes credit of unusually high proportions (50 percent). Even the repayment procedures proved to be extraordinary: the Soviet Union provided only 1/11 of the value of the trade deal as down payment and did not have to start repaying the loan until roughly three years after delivery—and then at an interest rate that was 1.5 percent below the customary rate. Additionally, installments would increase significantly toward the end of the loan, providing further financial flexibility for the Soviet Union.[136] In short, the Brandt administration had bent over backward in order to make the deal as lucrative as possible for the Soviet Union and quietly made up the difference between the customary market rate of 6.5 percent interest and the 5 percent the Soviet Union had demanded and received.[137]

Undersecretary Harkort voiced an even stronger condemnation of the deal in regard to the repercussions on inter-allied relations.

> 1) It can be that special conditions become necessary for trade deals with the East if they exceed common standards. But in that case they should be chosen due to their unusual size, not because they are deals with the East— unusual deals with the West should then receive the same treatment.

> 2) One and a half decades have we fought against a race to undercut credit rates and conditions in the trade with the East, among others. If new conditions have now become necessary, one should try to coordinate them with the other large export countries.[138]

According to Harkort, this deal also demonstrated a clear preference for business deals with the East over those with the West. This, of course, was true in the sense that German deals with other Western European or American companies were not subsidized with such outstanding credit conditions. Broadly speaking, Harkort criticized the pro-Eastern and anti-Western attitude of the German government in general. Political intervention to help a business deal along seemed acceptable when dealing with the East, while a deal with U.S. companies would be heavily scrutinized. Back in 1966 the CSU leader Franz Josef Strauß had pushed for a German opening to the Soviet Union as a means to balance the American purchase of the German DEA petroleum company.[139]

Brandt's own blunt refusal to consider U.S. objections to the preferential trade system set up by the European Economic Community also indicated his unwillingness to consider U.S. economic interests.[140]

Lack of intergovernmental and international consultation on a deal of such political consequence was the final point of criticism advanced by Herbst and Harkort. No specific reference to the U.S. is made here, which in and of itself is significant in that even the faction of the German government that was critical of *Osthandel* did not feel a special obligation to the Western superpower.

Nixon might have sensed the spirit of European independence as he suggested to Kissinger an informal meeting with "some major European ambassadors" to restore U.S. moral authority and leadership within the alliance.[141] Kissinger rejected Nixon's concern and assured him that his European policy was "on the right track." Nixon, however, was not as convinced and suggested the possibility of another visit to Europe.[142] On 19 January 1970 Nixon reiterated his desire to retake the initiative in alliance politics rather than "stand by and let Italy, France and Germany go off in all directions," and National Security Council (NSC) member Alexander Haig noted that the president had raised similar concerns several times previously.[143] Nixon's somewhat disillusioned view of Western European foreign policy initiatives must have been informed, at least in part, by the unsuccessful European intervention in Middle Eastern diplomacy.[144] Yet Nixon's vision of reasserting strong transatlantic leadership was falling on deaf ears within his own administration. By late January, the NSC had not even managed to conduct a systematic review of U.S. policy vis-à-vis its European allies, despite Nixon's prodding "for some months."[145]

Essentially, the discrepancy between Nixon's wishes and their implementation by the National Security Council stemmed from a difference in opinion between Nixon and Kissinger. Kissinger did not advance a tough ideological line in the NSC but embraced the flexibility offered by Brandt's *Ostpolitik*. The National Security Council staff also took a lax stand on European issues, arguing that "there may be no particular urgency to a reexamination of our European policy, nor any clear ordering of issues that must be decided" as the United States faced "no imminent crisis" in Europe.[146]

This approach, however, left the Nixon administration somewhat dumbfounded when Brandt scored sweeping successes within his first hundred days in office. In a perfect example of how to deal with the Soviets, the qualitative shift in West German–Soviet relations was inaugurated by a sizable trade deal, the first natural gas pipeline deal. In using *Osthandel* as a cornerstone of Brandt's *Ostpolitik*, this trade deal was the first of many, fostered and financially backed by the Brandt government, to pave the way for closer economic and political cooperation between the two nominally hostile powers.

Brandt followed this trade deal up with political successes. In the first move that exceeded Kissinger's expectations of German diplomatic maneuverability, the FRG intensified diplomatic contacts with the Soviet Union, conducting high-level talks between Bahr and Soviet foreign minister Gromyko from 30 January through 18 February 1970. Despite this flurry of activity, Kissinger stood behind Brandt's integrity. In a memo to Nixon he wrote:

> He [Brandt] rejects the idea that Germany should be free-floating between East and West and he remains strongly committed to NATO and Western European integration. Indeed he believes his Eastern policy can be successful only if Germany is firmly anchored in the West. He has in effect renounced formal reunification as the aim of German policy but hopes over the long run to achieve special ties between the two German states, which will reflect the fact that they have a common national heritage.[147]

He followed this up with a concluding assessment that Brandt, and the other two leaders within the SPD, Herbert Wehner and Helmut Schmidt, were "conducting a responsible policy of reconciliation and normalization with the East."[148] Kissinger's concern was therefore directed not toward Brandt or his *Ostpolitik* but toward the Soviets' ability to use this new approach to their advantage.[149] Unlike Nixon, he saw no necessary incompatibility between Western integration on the one hand and some degree of normalization with the East on the other, but he did warn of the possibility of long-term leverage for the Soviets.

> The Soviets, having achieved their first set of objectives may then confront the FRG with the proposition that a real and lasting improvement in the FRG's relations with the GDR and other Eastern countries can only be achieved if Bonn loosens its Western ties. Having already invested heavily in their Eastern policy, the Germans may at this point see themselves as facing agonizing choices. It should be remembered that in the 1950s, many Germans ... enthralled by the vision of Germany as a "bridge" between East and West, argued against Bonn's incorporation in Western institutions.[150]

Kissinger feared that the Soviets could use *Ostpolitik* to pursue selective détente, which would create more demands and concessions from Brandt.[151] Brandt must indeed have felt this pressure as he tried to reach the Soviets through both economic and political avenues. While Kissinger was certainly correct that the Soviets felt more comfortable with the new West German government and its economic gestures, *Ostpolitik* did not result in the stability the Soviets desired from East-West relations.

The Inter-German Summit Meeting: A Rude Awakening

Upon Brandt's insistence, a meeting between the heads of the two German states, Willy Brandt and Willy Stoph, occurred on 19 March 1970. Brandt had responded to one of Walter Ulbricht's propaganda tools, a proposal for a summit meeting to ratify a treaty on basic relations between East and West Germany. One day before Stoph invited Brandt to the GDR, the Soviet Union had also expressed interest in talks with the three former allies, to commence in only eight days time.[152] For Kissinger, the idea of new "partnership" between Germany and the U.S. turned sour over those proposals. Both Bahr and Brandt rejected American advice on when and how to negotiate with the East.

Kissinger had viewed the short time frame as impossible and thereby clashed with an eager Brandt, who wanted to see this through without giving the East Germans an out. As mentioned previously, Kissinger had had concerns about *Ostpolitik* all along because he felt that it might revive the "vision of Germany as a bridge between East and West" as well as "generating suspicions among Germany's Western associates as to its reliability as a partner."[153] Brandt's willingness to initiate talks with East Germany, against Kissinger's advice, demonstrated a level of inter-German independence that was clearly uncomfortable for the Nixon administration.[154] More importantly, the Americans' loss of control over the West German–East German dialogue eliminated intervention against a pan-German nationalism. This might have threatened the division of Germany, which was seen as crucial to the status quo of the Cold War.[155]

In a memorandum to Nixon on 10 March 1970, the very day the discussion over the eight-day time limit would arise between Kissinger and Brandt, both Nixon and Kissinger agreed that there was little chance of success for West Germany's negotiation. Nixon summed this up the following way: "It looks like Brandt is over his head. He has very little to offer and they have a great deal." More importantly, though, he already saw an opportunity in these negotiations for the fall of Brandt's government. Next to Kissinger's concern that there were "serious misgivings" over Brandt's policies—Brandt might feel compelled to give away more than would be prudent in order to succeed and keep his coalition with the Liberals in place—Nixon remarked on the memo that "if Brandt continues on this soft headed line—this would be in our interest."[156]

Yet it was Kissinger's other fear—of a revival of German nationalism—that ultimately brought him to side with Nixon in opposing *Ostpolitik*. Despite heavy security precautions by the feared East German secret police, the Stasi, East German citizens in Erfurt broke through the roadblocks to cheer Willy Brandt on for his attempts to establish inter-German dialogue. This unusually emotional response by the German people sent a warning signal to all involved parties that German nationalism was alive and well. Little was achieved on the diplomatic level during the summit, but the people's reaction showed how destabilizing inter-German rapprochement could be. An alliance between the two Germanys could create a situation in which Germany would maneuver between the East and the West in the tradition of Bismarck.[157] Kissinger's emerging reluctance toward *Ostpolitik* can be seen by his "Baloney" remark in response to Sonnenfeld's statement describing *Ostpolitik* as advantageous for the United States.[158]

To Kissinger, the Erfurt meeting must have demonstrated that the very opposite was becoming more and more likely. Nixon, however, viewed the Erfurt summit as a problem for the East. His acceptance of Cold War realities, i.e., the Soviet sphere of influence, was rather obvious in his remark on the popular reaction to Willy Brandt's visit in Erfurt. On his daily news summary, next to the report of "shouting and cheering East Germans" in Erfurt, he noted "K[issinger].- Good. This will scare [the] hell out of the Soviets. They have their problems and may now come to us to pull them out."[159]

The American media had also begun to voice objections to *Ostpolitik*. Even the leftist magazine *The Nation* highlighted the emotional atmosphere in which the East Germans welcomed Willy Brandt, and pointed to the role of the superpowers in "watching developments with interest—and a certain trepidation" as well as asking the rhetorical question whether the division of Germany was necessarily bad, considering "the exploits of German militarism over the past hundred years."[160] In response to the second meeting of the two German heads of state in Kassel on 21 May 1970, the *National Review,* a magazine more representative of Nixon's voters, had an even more negative reaction to *Ostpolitik*. Under the heading "Willy Brandt turns East," Brandt was depicted as a spineless politician who was being influenced by "radicals" such as Bahr, Bauer, and Wehner, who wished to appease the East and sought eventual neutrality. This article predicted that in the long run, *Ostpolitik* could cause the line between free world and totalitarian regimes to be eradicated, and called for a check on "the destruction of the Western defenses in Europe and the Soviet penetration of the European West."[161]

Nixon's views of Brandt's *Ostpolitik* were consistently negative. He saw the East-West conflict in a strongly ideological light and later belabored in his memoirs that "never once in my career have I doubted that the Communists meant it when they say that their goal is to bring the world under Communist Control."[162] What changed in the spring of 1970 was Kissinger's stance on *Ostpolitik*. Kissinger had felt confident that through the back-channel negotiations conducted between Bahr and himself he could contain Willy Brandt and his *Ostpolitik*, even use them in pursuit of U.S. foreign policy goals. For Brandt's honeymoon period—his first hundred days in office—this approach had certainly worked well, and Kissinger was able to moderate Nixon's ideological dislike for Brandt and his *Ostpolitik*. However, overconfident in his ability to control Germany's foreign policy and underestimating Brandt's political successes with the East, he had ignored Nixon's repeated call for a more assertive American leadership within the alliance. The very fact that Brandt had managed to arrange an inter-German summit meeting, let alone the stunning display of latent German nationalism, forced Kissinger to reevaluate his stance on *Ostpolitik*. But lack of a long-term concept of how to deal with the display of German nationalism in Erfurt, or the threat of a selective West German détente with Eastern Europe, left the Nixon administration without an effective strategy to address the issue. The end of March 1970 finally saw Nixon and Kissinger in agreement on the undesirability of *Ostpolitik*.

The German-American Summit on *Ostpolitik*, April 1970

Effective U.S. control of West Germany's new foreign policy was still impeded on the economic front. Kissinger continued to miss the apparent link between *Osthandel* and *Ostpolitik*, despite such a suggestion on the part of the U.S. embassy in Bonn.

> The SPD/FDP government continued the previous government's support of the negotiations, and some believe that the signing of the agreement (February 1, 1970) was arranged to lend atmospheric support to the Moscow visit of Egon Bahr, the State Secretary in the Chancellor's Office …
>
> It is clear that the FRG hopes for an improvement in the political climate from improved economic relationships. It regards the gas deal as the first big step toward closer economic relations with the USSR.[163]

The embassy report also cited a CDU expert as opposing the deal on the grounds that "one should not entrust to one's 'foe' the responsibility for providing basic energy supplies" and that "it is foolish to finance Soviet economic development at the cost of the FRG."[164] Yet Kissinger, only concerning himself with political diplomacy, expressed little concern for the intensification of trade with the Soviet Union, and even pushed Nixon to be more lenient on COCOM export controls.

Kissinger clearly did not appreciate the emphasis that the Soviets placed on trade as a sign of goodwill and as a means to complement any deficiencies in the Soviet five-year plan. In the ninth Soviet five-year plan (1971–1975) Western imports on credit played a key role in adding production capabilities and improving the efficiency of already existing structures.[165] In fact, foreign trade was supposed to rise by 33–35 percent during those five years. Apart from an emphasis on computers and automobiles, this five-year plan called for priority development of atomic power, machinery, the chemical and petrochemical sectors, and natural gas.[166] In all of these priority areas, the Soviet Union lagged behind the West. East-West trade, then, would be the key to satisfying these five-year goals. Large-scale contracts offered to Western companies with little or no down payment, to be paid for with the products of these manufacturing plants, was the Soviets' strategy to meet these goals without depleting their own hard currency resources.

Brandt hoped that West Germany would be heavily involved in meeting these goals. The German-Soviet natural gas pipeline deal would be the model, the cornerstone for a much-desired trade agreement. The interdepartmental communication between the chancellor's office and the Economics Ministry revealed the importance Brandt placed on these economic dealings. When Economics Minister Schiller seemed reluctant to take further steps to intensify trade with the East, as he saw significant problems in trade liberalization and the inclusion of West Berlin, Brandt intervened, asking that the chancellor's office be involved in any consultations between the Economics Ministry and the Foreign Office on this trade issue.[167] After consultations between Schiller and Brandt, an understanding was reached that a trade agreement would be in the general interest of the FRG but seemed too unrealistic at the moment.[168]

For West Germany, economic ties and incentives had to be the key to rapprochement with the Soviet Union. The FRG was in no position to offer a meaningful military or strategic concession that in and of itself could have enticed the Soviet Union to pursue détente. The special emphasis the German government placed on intensification of East-West trade was also reflected in the fact that Egon Bahr would become a special envoy for international business relations under the Schmidt government.

Brandt's emphasis on relations with the East also created discomfort on a political level, among the opposition as well as within his coalition. He had demonstrated Germany's newfound independence by postponing the customary White House trip for any new German chancellor, which traditionally occurred soon after the October inauguration, until far into the New Year. As Kissinger explained to Nixon, "Brandt is trying to carve out for himself an image of greater independence from us (he referred to this in his inaugural address) and ... for this reason, he does not wish to seem to be rushing to see you."[169] Yet this greater independence only went so far. Unlike U.S. presidents, who wield absolute power over their secretaries, a majority of German ministers have to agree to a policy before it can be implemented. After the Erfurt meeting in March 1970, the German cabinet forced Brandt to "postpone a decision on whether to move into full-fledged negotiations with Moscow on renunciation of force or merely to continue exploratory conversations" until Brandt had coordinated his foreign policy with Nixon. An American assessment of the chancellor's trip also suggested that Brandt's association with the U.S. president would help him silence the conservative opposition in the FRG.[170] Brandt's visit to Nixon was of paramount importance to the new German chancellor. Brandt needed to come away with Nixon's blessing of his *Ostpolitik* in order to quiet concerns among both the opposition and his own ranks. In a way, the German public wanted to see how the U.S. president would react to Germany's independent maneuvers.

Brandt had a very clear sense of what this summit meeting should look like. For one, he wanted it to happen in April, which caused a scheduling conflict for the White House. Nixon had implemented a new rule restricting the visits of foreign dignitaries to two days per month in order to cut down on the number of foreign visitors to the White House. As the Danish prime minister had already been invited for two days in April, Nixon had to make an exception to this rule so they could schedule the German chancellor.[171]

Brandt further caused uproar by insisting that the time he was allotted for his appointment with Nixon was insufficient. Nixon proved intransigent. In a memo by Al Haig, Special Assistant to the President, to Dwight Chapin, offered Brandt a time that did not please the visitor and noted, "Let's work out Saturday [the day of the meeting] problem—but the P[resident] won't do 9 am and maybe not 9:30 [the originally scheduled time]."[172] The way Chapin worded the note provides a hint of how difficult it must have been to convince Nixon of the necessity of a longer meeting with Brandt.

Kissinger recalls the summit between Brandt and Nixon in early April 1970 as "surprisingly cordial, given the fact that neither man would have sought out the other's company had not fate thrust the leadership of great nations upon them." Kissinger then elaborates on the ideological reasons for this, pointing out that "Nixon had genuine doubts about those he saw as personalities of the left."[173] In this, Kissinger's assessment was probably accurate. For Nixon, close ties with the communist bloc were problematic and Brandt, as a person of the left, highly unreliable. Nixon's two memoirs, *The Memoirs of Richard Nixon* and *In the Arena*, confirm this point. In them, Brandt is only mentioned once in passing, whereas Nixon treats other Germans, such as Otto von Bismarck, with reverence.

The summit meeting between the two heads of state demonstrated a conceptional difference between the German and U.S. leadership that could almost be described as "generational." Chronologically, this would of course be inaccurate as both leaders were born in the same year, yet the ideological constructs that clashed during the summit meeting are reminiscent of the deep divide between the conservative "silent majority" of Nixon voters and the progressive movements of the '68ers. While Brandt did not associate with the protest movements directly, his attempts at overcoming the Cold War stalemate with gestures such as the *Warschauer Kniefall* won him immense popularity among this newer generation.[174] Clearly, the most significant difference was between the two statesmen's approaches to Vietnam. To Nixon, support for his conduct of the Vietnam War would have been the greatest political "gift" Brandt could have brought with him from Europe. Brandt, on the other hand, while never openly criticizing Nixon for the conduct of the Vietnam War, was unwilling to offer more than tacit support.[175]

Given this wary approach to Brandt and his delegation, disagreement was unavoidable. Brandt clearly saw himself speaking for a new generation in a speech at a White House dinner given in his honor.

> Our primary goal has to be to conceptualize the 1970s in such a clear way that it helps the younger generation create an appropriate and convincing perspective. You in America and we in Europe ... are dealing with a new generation. It is full of movement ... experiences the many transitions of our time and searches for long-lasting concepts. It is our task to achieve this goal.[176]

Brandt probably did not mean to insult Nixon. Later in a letter to a member of the Bundestag, Horst Krockert, he explained his lack of criticism over Vietnam as follows:

> Since then [Brandt's inaugural address] I have declined to publicly comment [on Vietnam], not even to the reports on the events of My Lai. I think it inappropriate to comment on this in light of the strong condemnation by President Nixon and in light of the moral debate that the media coverage has triggered within the American nation. ...
>
> The American government under President Nixon seeks peace in Vietnam. There can be no doubt about this. ... I believe we should support the American government in its will to end this war on that basis [self-determination of the Vietnamese people].[177]

Nonetheless, as Nixon was facing student riots and the U.S. population viewed domestic unrest as the most important problem facing the nation at the time, this was not the supportive statement Nixon would have hoped for.[178]

Even worse than a lecture on Vietnam was that Kissinger soon learned that Bahr was not fully revealing the extent of Germany's secret negotiations with the Soviet Union. While certainly no Rapallo, Bahr had nonetheless been in negotiations on a German-Soviet friendship treaty. Only when confronted by Kissinger about papers that were exchanged during Soviet-German talks did Bahr admit to "holding in writing formulations that had been discussed." He summarized these "formulations" as drafts dealing with "the renunciation of force," and the "respect for (not recognition of) all European frontiers."[179] In short, Bahr had withheld drafts of key elements of the Soviet-German negotiations.

Despite this lack of trust, the Nixon administration would not openly oppose *Ostpolitik.* No U.S. administration could publicly stand in the way of West German efforts to reestablish economic and cultural links with the East, especially after Nixon had campaigned on that very idea himself. As a result, the Nixon administration was forced to resort to offhand comments that hinted at U.S. reservations about the divergent German policy. Kissinger indirectly conveyed his fears to Defense Minister Schmidt when he questioningly stated that "*Ostpolitik* surely would not jeopardize German loyalties to the alliance," following this with an implied threat of political repercussions should Brandt stray from the Western line.[180]

Nixon duly reiterated this point in a private conversation with Brandt on 11 April. He confessed faith in Brandt's policies and "was certain that [the Germans] did not think of jeopardizing proven friendships." Similarly, he warned that "insecurities" might arise in France, England, and the United States with regard to *Ostpolitik,* and that the German agreement needed "to stay in close contact in all East-West issues."[181] Even more bluntly, Nixon advised Brandt not to ever drop an old friend for a new friend unless he was sure that the new friend was better than his old one.[182]

Officially, Brandt left the summit with the White House's blessing for *Ostpolitik,* not because Nixon began to appreciate Brandt's ideology but simply because the Nixon administration could not afford to be portrayed as the one ally obstructing either détente or a rapprochement of the two Germanys. Despite its misgivings about the ultimate direction of Brandt's foreign policy, the Nixon administration had little choice but to publicly endorse *Ostpolitik*. Brandt's later claim that Nixon and Kissinger did not understand the novelty of his policies is symbolic of the White House's approach. Kissinger responds to this claim in his memoirs: "He was wrong. We got the point. We were simply not persuaded by the argument and we thought it more tactful not to pursue it."[183]

Kissinger's reminiscence on the tactfulness with which the Nixon-Kissinger team pursued its diplomacy may or may not be accurate. In either case, there were more significant forces that impacted Nixon's decision to grin and bear it. Undoubtedly, if U.S. foreign policy had been determined by Nixon's personal convictions alone, he would have reined in Brandt and limited him to a restrictive détente in the wake of Nixon's own approaches to the Soviet Union. As it was, Nixon thought it politically unwise to oppose Brandt in public. The obsession with Brandt's popularity and his policies may be one of the best illustrations of outside forces affecting Nixon's decision making.

As indicated in the first chapter, with the Kennedy or Johnson administrations it is imperative to understand the interactions between different administrative branches in order to pinpoint the White House position on a matter. Nixon and Kissinger's obsession with maintaining control and secrecy, however, short-circuited this type of administrative dialogue during Nixon's tenure. Instead, Nixon paid careful attention to public opinion and news media. Brandt enjoyed benevolent press coverage and tremendous public support in Germany and the United States alike. Had Nixon hindered Brandt in carrying out his *Ostpolitik*, he would have run the risk of being branded a hypocrite. After all, it was Nixon himself who had proclaimed his tenure an era of negotiation. Unable to stop Brandt, Nixon thus could not sideline his German ally by exerting the leadership that he sought in the transatlantic alliance.

Eastern Dilemmas over Détente

Oddly enough, the "new friends" in the East had troubles of their own in sorting out foreign policy priorities. As it turned out, Nixon was correct in his assessment of the Erfurt meeting. The forceful display of German nationalism shook the Eastern alliance. Pursuit of détente would increasingly heighten the risk of independent-minded allies. East Germany, with its independent-minded General Secretary Walter Ulbricht, was a prime example. Ulbricht, fascinated with cybernetics, had traded tight control of scientific development for a modern, Western-style bureaucracy with a focus on innovation and results. To that end, he had entertained ideas of limited cooperation with the West.[184] This "New Economic System" shifted power from party ideologues to "specialists," leaving the Communist Party with less influence. More importantly, though, such "specialists" could intensify political and economic contacts with West Germany to a much greater degree than the Soviet leadership felt comfortable with.

Conversely, just as the Soviets had concerns over East German *Westkontakte,* East German officials believed Soviet relations with West Germany were strengthening the wrong Germany. Despite cybernetics, East Germany expected its allies to place the political aspects of their foreign policy over the economic ones. As the Soviets embraced *Westhandel* under Brandt in large volumes, the East German position on allied trade became more reserved.

> Recent experiences in regard to the foreign trade of the FRG have shown that the leadership has not abandoned the totally hopeless attempt at using economic relations as a means to exert political pressure and use as a propaganda tool. Thus, we must increase our caution and may never forget that the FRG will try everything to harm the GDR. We want to and must only import from the FRG as much as we export. It is in the interest of the GDR to increase trade with other capitalist industrialized countries quicker than with the FRG. ...
>
> There is still a contradiction between demands for too many imports and an insufficient willingness to focus on high and effective exports.[185]

As "West German imperialism attempts to gradually destroy the socia[186]list order of the GDR," the "socialist economy of the GDR has to be protected" and "these are not the conditions in which cooperation between the GDR and the FRG in regard to industrial production, scientific or technology can be undertaken."[187] In this sense, East Germany advanced the concept of dealing with a vilified West Germany, the very same strategy the Soviets would later use in a similar attempt to maintain alliance cohesion. Ulbricht sought to strike the very same balance Brezhnev had achieved: while East-West trade was necessary to improve the East German balance of payment, the socialist state and its organizations needed to counter the "constant exposure with the dangerous West German imperialism and its new forms and methods" through tighter political control.[188]

East Germans were familiar with the balancing act of allowing Western products to enter the country on one hand but trying to keep out Western influences on the other. A good example of trade containing such infusion of Western ideas along with Western technology quickly arose at the chemical factory "Friedrich Engels" in Premnitz. East German workers there had established "personal contacts" with West German engineers, necessitating the removal of the factory supervisor and a factory-wide reeducation conference to stress the "necessary unity and combined strength of the party collective."[189] Nonetheless, the East Germans wished to continue this restrictive trade with the FRG for its economic benefits. The Soviet leadership thus had to choose between "press[ing] forward with its détente with the West German government (FRG) in the hopes ultimately of weaning Bonn away from a dominant place in the economic and military structure of Western Europe," or alleviating the fear of a German reunification by and continuing to vilify West Germany as revanchist and thereby making a rapprochement an impossibility.[190]

Brezhnev sought to have his cake and eat it, too. Two weeks after the Erfurt meeting, in April 1970, he informed the Poles of Moscow's suspicions that East German nationalists were gaining strength and called for Polish help to check East German forces that sought to unify Germany. Hoping to thus check the possibility of German reunification, Brezhnev moved ahead with West German–Soviet reconciliation, signing the Eastern Treaties in August 1970. Ratification of these "Eastern Treaties" on political friendship and economic cooperation came with immediate benefits. Within a week of the signing ceremony, the Brandt government removed import restrictions on over 4,700 products from Eastern Europe.

Poland's "checking" of East German ties with West Germany, however, took on a life of its own. Frustrated over perpetual East German refusals to share the economic and technological advances the East Germans reaped from Inter-Zonal Trade—privileged trade between East and West Germany—the Poles expressed harsh criticism of East German economic diplomacy. In a prime example of alliance rivalry over economic benefits, the Poles accused the East German military of being ideologically impure and containing some elements that sought to retake the formerly German territories as well as reestablish a single German superstate. More realistic accusations, however, included an indictment of East German economic discrimination against Poland and allegations of East German efforts to establish close economic ties with West Germany while excluding the rest of Eastern Europe from similar economic benefits.[191] Polish criticism certainly fit Brezhnev's plans as such a public outcry gave the East German pro-détente camp pause and strengthened Erich Honecker's hard-line position.

The unexpected consequence of the Polish criticism, however, was that Polish First Secretary Wladyslaw Gomulka looked to reap his own détente bonus. Rather than reining in East-West trade within the Warsaw bloc, Gomulka utilized Brandt's overtures to secure his own agreement on trade and economic cooperation when West German Economics Minister Schiller visited Warsaw on 23 June 1970. Gomulka even gave way on the politically dicey question of whether to include West Berlin, handing the West German government a decisive political victory.[192] This trade agreement would be supplemented in December 1970 with West Germany's acceptance of the Oder-Neisse border in the Warsaw treaty. Thus did the Soviet modeling of détente open the door for Poland to seek the economic benefits of East-West trade.

Overall, Brandt's policy of approaching Eastern Europe by first engaging the Soviet Union seems to have been a sensible one. Without the lure of *Westhandel* for the Soviets, Brezhnev would never have accepted the destabilizing effects of selective détente among his Warsaw Pact member states. As it was, both superpowers viewed the détente policies of their respective European allies with a healthy dose of suspicion but felt unable to effectively subjugate such policies under the larger mantle of superpower détente.

3

WESTHANDEL AND THE ALLIANCE (1970–1972)

The Need for Soviet *Westhandel*

Even when one considers the divisive effect of selective détente within the Warsaw Pact, the *Osthandel* ledger for the Soviet Union is, on balance, more positive than negative. Historian Keith Nelson has convincingly argued that it was economic exhaustion that drove the Soviet Union to pursue the more conciliatory policy of détente.[1] As such, the economic benefits of *Osthandel* were exactly what the Soviet leadership desired. Other historians, such as Mikhail Heller and Aleksandr Nekrich, add a political component to the equation, allowing the Soviet leadership to maintain credibility by supplementing moribound agricultural performance with purchases of Western foodstuffs at favorable prices.[2]

Other historians, however, have questioned the usefulness of East-West trade for the Soviet economy. Economic historian Philip Hanson, for example, sees foreign trade as facilitating improvements in the Soviet Union only "to a modest extent"[3] because of the negligible overall percentage of Soviet *Westhandel* and the perceived inability of the Soviet economy to rise to the qualitative level of Western production.[4] Historian Andrey Edemskiy instead sees the reason for a frustrated resignation over East-West trade in Soviet "bureaucratic inertia" and a "sense of superiority, particularly in the nuclear industry."[5] Such critical perceptions of East-West trade from either a teleological perspective or, especially, from Soviet primary sources must be viewed with caution. Naturally such developments caused opposition. Edemskiy illustrates nicely that Soviet détente and economic cooperation were by no means unequivocally supported by the members of the Politburo.[6] When East-West trade sparked dissent among the Warsaw Pact countries over indebtedness, as we will later see, a reemphasis on trade within the Comecon countries—and the accompanying anti-Western rhetoric—seems only logical, if not realistic.

Thus, the efficacy question of East-West trade for the Soviet Union still remains. While it is certainly true that the Western share of Soviet trade remained in the single digits, this by no means necessitates insignificance. The Soviets had learned from their mistakes of the 1950s, in which they had conducted espionage but were unable to reproduce the desired items. Ordering turnkey industrial plants in key sectors of heavy industry benefited the Soviet economy for the entire lifetime of these plants. Especially machine tooling plants allowed production of high-quality machinery that would not have been possible without Western technology. Similarly, the order of large-diameter steel pipes allowed for the construction of pipelines in areas that would have been inaccessible without the high-quality steel from the West. Even though the Soviets were never able to produce such pipes themselves, they benefited greatly from the technology. In other words, the purposeful transfer of Western technology facilitated Soviet economic growth even without full Soviet mastery of each technology. Since most plants were designed to facilitate industrial growth rather than consumer end-products, they served as multipliers in their respective industrial sectors. Thus, even with a limited percentage of the overall trade, they stood to facilitate Soviet economic growth significantly.

As such, East-West trade perfectly supplemented the Soviet Union's foreign policy goals. As Soviet Foreign Minister Andrei Gromyko explained time and time again, the ultimate goal of "weakening U.S. positions in Western Europe" would be achieved by "tirelessly promot[ing] the ideas that Europe itself can and must ensure its security."[7] This, of course, speaks to the overall strategy of strengthening Soviet gains from the Second World War and preventing a nuclear escalation through détente in the 1970s, specifically focusing on the reduction of military expenditures.[8] A necessary corollary of this belief, which was also shared by Brezhnev, was the need to extract trade concessions from the West in the service of economic development. Shevchenko, in his memoirs, explains the Soviet Union's emphasis on trade as a supplement to the political process even more vividly: "Soviet policy was to encourage Bonn to think that only the U.S.S.R. ... could alleviate the terror of nuclear war. We intended to support the theme with a refrain that Moscow was Germany's natural and historic economic partner."[9]

For the Brezhnev regime, though, trade with the industrialized West was a necessity, not only for its military and political benefits, but also in terms of credibility of the Soviet leadership before its own people. The eighth Soviet five-year plan, about to draw to an end in 1970, had resulted in significant growth in heavy industrial production (50 percent). Nonetheless, growth occurred largely in the earlier years, and large investments and labor allocations were required to sustain these growth rates. Although the initial target rates had been scaled down for the 1970s, they would remain largely unmet. These industrial short-falls were felt most sharply in the sphere of consumer goods, where the public steadily demanded improved quality and increased quantity. Overall, it was apparent by 1968 that the Soviet standard of living had stagnated at a level well below that of many Western countries.

Agricultural production continued to present a problem in its own right—and in ever increasing magnitudes. During the late 1960s, Brezhnev finally had to resort to raising prices for agricultural products, and the Soviet Union was forced to import an increasing amount of grain from the West.[10] As industrial deficiencies so directly affected Soviet citizens, the credibility of the planned economies and Brezhnev's leadership were at stake. Brezhnev homed in on the topic in mid April 1970 by revamping a nearly completed draft of the ninth five-year plan. In a memorandum "On the Agricultural Situation," Brezhnev shifted the emphasis of the new 1971–1975 five-year plan to accelerate the production of machinery and supplies for the agricultural sector.[11] The "great and noble cause" of boosting agricultural production would be a top priority, with all other sectors contributing what they could to the manufacture of agricultural equipment.[12] Underscoring the pressing nature of the problem, Brezhnev highlighted that "naturally, a certain time is needed to do all this work [creating industrial machinery for agriculture], but the countryside needs machinery <u>now</u>."[13]

East-West trade restrictions and Western embargos, then, were seen from a Soviet perspective as limiting growth and even beginning to affect social stability in the Soviet Union. Gromyko went so far as to decry Western trade restrictions as not only unnecessary discrimination against the Soviet Union, but also a primary reason for economic stagnation in the early 1970s. He complained to his son: "Using trade discrimination in the 1970s the West weighed down economic and socialist development in the Soviet Union, and consequently, chained our foreign policy."[14] Incidentally, Vladislav Zubok, in his most recent account of the inner workings of the Kremlin, depicts Gromyko and the KGB head Andropov as Brezhnev's two key allies in opening West Germany to East-West trade.[15]

Osthandel offered a way out of the agricultural quagmire. For the ninth five-year plan (1971–1975), the Soviet leadership counted on Western imports—on credit—to add production capabilities and improve the efficiency of already existing industrial structures. Offering Western companies large-scale contracts with little or no down payment that were to be paid off with the to-be-manufactured products became the strategy the Soviet leadership pursued to increase domestic output without depleting hard currency reserves. For Soviet officials, the beginning of 1970 seemed an ideal time for an intensification of West German trade with the Soviet Union.

Such close cooperation between two diametrically opposed economic systems brought challenges on both sides, however. To avoid "contamination" of the socialist society through Western trade, the Soviet government tried to minimize contact between Western companies and Soviet society. The result was a tightrope act that used Western technology to build Eastern communism while curtailing accompanying societal, economic, or political consequences. Thus the Soviets consistently refused the creation of joint ventures, investment of foreign capital in the Soviet Union, or dealings with multinational corporations. Systemic differences even existed in the day-to-day implementation of economic cooperation. Despite confirmed business meetings and schedules, Western businessmen frequently had to return home the same day they arrived because their hosts had not reserved a hotel room for them. Even Economics Minister Schiller ran into logistical problems on his visit to Moscow in late 1970. His pilot was unable to pay for the refueling of his plane with the internationally accepted vouchers and thus had to involve the German embassy to cover the incurred expenses.[16]

The Soviets countered these negatives by offering large-scale orders for industrial goods that reached the capacity of a single Western European country. The prestige and benefits of such projects were often too significant to overlook. Another quite effective practice was refusing to deal with multinational corporations, thereby playing one Western country and its industry against another. Patolichev, for example, spelled out quite clearly that he had to "take a business approach and compare whether credit offers from the FRG are worse than those of other countries. ... If the FRG is not competitive here, it will lose big and lucrative deals."[17]

Western Imports: The Kama River Plant

A typical example of Soviet Western trade was the Kama River truck manufacturing plant. German involvement in the planned Soviet plant not only exemplifies the difficulties West Germany faced in dealing with the Soviet Union, but also indicates the policies the Soviets pursued in dealing with the West.

The Soviet Union managed to exert enormous pressure on various Western countries despite its dire need for such a plant. A necessary step in overcoming its agricultural quagmire was the need for more trucks. In 1968 and 1969, a truck shortage had prevented the gathering and storing of the harvest, resulting in the large-scale waste of perfectly good crops. Even beyond agriculture, the lack of appropriate means of transportation crippled progress in various industrial sectors of the Soviet economy.[18]

Initial German attempts by representatives of the Daimler Benz Corp. to engage in a dialogue with Soviet industry representatives in 1968 failed over the Soviet refusal to deal with West German firms. After the reversal of that policy, the Soviets sent a high-level delegation to visit the Daimler Benz manufacturing plant in September 1969 and presented their vision to Daimler during a follow-up meeting in Moscow in 1970.[19] Daimler Benz was to build a turnkey plant and act as general contractor as well as financier. The creation of a multinational consortium or a joint venture with a Soviet company was categorically ruled out. There was to be no penetration of the Soviet economy, ownership of Soviet capital, or even interaction with the Soviet population. The Soviets wanted Western technology and labor to design, construct, and develop the manufacturing plant.[20] Essentially, the Soviets sought to create a small, insulated, capitalist bubble within the Soviet Union, where Western capital and know-how would construct a high-tech plant that would then be turned over to the Soviet Union for the good of the socialist cause.

Yet already the issues of financing the deal offered a glimpse at how illusionary such a concept was. This was particularly apparent in regard to the Soviets' insistence on low-interest loans. Rather than judging a proposed deal in its entirety, Soviet negotiators zoned in on interest rates, demanding a federally subsidized loan comparable to that of a French offer. Economics Ministry Undersecretary von Braun then suggested to Soviet ambassador Zarapkin that it was not the interest rate per se, but rather the overall cost to the Soviet Union that should be the deciding factor. In other words, if a German company could sell a product cheaper, the interest rate made no difference, as the German company was the debtor, not the Soviet Union. Von Braun concluded his account of the meeting with the assessment that "this consideration had apparently never crossed Mr. Zarapkin's mind before."[21] As Shevchenko explains, Soviet negotiators usually would not have a fallback position in these negotiations. Even a new insight such as this would leave them "singing one stubborn note at the bargaining table."[22] Not surprisingly, Zarapkin continued to insist on low-interest loans.

The generous conditions of the first gas pipeline deal also made for a stumbling block, as the financing of the deal had apparently heightened the Soviets' expectations of low-interest long-term financing. Soviet Minister for Automobile Industry Aleksandr Tarasov was intransigent in a meeting with Economics Minister Schiller on 30 September 1970, demanding with every statement that he desired the same interest rate (6 percent) as that arrived at in the gas pipeline deal, despite a recent rise of interest rates to 10 percent. He also insisted on a flexible bank loan rather than a much more controllable line of credit, again as in the gas pipeline deal.

Such financing terms had become untenable for the German side. The long-term, low-interest financing had already sparked heavy criticism from other EC countries, and German banks, recalling Soviet spending behavior during the gas pipeline deal, balked at granting another flexible bank loan.[23] Indeed, the Soviets had used a third of the flexible bank loan of 1.2 billion marks, earmarked for steel pipes, to purchase unrelated Western goods. This had created not only consternation but also numerous administrative difficulties, as the vendors of the smaller orders were reluctant to accept the ten-year repayment terms connected with the loan.[24]

Beyond that, Daimler Benz was able to gain valuable insights from the difficulties that Italian car manufacturer Fiat had experienced as the general contractor of a turnkey car manufacturing plant in Togliatti. While the Soviets had proven cooperative in spirit, renaming the entire town in which the plant was to be built after the Italian communist Palmiro Togliatti, poor or delayed Soviet workmanship in constructing the infrastructure for the plant had turned the entire project into a nightmare. At Togliatti, the Soviets were not even able to keep the deadlines for moving earth and pouring foundations, putting Fiat, as the general contractor, in an awkward position. Daimler Benz remained reluctant, as the entire project was simply too risky for one company alone, and delivered the decision to Brandt, who had been kept personally informed about the developments on Soviet trade through the German Industry Committee on Trade with the East.[25]

Faced with this initial rejection, the Soviets did not surrender but took another tack: rather than focusing on the economic aspects, they increased the political pressure. The Soviet negotiating style turned into a highly politicized exercise that pitted the Western European allies against each other. Out of "concern" for German industry, Minister Tarasov informed Schiller that both France and Italy had agreed to a flexible bank loan of 6 percent (subsidized by the national governments) and that since the Soviet side had to "unify" their financing, he was afraid that the German firms would not be competitive.[26] Indeed, the Russians had already concluded deals valued at over 350 million marks for equipment from the French, destined for Kama. A prospective cooperation between Daimler Benz and Renault for the complete plant failed because Renault was unwilling to be a minor partner working under the supervision of Daimler Benz.

To gain the upper hand in this deal, both the French government and French industry brought security and efficiency concerns to the Soviets' attention. In an absurd twist on security concerns from an ideological point of view, the French argued that it would be in the Soviets' best security interest to build several small plants, rather than one big one, thereby creating a less strategic target (presumably for NATO forces). The first of these smaller plants, furthermore, could be in operation much more quickly, providing a first batch of badly needed trucks. This smaller plant could be provided entirely by the French company Renault, and other European firms would only have to be involved to the extent that the other plants exceeded French capacities.[27]

Another interesting aspect is the U.S. position on this deal. In the 11 May 1970 issue of *U.S. News and World Report,* Secretary of Defense Melvin Laird moved the debate about the possible involvement of the Ford Motor Co. in the Kama River project to the center of public debate by voicing concern about such a deal.

> Before giving away the technology to construct trucks in the Soviet Union, and establishing plants for them, there should be some indication on the part of the Soviet Union [that] they're not going to continue sending the trucks to North Vietnam by the shiploads for use on the Ho Chi Minh trail.
>
> We have many American pilots who are today prisoners of war in North Vietnam because they had to attack trucks provided by the Soviet Union to North Vietnam.[28]

Democrats questioned this highly politicized and emotional line of reasoning only in form, not in substance. Senator Edward Kennedy (D-MA) thought the criticism was heavy-handed and that the plant would become operational only in 1974; by then, Kennedy hoped, the Vietnam War would be over. However, no one voiced criticism concerning the general problem of whether trade sanctions were a valid tool in achieving a foreign policy goal. Laird countered Kennedy's criticism with the statistic that 80 percent of all the trucks in use on the Ho Chi Minh trail were Soviet-made.[29] Despite this controversy and Ford's rejection of the proposed deal (in response to pressure from its shareholders), there was no similar concern on the part of the European governments or industry about its involvement in the project.[30]

Concerns over U.S. unhappiness with German exports had waned. Two CDU/CSU members of the Bundestag inquired whether "the federal government is willing to consult about the deliveries to the East of strategically significant value, such as a truck manufacturing plant, with our allies, so as to find a common approach."[31] Dr. Klarenaar of the Economics Ministry laid out the answer for Minister Schiller, which stated that the truck plant did not fall under export controls and that "furthermore, we will consult with our allies should the negotiations of German companies lead to concrete agreements." This formulation was crossed out in the draft and replaced by a noncommittal "furthermore, we will research the necessity of consultations, should the negotiations of German companies lead to concrete agreements."[32]

With the major Western European industrial players balking at such a huge project, the Soviet Union assumed the mantle of a general contractor outsourcing high-tech individual plants and elements to various Western companies. In this scenario, West Germany provided the parts of the plant that the U.S. deemed too sensitive to export.[33] This clearly conflicted with Nixon's interests and ideas. Kissinger, on the other hand, had little ideological interest in maintaining export controls. In several instances, Nixon not only went along with Kissinger's recommendation to continue a policy of restricting trade with Eastern Europe, but even disapproved some of Kissinger's suggestions on moderately liberalizing trade with communist countries.[34] This did not reflect a firm belief in the effectiveness of existing prohibitions on trade, as Nixon had repeatedly voiced his convictions that "the present prohibitions on trading with Communist countries are obsolete."[35] Instead, it demonstrated a moral conviction in doing the "right thing" by maintaining export controls vis-à-vis communist countries.

Despite awareness that the Soviets would simply purchase these components from Western Europe, Nixon partially blocked the Kama River foundry plant, assembly plant, and gear and transmission plant, the three most technologically complex elements of the proposed Soviet Kama River truck manufacturing plant.[36] But Nixon went further than just blocking manufacturing capabilities in the Soviet Union. Following political rather than economic instincts, he also blocked a proposal for the construction of oil and natural gas pipelines in the Soviet Union.

Soviet Exports: Energy Resources

Energy trade would constitute the most enabling and long-term element of East-West trade. Soviet grain imports catapulted hard-currency revenues to the top of the export agenda. Maintaining the axiom that economic priorities were not to change for the benefit of East-West trade, the Soviet Union found it increasingly difficult to produce commodities that could be marketed in the West for the necessary hard-currency inflow. As debt ceilings climbed, the Soviets looked more and more toward energy sales as the means to finance trade.

Because West Germany limited the import of energy through the use of quotas, Soviet officials found themselves continually pushing for liberalization of the German energy market. Without true political clout in the German Economics Ministry, they used German industrialists to do their bidding for them. Soviet importers simply made the purchase of German machinery contingent on the German seller obtaining import licenses for Soviet products of equal value. Especially in the 1960s, when the German oil market was saturated, German companies often tried to make a deal by petitioning the Economics Ministry for import licenses, which were usually declined to stabilize the domestic energy market.[37]

In 1969 the Soviets began to tout large-scale orders for trade liberalizations in the energy sector. A prime example was when Soviet Trade Commissioner Volkov, visiting the Economics Ministry on 2 February 1969 "after a hiatus of several years," indicated that the Soviet Union was prepared to provide orders worth 300 million marks to German companies in order to partially equip the car manufacturing plant in Togliattigrad that Fiat had been contracted to build.[38] Here, the Soviets sought to penalize the Italians for stalling over the extension of a natural gas pipeline from Austria through Italy into France, which would have provided a sizable hard-currency inflow.[39] But it also enabled Volkov to negotiate an increase in German import licenses, as he indicated that only with increased exports to Germany could the Soviet Union afford to order the proposed machines from the FRG. After Volkov's visit, the FRG granted the Soviet Union a sizable increase in import licenses (heating oil from 0.7 to 1 million tons and gasoline from 0.1 to 0.3 million tons), which the Soviet side received "with satisfaction."[40]

Even so, the Soviets continued to push for ever more import concessions, seeking to realize the sales of the total 1.8 million tons of heating oil they had arranged with German firms despite the 1 million–ton ceiling the German government had issued. The Soviet trade commissioner promptly repeated his concern that the order of German machinery, now increased to 400 million Marks, would be in jeopardy if no more concessions were granted to the Soviet side.[41] Volkov wasted no time waiting for the initially negative response from the Economics Ministry.[42] Rather, he visited numerous trade and industry associations, such as the German Machine Tooling Association (Verein Deutscher Maschinenbau-Anstalten), and requested "in a persistent manner" that private German industry pressure the German government into allowing an increase in heating oil and gasoline imports from the Soviet Union.[43]

This near-total dependence on increases in heating oil exports to finance additional manufacturing capabilities from the West was very troublesome for the Soviets, as the heating oil market in Germany was completely saturated and the German government had already hesitated to increase import licenses from 0.7 to 1 million tons. When the Soviets played their trump card, a prospective pipeline deal with the German companies Mannesmann and Thyssen, they linked any future prospects of this deal to the increase in heating oil imports to the desired 1.8 million tons.[44]

The trump card worked. During his visit to Moscow in May 1969, Undersecretary von Dohnanyi promised Patolichev another increase of 0.3 million tons in heating oil imports and 0.15 million tons in gasoline imports. At a subsequent visit by Volkov to the Economics Ministry on 19 August 1969, the Soviet trade representative continued to indicate his unhappiness regarding the gap between the 1.3 million ton heating oil quota and the 1.8 million tons desired by the Soviets. When the Economics Ministry mentioned that the Berlin-based company Brenntag GmbH was having trouble getting the Soviet company Sojuznefteexport to fulfill its deliveries of 50,000 tons of oil, the Soviet delegation declined to speak about it since West Berlin was not part of their responsibility. Only after the Economics Ministry promised to increase the import quota by another 0.25 million ton of heating oil did the Soviets promise to honor Sojuznefteexport's agreement with Brenntag.

The Soviets did not want a further increase in the gasoline quota, as the Soviet Union had made good on deliveries of only 60,000 of the 150,000 tons of gasoline for which von Dohnanyi had issued Soviet import licenses in May. Furthermore, the Soviets were very interested in maintaining the then-negotiated quotas for heating oil for the year 1970.[45] In summary. the Soviet Union had a clear interest in Western imports but could not find the means to acquire them. Only through coercive pressure on German companies, as well as concessions on Berlin, was it possible to get heating oil exports to Germany to anywhere near the level necessary for the completion of existing trade deals. The Soviets were also unable to fulfill the quota that the German side offered on gasoline exports, leaving virtually no trade goods that the Soviets could have used to boost their export balance. Despite a heavily saturated market that had already led to a price deflation of 4.5 percent compared to the previous year, the German Economics Ministry was very liberal with its import quotas over the next two years.[46]

Contextualizing the impact of the previously discussed natural gas pipeline deal in February 1970, it becomes apparent that this new hard currency revenue for the Soviet Union cannot be overestimated. With the first pipeline still under construction, negotiations for a second pipeline began; seeking to deliver another four billion cubic meters of natural gas per year in addition to the three billion from the first contract.[47] With the proposed pipelines' capacities fully utilized, Soviet gas was estimated to provide roughly 11 percent of the total German natural gas supply by 1980. The yet-to-be constructed gas pipeline would further use roughly one-third of its capacity to support Eastern European allies, offering benefits of Soviet–West German energy trade to Warsaw Pact allies.[48]

Western support for this proposed second deal was shakier than it had been for the first one. Helmut Schmidt, Germany's finance minister at the time, was particularly opposed to the heavy subsidies demanded by the Soviet Union. Even though political and economic situations had changed, the Soviets demanded the same favorable conditions they had received for the first deal. Soviet Vice President Kirill Novikov was very reluctant to commit to an increase in steel pipe orders without concessions on the financing. Highlighting the need for Soviet exports, he remarked to Brandt that "one has to first look at the figures of the natural gas deal because the Soviet Union only wants to make commitments it can keep." Novikov, trying to play different Western countries against each other, further added that the U.S. had expressed interest in Soviet natural gas as well.[49]

In his position as finance minister, Helmut Schmidt was able to block an interest rate subsidy by the German government and the lowering of the customary fees in connection with federal loan guarantees.[50] Otherwise though, the cabinet bent over backward to make the second gas pipeline deal lucrative for the Soviet Union. To equip Economics Minister Schiller with incentives for the deal, on 18 September 1970 the cabinet approved a loan guarantee volume for the Soviet Union of 1.5 billion marks annually. The unprecedented size of such a guarantee troubled many, as a default on the loan would have necessitated a parliamentary vote to increase the debt ceiling of the federal government.[51]

With Brandt's support, though, a general consent for a second pipeline deal was reached in April 1971. The financing, however, continued to present problems as the Soviets again insisted on the same financing as in the first deal. Completely ignoring the changed market conditions, Deputy Foreign Trade Minister Victor Osipov stated demanded an "improvement in the financing conditions. We cannot agree to worse conditions." Here again, the Soviets made the purchase of 1.5 billion marks of German steel pipes contingent on the successful completion of the financing of the second gas deal.[52]

From the German perspective, the Soviet demands appeared outrageous. With the market rates at 9 percent, the 6 percent rate the Soviets wanted seemed unrealistic. Furthermore, the Deutsche Bank consortium sought to limit the debt ceiling and shorten the life of any proposed loan. The second credit, they argued, should only range between five and eight years because the Soviets would be able to pay higher installments as they realized natural gas sales from the first pipeline. Lastly, the Economics Ministry was not inclined to grant the same thirteen-year life of the loan, since the first gas pipeline deal had caused a "severely critical reaction of our EC partners to the 'exotic' conditions of the first pipeline deal."[53]

The second pipeline deal finally reached fruition in 1972 with the Soviets getting what they wanted. As the U.S. consul in Düsseldorf reported, German industry eventually would have to concede to Soviet demands "in order to keep the Mühlheim operation going after the end of the year."[54] The Mühlheim plant, which had been specifically constructed for the large-diameter steel pipe orders from the Soviet Union, now depended on continued Soviet orders. The welfare of certain German industrial sectors, such as steel, had become more and more intertwined with the development of the Soviet economy and the political climate between East and West.

Schmidt quickly tried to alleviate U.S. fears of German dependence on Soviet energy during his next visit to the White House. In a conversation with Secretary of Commerce Peter G. Peterson, Schmidt tried to emphasize the minimal commitment on the part of the German government: even with the second gas pipeline deal, the proportion of Soviet gas to total energy consumption would amount to no more than 7 or 8 percent. Germany, Schmidt said, did not grant government-sponsored loans, just loan guarantees. This distinction did not convince Peterson, as the U.S. did not grant any loan guarantees. To Peterson, America's restrictive trade policies kept the U.S. at a disadvantage, and Peterson was eager to coordinate such loan policies. He changed the summit meeting schedule so that U.S. experts could consult with Economics Undersecretary Mommsen on East-West loan policies during the visit.[55] Ironically, it was Schmidt, who initially had objected to government-sponsored interest subsidies for East-West trade but had been overruled by Brandt, who now had to defend the generous loan guarantees to the American allies.[56]

Another example of the erosion of West German fears over too much energy dependency on the Soviet Union concerned potential Iranian natural gas deliveries, touted as a diversification of imports, that were scheduled to be shipped via the Soviet Union. As early as 1971, the FRG had planned on importing natural gas from Iran via a pipeline. The pipelines would be routed either through the Soviet Union or through Turkey, Greece, and Yugoslavia. Clearly, the latter route provided more potential for strengthening the alliance: it could have tied the NATO countries Greece and Turkey closer to the West and realized considerable transit revenues for these economically weak countries. It would have also been an ideal means to foster the independence and Western orientation of Yugoslavia and ultimately offered a truly independent source of natural gas.

Instead, the Brandt government chose a route through the Soviet Union, making it a transit country that would collect hard-currency revenues. The Soviets insisted, however, on not just functioning as transit country but also becoming the middleman, i.e., the buyer of Iranian gas and in turn the seller of Soviet gas to the FRG. Here, the FRG would once again increase its reliance on Soviet natural gas rather than gain access to an independent source. Despite such dependencies, Bahr, in a conversation with Soviet Minister Kulov, agreed to negotiate with the Shah of Iran for the Soviet option.[57] Chancellor Brandt also expressed pleasure regarding the stance that the Soviet delegation was taking toward the planned triangular agreement with Iran "because such a joint agreement demonstrates what such different countries could accomplish if a perspective of a secure peace exists."[58] In the end the prospective deal did not come to fruition because of the Iranian revolution, but the planned project demonstrates Brandt's focus on increasing economic ties with the Soviet Union.

The German Paradigm Shift of the Soviet Union toward a "Normal" State

Beyond the issue of energy dependency, however, East-West trade deals increasingly altered the perception of the Soviet Union in Western Europe. High-level communications, meetings, and the sense that the Soviets were in need of West German know-how created the impression of a more "manageable" Soviet Union. As a result, a sense of ownership in the new *Osthandel*, the necessity of its success, desperation over the status quo, and a healthy dose of wishful thinking led German business representatives to envision the Soviet Union as a benign power with virtually unlimited economic potential. This aspect of the gas pipeline deal, perhaps the most profound one, was not readily apparent at the beginning of 1970. No one could seriously argue that 2–3 billion cubic meters of natural gas per year could make the FRG dependent on the Soviet Union.

However, by intertwining German business and governmental interests with the successful development of the Soviet economy, the FRG acquired a vested interest in the prosperity of the Soviet Union. The old adage "Lend a man a dollar and he owes you, lend him a million and he owns you" rings true here. Once the natural gas pipeline had been constructed (it was scheduled for completion in October 1973), the FRG would have to trust the Soviet Union to keep the gas flowing. The financial investment of German industry as well as the political viability of the Brandt government now depended on maintaining a healthy East-West climate. This investment by industrialists and politicians alike led to much wishful thinking, often glossing over harsh Soviet economic realities. This is also evident in the West German public's rising willingness to see the Soviet Union as an acceptable international partner.

This paradigm shift occurred in the course of repeated visits of German government and industry representatives to the Soviet Union. Upon analysis of the reports of these trade visits, two somewhat contradictory images begin to emerge: that of a poverty-stricken third-world economy and, conversely, that of a booming and flourishing, yet foreign, economic system with seemingly infinite resources. While these images constantly collided with one another, the wishful thinking usually tipped the scales in favor of an upbeat assessment. As Foreign Minister Walter Scheel observed during a tour of the Togliatti auto plant:

> Eighty percent of the presses are from the West.... Just 10 percent of the presses were manufactured in the Soviet Union, in Barnaul. They work only smaller pieces and are not comparable to the finished product of the Western presses.[59]
>
> Often, German specialists complain that the—generally stringent—Soviet work environment regulations are not enforced so that there have already been many deadly accidents among the Soviet workers. Fortunately, they [German workers] have been spared so far. Indeed, there are many deep open holes on the production site. People are welding in the factory buildings while the machines are already running. Mr. Poljakov, the plant director, commented that if someone believed that the regulations are not kept, he could quit his job.[60]

Yet, ironically, Scheel actually marveled at the Western technology of the plant, incomprehensibly using it as evidence of Soviet advances:

> It is impressive to witness how the chassis and the chassis production line flow into each other. Through hydraulics the transmission and the front axle are lifted into the chassis from below and then installed. On this point, this plant is more modern than the VW-plant in Hanover.[61]

Other observers reported the total dependence on foreign technological assistance even more pointedly:

> The ardent observer should notice immediately that many plants and equipment are of foreign origin. Various large lathes, among them torrent lathes, carried the logo of a West German company. The surface preparation for rotors (drive shafts) is conducted with the highest demand for precision. Over and over it is quite disarming that for Soviet experts it is a matter of course that these demands on quality can only be fulfilled with foreign assistance.[62]

Potentially destabilizing social problems were also readily discarded, as in this report:

> Basically, you cannot begin to compare the economic tasks that the Soviet Union has to complete with the ones of a market economy such as the West German one. The Soviet Union commands a population of 240 million and incredible natural resources, which it can only mobilize one at a time but which it will mobilize, even if it takes longer. ...
>
> It is wrong to assume that Russia would be influenced by the discontent of its population. The Russian people do not compare their standard of living with that of the Western countries. Instead, they contrast it to their worse life of the past, recognize gradual improvements, and save money so they can buy once the offering is more plentiful and qualitatively better.[63]

A premier example of the German fascination with the Soviet economy, akin to the California Gold Rush, is the dealings of the Dieffenbacher GmbH, which delivered three plywood-manufacturing plants to the Ukraine. Due to the revaluation of the mark in 1969, these contracts were completed at a heavy loss to the Germans.[64] The company, however, considered this a proverbial loss leader since the Soviets expressed interest in more large-scale orders should the plants work to satisfaction. Although the plants did work to Soviets' satisfaction, a perplexed company owner wrote to his Bundestag representative complaining that the desired large-scale orders instead had been given to a Finnish firm that produced inferior products but could operate under a Soviet-Finnish barter trade agreement (oil for machines).[65]

The usefulness of a policy that relies on trade to encourage a hostile government to cooperate is a matter of debate. Undoubtedly, economic ties with the Soviet Union and the political capital Brandt had invested in his *Ostpolitik* drove the FRG to ever-increasing cooperation with the Soviet Union while at the same time virtually disregarding U.S. and/or NATO interests. The perception of the Soviet Union, fostered by Soviet representatives and the soft-pedaled reports of German observers, became one of an economic wonderland that, as a result of its planned

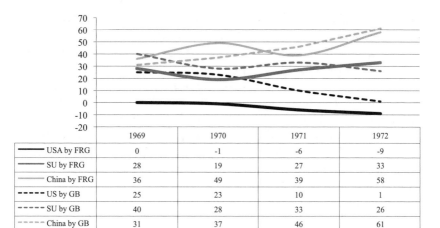

	1969	1970	1971	1972
—— USA by FRG	0	-1	-6	-9
—— SU by FRG	28	19	27	33
—— China by FRG	36	49	39	58
- - - - US by GB	25	23	10	1
- - - - SU by GB	40	28	33	26
- - - - China by GB	31	37	46	61

Figure 3.1 Gallup/EMNID Poll in West Germany and Britain: "Will the next year bring an increase or decrease in power for the following countries?" (1968–1971) taken from S. H. Drescher, ed., "Jahresend-Befragung in 7 Ländern (End of Year Poll 1968)," *EMNID-Informationen* 21, no. 1 (January 1969): A1–A3; S. H. Drescher, ed., "Jahresend-Dokumentation von Gallup-International," *EMNID-Informationen* 21, nos. 11/12 (November/December 1969): 5–6; S. H. Drescher, ed., "Internationale Gallup-Jahresendbefragung 1970," *EMNID-Informationen* 22, nos. 11/12 (November/December 1971): 5–6; S. H. Drescher, ed., "Internationale Gallup-Jahresendbefragung 1971," *EMNID-Informationen* 23, nos. 11/12 (November/December 1971): 5–6.

economy and large-scale orders, could provide Germany with an economic stability that was much more reliable and advantageous than the fickle throes of a weakening U.S. economy. Thus, in the FRG the perception of the Soviet Union changed drastically.

Using *Westhandel* as a Wedge in NATO

The Soviet leadership was not one to shy away from a chance to use that positive climate with West German officials to sow seeds of discord. In one of the earliest high-level negotiations with the SPD leadership in 1970, Kosygin indicated to Bahr that he preferred to conclude the negotiations with the FRG during the next three to six months, while the Americans were still involved in Vietnam.[66] The wish to finalize negotiations while an ally was otherwise occupied should have sent up more than a few warning flags. The fact that it did not is indicative of West German diplomats' and industrialists' acceptance of Soviet anti-American rhetoric as an unavoidable part of negotiations.

In one of the most striking instances of these Soviet machinations, Kosygin used German Economics Minister Schiller's visit to Moscow to sow discord within the alliance. In one of his initial comments he stated that "the Dutch sell their gas pretty expensively. We took note of this but of course do not mind."[67] This provocative comment was followed by an abrupt change in topic when he inquired if the German payment for U.S. troops was an unduly heavy burden on the federal budget. After Schiller explained that these payments were measures intended to balance payments, a well-informed Kosygin objected that German offset purchases were used to acquire weapons and U.S. bonds, which the FRG could not resell.[68] While Kosygin's statement was not entirely accurate, it nonetheless demonstrated a strong Soviet preoccupation with the German-American relationship and a readiness to remind the German visitor of sore points that existed within the transatlantic alliance.

Kosygin, however, went one step further and outlined his vision of a future German-Soviet nuclear energy policy that would alleviate the "one-sided orientation toward the West in these matters." He recalled statements made by Chancellor Brandt after signing the Moscow Treaty, in which Brandt had floated an offer of cooperation in the area of nuclear technology. Without mentioning the U.S. by name, Kosygin argued that "other countries might be angered by such cooperation or might fear it." In fact, he went so far as to suggest that "we can work without much noise and want to build our economic relations on a firm basis."[69] Schiller actually played along and reiterated the FRG's interest in nuclear cooperation with other countries. He "agreed with this [Kosygin's] presentation of economic issues and declared bravery and patience as necessary preconditions for the solution of economic and political tasks of the treaty of August 12th [Moscow Treaty]."[70]

In yet another instance, Kosygin postulated that a continued U.S. devaluation of the dollar could turn the U.S. into a strong competitor for the Europeans but uniting the resources of European countries such as the FRG, France, Italy, and the UK would create a firm foundation for continued negotiations.[71] Furthermore, he elaborated on the theme of U.S. economic weakness: "today, the FRG credits the USA—just like a reverse Marshall Plan." After sufficiently maligning the Western economic system, he portrayed the Soviet Union as the steady rock that would continue to expand according to plan and, benevolently, engage in trade with the FRG, even if the dollar-devaluation adversely affected the competitiveness of West German products.[72]

While it is debatable whether the Soviet rhetoric that took place during these talks had any impact on German foreign policy per se, the economic shift toward the Soviet Union certainly did. The transatlantic alliance had nothing to gain and stood only to lose from this development. Despite strong proclamations to the contrary, in the bipolar world of the Cold War any movement toward the Soviet Union precipitated a distancing from the United States. Even though the two poles were themselves coming closer together, Brandt's administration moved more quickly and with a different purpose from Nixon's, resulting in a profoundly different approach and attitude toward the Soviet Union, one that had the effect of altering the perception of German industry and society alike. Despite a stagnating economy, a lack of the financial resources, and the technological inability to exploit its own natural resources, the Soviet Union managed to maintain the upper hand in its dealings with the Western Europeans. As a result, Western European countries were more than willing to trade under the yoke of Soviet preconditions and barter deals. Western Europeans' willingness to ignore commercial disadvantages for potential political gains, however, created a schism in the transatlantic alliance with the United States, which was not willing to undertake such steps.

It seems appropriate here to address the myth of an apolitical West German trade pattern obediently following the mantra "trade is trade and politics is politics." In a sense, one could argue that such a stance, namely the willingness to trade with any regime regardless of its political stance, is a political decision in and of itself. Beyond that, however, no matter how much West German businessmen tried to remain focused on purely economic matters, the Gordian knot that interwove politics and trade with the Soviet Union and the United States alike made any trade deal a political act and any negotiation a political opportunity. The memoirs of the Deutsche Bank representative for Soviet-German trade, F. Wilhelm Christians, illustrate his efforts to remain a "private negotiator for strictly commercial affairs," only to be thrown time and time again "into the complicated political context of West-East tensions."[73]

This is not to imply purposeful intent on the part of German businessmen to create political realities. More often than not, political implications were unintended, and appeared bothersome and troubling. Christians rationalized the "expectations of statements on [political] questions that had nothing to do with my task" by viewing them as a trust-building measure. As he recalls, "it might have seemed convenient to the Soviets to involve me as a representative for German politics in problems that I could not and wished not discuss in an official or political capacity."[74] It was thus the Soviets, using business meetings for political purposes and intermingling politics and economics with or without the intentions of German businessmen, who made trade a "politicum" and enabled *Ostpolitik* to succeed.

Clashes within the Alliance over East-West Trade

The Soviets clearly intermingled politics and economics. They dem-
onstrated a much less forthcoming approach toward trade with the
United States than with the FRG during the early 1970s. The Germans
obviously recognized this difference in approach. German ambassador
Pauls reported several fundamental elements that tended to make the
Americans suspicious of Soviet trade policy. Among them was

> Moscow's lack of willingness to compromise in the question of Berlin
> despite the advantages that the German *Ostpolitik* promises for the Soviet
> Union and the Soviet policy toward a "Europe from the Ural Mountains
> to the Atlantic," which includes the CSE [later the CSCE] initiative as well
> as bilateral agreements.[75]

Ultimately, this led to an American suspicion that "the Soviet policy
is focused on eroding NATO much more so than previously thought.
This is done by applying a split-level policy with promises of détente
for Central Europe all the while maintaining at the same time a hostile
stance toward the American rival."[76] Despite this clear recognition that
U.S. perceptions regarding the Soviets' split-level policy—"Smiles for
Europe, Frown for Washington"—was cause for concern, the German
government did not alter its course of developing intense economic cooperation with the Soviet Union.[77] In a sense, however, this reflected
the growing American fear of Western Europe moving away from the
United States as a whole. Reports of German and French heads of state
coordinating their policy when dealing with the U.S. further strengthened this troubling perception.[78]

Consequently, *Ostpolitik* had become a highly divisive issue and part
of the overarching ideological debate between liberals and conservatives. Jabbing at the "liberal news media" for approving of Willy Brandt
simply because he was a Social Democrat, the conservative *National Review* criticized Willy Brandt for giving in to the East as early as June 1970.
Portraying Brandt as flip-flopping between an anti-American left-wing
position with an emphasis on the "Social" and a pro-American right-
wing position that emphasized the "Democrat," the author, Norbert
Muhlen, saw Brandt encircled by left-wing Social Democrats. *Ostpolitik*
was viewed as a dangerous policy of appeasement, as "Willy Brandt
could be preparing the way for the destruction of the Western defenses
in Europe and the Soviet penetration of the European West."[79]

After the signing of the Moscow treaty, conservative U.S. opposition became fiercer, and comparisons were drawn between *Ostpolitik*
and the Treaty of Rapallo. An article in the *National Review* portrayed a

vision of a Europe free of U.S. influence, seeing many advantages for German industry in expanding into the Soviet Union and remembering Lenin's dictum that German technology combined with Russian space, resources, and manpower would rule the world.[80] By September 1970, conservative criticism focused on Brandt. Chiding the U.S. administration for not recognizing the fateful doings of Brandt—that "experienced and resourceful Marxist"—the Moscow Treaty was now portrayed as an even more damaging agreement than the Hitler-Stalin pact. Brandt was portrayed as purposely trying to link Germany to the Soviet Union, destroy NATO, and expel the United States from the FRG.[81]

This damning critique was countered by the liberal magazine *The Nation*, which felt Brandt's policies did not go far enough. Joe Morris, editor of *The Nation*, applauded Brandt's overtures to the East as a long-overdue step designed to overcome the Cold War divisions brought about by the Dulles-Adenauer team, but wished for a more conciliatory German stance on the permanence of the postwar borders.[82] This turned into open praise and excitement over the Moscow in August 1970.[83] To *The Nation*, Brandt was the hero who had implemented badly needed détente policies yet was being undermined by Nixon and other hawks in the U.S. Conservative critiques were brushed aside with the remark that these hawks operated under an antiquated Cold War philosophy that assumed that communism was evil and could not change.[84]

A year-end assessment conducted by the German embassy on U.S. media and its portrayal of coverage on *Ostpolitik* found that it took a turn for the worse in the mainstream media. A worsening Soviet-American relationship, resulting from the tense situation in the Middle East, Cuba, SALT, and reports of abuses of Soviet dissidents, changed the tenor of the media coverage. Citing comments like "Many Faces of Kremlin, Smiles for Europe, Frown for Washington" and "… keeping the American 'bogey' now that the Soviets' relations with China and West Germany are better," the media depicted a more aggressive Soviet stance that clearly translated into a more cautious and delicate approach to *Ostpolitik*.[85] The conservative arguments became more prevalent, ramping up the focus on U.S. interests concerning *Ostpolitik*. Issues such as threats to the Western alliance, the potential pitfalls of allowing high-tech exports, and whether West Germany was compensated adequately for its concessions were of crucial importance in the latter half of 1970.[86]

Despite the ideological division between conservatives and liberals in this debate, one of the most vocal opponents to *Ostpolitik* ironically came from a collection of American labor unions. The AFL-CIO Executive Council clearly recognized the link between *Osthandel* and Soviet influence. In a damning critique of Brandt's *Ostpolitik*, the diplomatic agenda of *Ostpolitik* was portrayed as giving away the store, leaving the Western powers with weakened diplomatic leverage after receiving nothing in return.[87] The depth of negative public opinion within American labor groups was clearly demonstrated by the German reaction to the article "Willy Brandt: Remaking the Face of Europe," published by the American Automobile Workers Union (UAW). The German embassy in Washington commented that this article "belongs to one of the relatively few comments from organized labor in the U.S. which finds the *Ostpolitik* of the [German] Federal Government to be positive."[88]

Some members of the U.S. Congress were also skeptical or downright critical of *Ostpolitik*. After a prominent SPD leader, Steffen, accused allied forces of being in Germany under precisely the same moral, political, and juridical auspices as the Soviet occupiers were in Czechoslovakia, conservative Congressman Philip M. Crane (R-IL) linked this attitude to Brandt's *Ostpolitik* and suggested "that Chancellor Brandt's party is being influenced by a far leftist faction whose intentions do not coincide with those of the United States or our NATO allies.[89] Still, it must be noted that not all members of Congress shared this point of view. Senator Jacob K. Javits (R-NY), for example, was adamant in his support for Brandt's *Ostpolitik*. In a conversation with von Dohnanyi, he assured the minister that his use of the term "Finlandization" in reference to German *Ostpolitik* had been politically abused and vowed that it would be stricken from the transcripts. He explicitly wanted to convey the message to Brandt that he "was in full agreement with the foreign policy of the German government."[90]

Criticism, however, was not limited to the public arena or Congress. Former Undersecretary of State George W. Ball criticized *Ostpolitik* for relying on the faulty West German perception that the Soviet Union was a peaceful nation. Claiming that the Soviet Union was only dormant, he discarded the diplomatic initiatives enacted by the Brandt government and questioned the long-term ability of the West German government to resist the Soviet Union's attempts "to push the boundaries of its empire farther to the West."[91] German observers cited the "long and agreeing applause" as an indication of how unpopular *Ostpolitik* had become.[92]

In one of the major misunderstandings between West Germans and Americans, the German ambassador predicted that a trade deal between the U.S. and the Soviet Union for $1 billion in grain deliveries for the years 1971 through 1973 should be viewed as a sign of a loosening of American opinion, largely precipitated by the shock over a negative trade balance.[93] German observers hoped that Americans and West

Germans would now speak the same language on East-West trade, i.e., economics rather than politics. Consequently, German officials often pointed to the Soviet-American grain sale as an argument that the U.S. pursued a policy very much akin to the West German position. Moreover, the magnitude of the grain sales was so immense that within a year the U.S. trade balance rivaled that of West Germany.

Yet American officials did not view grain sales as having strategic value—certainly not when compared to the boosting of Soviet manufacturing capacity or improvements in Soviet energy infrastructure. Furthermore, the Nixon White House believed that the creation of steel processing plants (as done by the Mannesmann AG) or the construction of a natural gas distribution system in Bavaria created much stronger and more lasting ties with the Soviet economy than selling surplus grain. If there was indeed a quantitative similarity with the Soviet Union in terms of trade volumes, the American public did not view the quality of goods exported as comparable.

As a result, by mid 1971 *Ostpolitik* had lost much of its initial attraction for the American public. As the U.S. seemed to be slowly extricating itself from Vietnam, Brandt's maverick approach to overcoming the Cold War—once cherished—no longer held appeal. With the fate of Brandt's government riding on the outcome of the Four Power Agreement and public opinion more or less ambiguous toward *Ostpolitik*, it should have been relatively easy for Nixon to boycott the process and end Brandt's overtures to the East.

A parallel process of disenfranchisement occurred within the Nixon White House. By fall 1970, both Nixon and Kissinger had come to the conclusion that *Ostpolitik* contained significant risks, especially since it gave the Soviet Union a lever to pry the alliance apart.

> [t]he objective obstacle facing Brandt is that he cannot keep Soviet friendship if he emphasizes West Germany's ties to NATO. ... Brandt has manoeuvred the situation so that we have been pushed into the position of being responsible for both Berlin, and for the success of his Eastern initiative ... The impact of the German-Soviet treaty might very well lead to an increased interest on the part of the Europeans to deal more independently with Moscow. Moscow, in turn, will find it useful to encourage this in order to split off the various Western Allies from each other.[94]

Nixon deemed this a "decisive" and an "excellent perceptive analysis (and somewhat ominous)."[95] The alternatives to the SPD-led foreign policy course were clear. On 13 September 1970 Kissinger called the CDU "our friends" whom the U.S. must take care not to "demoralize" by openly supporting the policies of the SPD.[96] Ironically, Kissinger even expressed his regret that the German ultra-right party had not entered parliament, as this would have shifted political power in the German parliament toward the CDU.[97] This line was maintained when the CDU party chairman Rainer Barzel was assured that "we stand by our old friends."[98]

Nonetheless, a public endorsement of the opposition party in an allied country would be a tricky policy to enforce. Any display of public tensions between the Nixon administration and Brandt's government would have undermined the alliance and further exposed German Social Democrats to Soviet influence. West Germany was a key aspect in the American version of détente; therefore, great care had to be taken to not diminish U.S. influence. On the other hand, Nixon sought to avoid helping Brandt retain his chancellorship and thus offered only tacit approval of *Ostpolitik*. In short, the Nixon administration tried to pursue a course that sought to not offend the SPD while supporting the CDU.

In a National Security memorandum dated 6 November 1970, Kissinger pursued this policy to perfection. He outlined the need to

> develop a sense of confidence and trust in relations with the FRG, whether governed by the CDU or SPD … to avoid to the fullest extent feasible any involvement, either indirectly or directly, in the internal political affairs of the FRG and, in particular, to avoid any impression that we favor or support any political party in the FRG.[99]

While this document, at first glance, seems to have played toward the SPD interests, it was in fact a masterpiece of Kissingerian political maneuvering. Since Kissinger announced that "this policy will be communicated to the British and French governments and to the FRG as part of the normal consultative process," it gave President Nixon good reason to disparage any statement that supported Brandt or his *Ostpolitik*. The CDU could not be offended, as this policy welcomed relationships with either party. While it supported "the FRG's Eastern policy" in general, the United States did not obligate itself to "support particular tactics, measures, timing or interpretations." It further enumerated an assertive U.S. policy in which "our juridical position with respect to Germany as a whole is in no way impaired" and strengthened the Americans' negotiating position with the Soviet Union in that "a new four power agreement is, therefore, not an essential requirement in terms of <u>our</u> interests or <u>our</u> policy."[100] In essence, this policy severely limited practical American cooperation with Brandt's *Ostpolitik* while endorsing it in general terms.

With such clashing political discourses, it was only a matter of time before East-West trade became the center of attention and the FRG clashed with the U.S. in COCOM. Again diverging from the U.S. position, which saw no intrinsic value in the lifting of restrictions but rather preferred to use them as a bargaining chip with the Soviets, the Brandt government now advocated a liberalization of COCOM restrictions without any concrete Soviet concessions. In a meeting with Commerce Secretary Peter Peterson it became clear that the Brandt government considered Soviet moves at détente grounds sufficient for liberalization: "In light of the technological and scientific development in the East and the West and the desired increase in the exchange of goods and services between both regions I wonder if the volume of current COCOM restrictions is still reasonable."[101]

It is a telling insight into the internal dynamics of the FRG that Finance Minister Schmidt attributed the pressures aimed at liberalization to German industry and saw the German government in merely a supporting role—rather than the other way around. This demonstrates that the Soviet Union had managed to manipulate the dynamics between trade and politics to its advantage. While Brandt had pushed German industry to pursue trade with the East in 1970 with the intention of bringing about political concessions, now the Soviet Union could count on German industry to advocate its case in the political arena.

> The German industry views the many embargo rules as an intolerable export hindrance in these times and demands a stronger liberalization for computers, electronics, transistors, electronic devices, and communication equipment and parts, chemical products as well as ships with higher speeds. … The federal government supports this view.[102]

In short, East-West trade had managed to weaken Western Europe's political will to continue strict embargo policies and created public support for such a notion.

Solidifying Westhandel: The Fight for Détente in the Soviet Union

Despite such relative successes, the Soviets remained reluctant to solidify prospering East-West trade through official agreements. As mentioned above, this was mostly due to domestic reservations. Internally, Brezhnev had not yet consolidated his power to the point where he could rule without any opposition. Rather, he had to carefully to balance Kosygin's liberal views with the more Stalinist Kirilenko, favoring "sometimes Kosygin, sometimes Kirilenko, and occasionally neither."[103] While Kosygin often spearheaded negotiations with the West, Kirilenko offered only "cautious lip service to a policy of détente" characterized by "tough conditions which appear almost to rule out its application to the U.S."[104] As it happened, Brezhnev stood to lose significant clout in the eyes of the Politburo if his détente policies with the West resulted in either a Soviet diplomatic defeat or undermined the stability of the socialist regime in the Soviet Union.[105]

The newly adopted Soviet détente policies had already emboldened several Eastern European countries to strengthen ties with the West. However, no communist country showed more of an about-face from friend to foe than did the People's Republic of China. Observed from an East German perspective, an increase in strong anti-Soviet rhetoric during the 9th Party Congress in 1968 and a continuous softening of anti-American rhetoric marked a substantial shift in Chinese policy.[106] Since then, Chinese foreign policy had aimed at carving out a position between the superpowers by drawing in the U.S. as an ally on one hand and being outright hostile to the Soviet Union on the other.[107] Skirmishes between Chinese and Soviet border guards on the Ussuri River in March 1969 had demonstrated to the entire world that "that the PRC has broken with the Socialist bloc and the communist workers movement and through pressure against the Soviet Union has begun to fight for the status of an autonomous major power."[108]

This was followed up by many Chinese *People's Daily* articles condemning Soviet rapprochement with West Germany and its calls for a European Security Conference. The Chinese were perturbed over policies that they perceived as a means for the Soviets to free themselves from confrontations with the West "so that they may shift their force to coping with the anti-imperialist anti-revisionist struggles of the Asian people, and to performing more tricks in opposing China."[109] After observing an emerging pattern of prioritizing détente over alliance interests, as demonstrated in Moscow's negotiations with Bonn and the New *Ostpolitik,* the Chinese leadership sought to strengthen East Germany's diplomatic position. Fearing that the Soviet troops based in Eastern Europe could be redeployed to the Sino-Soviet border, the Chinese pursued a policy that CIA analysts dubbed "wedge-driving." Published statements in the *People's Daily* ranged from claims that West Berlin should belong to East Germany to statements that the Soviets had given Bonn tacit approval to annex the GDR. This all served to undermine Soviet leadership within the Eastern bloc In a bold move, Beijing even advised the East German ambassador to be more forceful in opposing the new West German–Soviet rapprochement.[110] The status of West Berlin thus remained the linchpin for East and West alike.

West Berlin, Trade, and the Eastern Treaties

Throughout most of the 1960s, the Soviet Union's use of trade issues was designed to undermine the status of West Berlin. One such example was the Soviet company Prodingtorg, which filed a complaint in regard to a West Berlin company's illegal reexport of Russian caviar to West Germany. As the sales agreement prohibited reexports to third countries and the Soviets considered Berlin a separate country, their view of this activity constituted a break in the sales agreement.[111] Upon receipt of this complaint, West German officials immediately panicked and consulted their allies to gauge their support of such matters. In this way the Soviets were able to employ the issue of West Berlin as a tool to keep the West German government in a permanent state of limbo.

In Bonn, a permanent trade agreement that included West Berlin was seen as the only solution to the quagmire. As the Soviet Union had little interest in solving the problem for the West Germans, a political understanding on the implementation of a trade agreement remained elusive. None of the prior trade agreements between the FRG and the Soviet Union contained any references to West Berlin. The only treaty still valid was the 1958 German-Soviet Agreement on Trade and Shipping. In this treaty the Germans had handed the Soviet delegation a letter stating that the FRG assumed that West Berlin was included in the treaty. The Soviet delegate apparently took the letter unopened, and as a result the Soviets, in a later negotiation, denied the validity of said treaty for West Berlin.[112] The 1967 negotiations on the reinstatement of a general trade agreement then faltered on the issue of Berlin.

The Soviets were also adamant that all trade taking place with German companies in Berlin was to be conducted in U.S. dollars. One consequence of this policy was that Soviet firms rejected German credit lines and even insisted that German companies have their trade with the Soviet Union funneled through branch offices in West Berlin. In one instance, when a German company did not have a branch in West Berlin, the Soviet firm involved recommended that the German owner find one.[113] The Soviets turned the issue any way they pleased. They gladly accepted West German import licenses issued to companies based in West Berlin, since these provided them with sought-after hard currency. In other instances, however, they strictly separated West Berlin and West Germany. Soviet trade statistics listed West Berlin and West German as individual entities, Soviet trade fairs displayed a West Berlin rather than a West German flag, and Soviet officials insisted on paying West Berlin companies in U.S. dollars.[114]

For the German government the inclusion of Berlin in any prospective trade agreement was of paramount importance. Even before actual negotiations on a trade agreement had begun, the German side stated "the work of the German-Soviet trade commission would take into account the ties between the Federal Republic of Germany and Berlin (West), especially in the area of economics, science and technology." Should this not be possible, it was concluded, "we will have to wait with the formation of the German-Soviet Trade Commission until the Four Power Agreement on Berlin comes into force."[115]

Once East-West trade stood to boom with the conclusion of the first natural gas pipeline deal, the need for a trade agreement became more pressing. For Brandt, including West Berlin in any treaty with the Soviet Union was not simply a priority but a tangible and politically significant measure of the effectiveness and validity of *Ostpolitik*. Failure to include West Berlin would have been tantamount to a public relations disaster for the SPD/FDP coalition. As Brandt explained to Bahr in August 1970 after failing to find satisfactory coverage of the Berlin issue in Bahr's account of his Soviet negotiations: "The [Berlin Declaration] is a substantial element and a crucial point domestically. ... The Soviet side has to understand that our government has to explain in parliament in which way the foreign minister has articulated our interest in this crucial question." He further explained that a de facto inclusion of West Berlin in the East-West trade agreement would be very helpful. Finally, he warned Bahr that "we need a substantial discussion, an agreed-on formal declaration and an agreed-on terminology."[116]

Brandt was further concerned about the spirits of West Berliners. He saw the current situation as unattractive, depressing, and devoid of youthful energy, warning that "time is working against us."[117] With such important political issues at stake, Brandt and his administration needed West Berlin to be included in the treaty. Economics Minister Schiller, for example, upon being asked by a journalist during his trip to Moscow in October 1970 whether he felt that the Russians had agreed to consider West Berlin as part of the FRG, answered that "West Berlin must be included in the territorial delineation of the treaty. The Soviet reaction to this was less than enthusiastic, as usual. The question of the territory will, therefore, be a major element of the upcoming negotiations."[118]

Despite Brandt's *Ostpolitik* and West Germany's willingness to bend over backward on East-West trade, the Soviet leadership remained intransigent in its approach to West Berlin. The chair of the Foreign Relations Committee, Jury A. Zhukov, explained in a speech on 22 September 1970 that "we are not of the opinion that the Federal Republic has a right to assume that West Berlin is part of it. It is not politically united with it. West Berlin is the only territory that still remains under occupation. No one can change these facts."[119] In backdoor negotiations, Soviet Premier Kosygin was even more direct. Prodded by Schiller about whether using the jurisdiction of the German Bundesbank would be an appropriate term for a new trade agreement, Kosygin simply replied: "This is a complicated question. I think it should not be included in parts of the trade agreement so as not to complicate the economic issues. I therefore ask you not to pose that question here."[120]

The FRG Foreign Office, however, seized upon Schiller's suggestion. Rather than insisting on an agreement that covered Berlin before negotiations could begin, the Foreign Office wanted to send the Soviet embassy a letter insisting that the FRG could conclude a trade agreement only if it referred to the jurisdiction of the "Währungsgebiet der Bundesbank."[121] In another German push for movement on the issue, Ambassador Allardt of the FRG informed the Soviet Foreign Ministry through Ambassador Valentin Falin that the FRG was willing to commence negotiations on a trade agreement with the caveat that an agreement on the jurisdiction over West Berlin would first be reached. Falin, on the other hand, presumably in accordance with a Soviet stance that was designed to leave the Germans sweating, stated that he could not comment on this, as the status of West Berlin was part of the ongoing allied four-power negotiations.[122]

More than that, however, the status of West Berlin was still part of the ongoing political struggle in the Soviet Union. Publicly criticized by hard-liners for being too soft on the West and selling out East Germany, Brezhnev repeatedly criticized the unnamed opponents of Soviet–West German rapprochement.[123] Despite such attempts, anti-German propaganda and a lack of commitment by Soviet diplomats threatened the successful conclusion of the Berlin negotiations.[124] What the West Germans were hoping for, the Soviets had not hashed out for themselves.

Even so, the West Germans could not afford to surrender the status of West Berlin. When the Soviet delegation for the negotiations finally met in Bonn on 25 February 1971, the German delegation leader, Dr. Hermes, reiterated that an agreement that failed to cover the inclusion of Berlin was out of the question, and the Soviet delegation leader, Manzullo, replied that this had nothing to do with the current negotiations. While the bulk of economic questions were resolved quickly, the question of Berlin remained the major sticking point. The delegation agreed to end the first round of negotiations on 5 March 1971 and reconvene in Moscow at some future date, presumably after the Four Power negotiations on Berlin had been concluded.[125] When the negotiations were aborted, there were only two issues that continued to pose substantial problems: trade liberalization for German imports and the issue of Berlin.[126] While trade liberalization was a matter of degree and quite negotiable, Berlin was a matter of principle. The Eastern Treaties, a trade agreement, and German domestic support of *Ostpolitik* all hinged on the issue of Berlin.

It was during the 24th Party Congress on 30 March 1971 that Brezhnev finally felt confident enough to overcome the opposition in the Politburo and focus Soviet foreign policy on détente with the West. Staking his political prestige and future on the assertion that peaceful coexistence should provide the basis of dealing with the West, he renewed the call for a Conference on Security and Cooperation in Europe and committed his regime to increased consumer goods allocation.[127] As the Eastern Treaties with West Germany hinged on the successful resolution of the Four Power talks, any infusion of Western capital into the Soviet economy was dependent on a speedy resolution of the ongoing talks with the West.

Westhandel policies would play a central role in this. Restrictive or protectionist approaches all over the East would be changed by cooperative East-West trade. As Brezhnev outlined, "the economic and scientific-technological cooperation [with the West] must be utilized for the fundamental strengthening of the states of the Socialist community."[128] But even though trade was embraced wholeheartedly, curtailing Western influences on communist society remained a top priority. As an East German delegation found out when visiting Moscow, the first rule of East-West trade was obviously to play "capitalist partners" against each other to maximize commercial advantages. Beyond that, the Soviet Union was counting on imports of industrial machinery, particularly machine-tooling plants. Such plants would eventually limit the need to import industrial plants. Otherwise, Western technology ought to be purchased in small quantities to be studied, improved, and then copied in the Soviet Union.[129]

The root cause for such cost-saving measures was the need to cut financial dependency on Western credits. Soviet goals in trade negotiation had moved beyond the model of the first gas pipeline deal. East-West trade should be financed through Western government credits alone, removing the link between credit repayment and the product of the industrial plant that the credit financed. In this way, increased dependencies on the West could be avoided.[130] Other Western influence, through joint ventures or business models of shared capital investment, would be refused, be they in East or West.[131]

Such policies again illustrate the tightrope act to which Brezhnev had committed the Soviet Union: meeting the desperate need for Western technology and credits while at the same time trying to limit the influence of Western industry on the East. However much consideration Brezhnev might have given the internal stability of the Soviet Union or the Eastern alliance, he needed East-West trade—and West Berlin stood in his way. Brezhnev needed to move on Berlin without appearing too generous during the negotiations, as this would open him up to the internal criticism of having sold out East Germany.

The Berlin issue stood to thwart Brandt's political goals as well. With his government holding only a razor-thin majority in the Bundestag, it was clear that it could not survive a contentious debate on the treaties without movement on West Berlin. The West German opposition had already expressed strong reservations over the Eastern Treaties. In a letter to Brandt, CDU opposition leader Rainer Barzel expressed concern that only with a "satisfactory solution in regard to Berlin and the inter-German problems" should the Eastern Treaties be ratified.[132] With both the West Germans and the Soviets poised to deal, everything hinged on the Americans. For the Nixon White House, the benefit of a possible understanding on West Berlin was not readily apparent. Kissinger aptly reflected that, for the moment, "we had harnessed the beast of détente."[133]

In December 1970 Brandt emissary Horst Ehmke had met with Kissinger and Assistant Secretary of State for European Affairs Martin Hillenbrand on short notice, intent on discussing the lack of progress made in regard to the Four Power Agreement on Berlin. "Reports of unhappiness in the Nixon administration over West German Chancellor Willy Brandt's Eastern policy" had filtered down to the news media.[134] The sentiment was certainly accurate with respect to Nixon personally.[135] In May 1971, two months before the conclusion of the Four Power talks on the status of Berlin, he still retained his aversion to *Ostpolitik* and the liberal German chancellor: "I don't want to hurt our friends in Germany [CDU] by catering to that son-of-a-bitch [Brandt]."[136]

Kissinger's stance was more oblique and ultimately carried the day. While he had been concerned about *Ostpolitik*, his trepidation was mostly due to the lack of his personal involvement rather than the policy's effects on international relations. In his memoirs Kissinger triumphantly outlined the linkage of the Eastern Treaties to the successful completion of a Four Power Agreement as a successful U.S. policy for retaining leadership in détente. Yet when it came to the Four Power Agreement, he failed to take the reins, instead relying heavily on Bahr for the actual negotiations. Bahr, who had apparently learned from past mistakes, continued to describe his talks with Soviet representative Falin in great detail, even recounting personal aspects of Falin's wife's illness.[137] Kissinger, for his part, involved Bahr extensively in the preparations for the talks. Kissinger remembered that he had given Ambassador Dobrynin a draft proposal that suggested focusing on practical aspects rather than legal issues as a way of overcoming deadlock in negotiations. Kissinger apparently did not modify many of Bahr's suggestions in this draft, which was discussed during a weekend retreat, since he simply gave Dobrynin Bahr's German version of the draft.[138] Furthermore, Bahr was invited to be a third party in back-channel meetings between Ambassador Rush and Falin, who was the key Soviet representative in the negotiations.[139] In summary, having "harnessed" Bahr, he consulted the West German side heavily when developing acceptable language and diplomatic solutions for the U.S. delegation during the Four-Power Agreement negotiations.

Nevertheless, it seems clear that the Nixon administration was less than enthusiastic about the Berlin talks. Fundamentally, Nixon viewed Berlin as a bargaining chip with the Soviets: "Berlin is something they need from us a hell of a lot more than we need it from them. ... We are going to make them [the Soviets] pay."[140] According to David Geyer, Berlin "was always a means and never the ends in Soviet-American relations."[141] The Berlin accords were used as a tool to speed up SALT negotiations and to help pressure the Soviets into providing assistance to the U.S. cause in Vietnam. Only when the Soviets made the Berlin talks a precondition for a Soviet-American summit did the Nixon administration ratchet up the pressure and move the negotiations into high gear. This had the desired effect of spurring forward the negotiation process on the Four Power Agreement.[142] Thus, Brezhnev ultimately purchased the Four Power Agreement on Berlin with a summit meeting in Moscow.

Even though all sides wanted to conclude the agreement, the inability on all sides to concede much left the final language quite malleable. The key provision of the Berlin Accords, signed on 3 September 1971, defined the West German/West Berlin relationship in such ambiguous terms that it could—and would—be interpreted quite differently by different political factions. The Four Power Agreement, then, failed to deliver to Bonn what it had desired: a clear and indisputable agreement that linked West Berlin with West Germany. Instead, the end result was a vague formulation that each side could manipulate in any manner it pleased. Even with the agreement in force, West Germany was dependent on case-by-case negotiations to include West Berlin in bilateral treaties.

An Independent West German Diplomacy?

Even with all their faults, the Berlin Accords proved sufficient for Brandt's *Ostpolitik*. The formal conclusion of the Berlin issue and the political goodwill in the wake of the signing of the document injected Brandt's foreign policy with a newfound sense of accomplishment and, indeed, self-confidence.

Following Brandt's ascendancy to the chancellorship, balancing Western cohesion with détente had become the new German foreign policy credo. According to both Brandt and Bahr, "the policy of a European unity [in this case not the EC but East and Western Europe] cannot be pursued without the support and the backing of the U.S.A."[143] On the other hand, there was a palpable sense of difference between the U.S. and Western European positions in world politics. The economic and political turmoil in the U.S. betrayed a sense of weakness and insecurity that begged for distancing. As Günter Grass, an intellectual leader and a confidant of Brandt, put it:

> The United States is in an apparent irreparable crisis. The signs are many: Overconfidence gave way to aggressive insecurity. The liberal minorities resign or place their hope in mostly short-lived political actions. The youth, which was still protesting yesterday, is now preoccupied with itself and drugs. ... Many predictions point to a second (creeping) civil war. Political assassinations occur daily in the countryside and have become entrenched practice. The country is sick. Europe, if it does not want to become infected, must distance itself.[144]

Distancing itself from the United States was impossible for West Germany in 1970, nor was it something that could have been considered during the Four Power negotiations. By autumn 1971, however, with the Four Power Agreement on Berlin all but completed, Brandt embraced a more independent stance.

Across the Atlantic, Nixon's actions had thrown the U.S. into an economic crisis that perpetually consumed the White House and hurt alliance cohesion. Following an ill-fated report by then Assistant to the President for International Economic Affairs Peter Peterson, Nixon began to recognize the importance of trade and international economics for domestic politics. Along with Secretary of Treasury John Connally, Peterson convinced Nixon in July 1971 to adopt a highly mercantilist view of international trade in which the decline of U.S. economic strength was directly linked to unfair import practices by foreign allies. Pairing the concept of economic warfare with illustrations of how declining U.S. exports led to domestic unemployment, Nixon began to foster economic nationalism heavily.[145] International trade and finance featured prominently in this context, and West Germany, in its role as Europe's economic powerhouse, became even more prominent.

At such a time of economic uncertainty, a positive gesture by Brandt would have gone a long way toward pacifying the Nixon White House. An opportunity to influence the American business community arose when Brandt was invited to give a short address to the U.S. Chamber of Commerce in Frankfurt. Strengthening inter-allied understanding at a time when the U.S. business community was paranoid over international economic relations would have been an appropriate move. Yet he declined the opportunity and instead sent then Defense Minister Helmut Schmidt to give the talk.[146]

Brandt displayed the same aloofness toward allied relations and American concerns over the issue of U.S.-German offset agreements. Again, the Nixon administration, concerned over the U.S. economic situation, was pushing for a more favorable offset agreement. Bundestag member Kurt Birrenbach of the CDU voiced his concern that the current year's agreement to offset the costs of U.S. military troops in Germany might fail, as the U.S. was facing a particularly difficult situation and the FRG had not agreed to the demands put forth by the U.S. (such as a larger percentage of payments rather than loans, and a 0 percent interest rate on the remaining loans). Birrenbach observed that election-year politics would blow the failure of an offset agreement out of proportion and strongly advocated committing to the increased payments as the lesser of two evils: "As we have to fear that the Democratic Party will not be choosy with propagandistic demands, one should try to support this president, who is truly an Atlanticist and shows concern for the problems of Europe."[147]

Chancellor Brandt replied, rather coolly, that the German federal government "has agreed to provide the Americans appropriate compensation for the currency expenditures for their troops in the Federal Republic." However, for "political, psychological, and economic/financial reasons," Brandt refused to commit to German offset-payments at the customary rate of 80 percent of U.S. expenditures. He did this in full recognition that West German unwillingness to continue the offset-payment at revious rates could jeopardize America's "continued military presence in Europe."[148] To the contrary, in his letter to Birrenbach he reaffirmed his beliefs that "we cannot buy an agreement with Congress to keep troop levels in Europe the same."[149] While Brandt certainly was correct in stating that he could not purchase the deployment of U.S. soldiers in Germany, his unwillingness to help finance expenses incurred in the FRG would most certainly strengthen the position of the more isolationist members of Congress. When compared with previous governments, to whom this issue was a top priority, it seems evident that Brandt felt less of a need to fret over U.S. troop levels in Germany. The success of his *Ostpolitik* afforded him an unprecedented level of independence from the U.S.

A more independent-minded Brandt now found it possible to be less forthcoming with his support for Nixon's Vietnam policy. A proposed letter by Brandt's staff commended Nixon on his policy:

> In your eight-point-plan of January 25, 1972, and most recently in your declaration of May 8 1972 you have shown the way by which the Vietnam problem could be solved in a short period of time. This, however, requires the goodwill of all parties involved. I hope your opponents realize this soon and act accordingly.[150]

However, Brandt revised this letter, removing the part that implied his support of Nixon. Instead, all that the letter conveyed was an assurance that he was closely monitoring the situation and appreciated those policies that led to an end of the conflict:

> I assure you, Mr. President, that I watch the developments in Southeast Asia with much care and that I fully appreciate those measures of yours, which aim at ending the conflict and lead to a negotiated solution.[151]

Later that year, after the "Christmas bombings," Brandt became even more critical, instructing his foreign minister to investigate the possibility of issuing a censure on U.S. foreign policy. He wished, however, for a European statement rather than a West German one. While Scheel viewed this prospect with justifiable misgivings, he nonetheless consulted with the other Western European allies. Nothing came of the idea, as the British refused to play along and the French were concerned to preserve their role as mediator in the Paris peace conference. One striking indication of West German self-confidence here is that even though Brandt tried to hide behind a European front in issuing criticisms of the U.S., the FRG government was fully aware that upon consulting its Western European allies, Brandt's attempt would be reported to Washington. Apparently, Brandt felt he was in a strong enough position to advance the idea anyway.[152]

Brandt's orientation shift toward Western Europe at the cost of a transatlantic emphasis can also be seen in his opposition to suggested regular consultations between NATO and the European Parliament under the auspices of NATO. As the Parliamentary Commission of NATO suggested, this would increase contact between U.S. Congressmen and members of the European Parliament. Brandt's view of this suggestion was far from enthusiastic. Using the unconvincing argument that Ireland was not part of NATO, he said that he preferred to leave any possible contacts under the auspices of the European Parliament.[153] Brandt did not want to strengthen the role of NATO in the European integration process. His position was explained very clearly in an accompanying letter, which clarified his reasoning:

> This draft avoids a commitment to support the political action committee's suggestion to recognize the North Atlantic Council as the official North American- European parliamentary body. In the past we have, in accordance with the Foreign Office, followed the principle that it would run counter to parliamentary tradition to elevate parliamentary groups that have no real electoral authorization.[154]

While this procedural objection was not explicitly directed against the United States, there can be little doubt that any increased consultation between the European Community and the United States would have strengthened transatlantic ties. As Brandt was anything but a stickler for formalities, the intent behind this objection must have been to limit the influence the U.S. would have on European decision-making. Quite confident in his belief that Europe could develop its own foreign policy, Brandt must have wanted to limit U.S. political influence.

With the Four Power Agreement settled, Brandt's *Ostpolitik* ledger listed one success after another. During a meeting between Nixon and Brandt at Key Biscayne in late December 1971, Nixon grudgingly recognized Brandt's successes in that "West Germany was no longer the Soviet Union's whipping boy." Brandt responded by referring to the Eastern European need for East-West trade, upon which Nixon lectured him that "U.S. policy assumes progress in political areas must precede progress in trade."[155] This echoed Kissinger's warning, expressed in the briefing for the summit meeting, that "improved East-West trade and economic arrangements must not dilute the unity of the EEC, or our Atlantic partnership."[156] Nonetheless, Nixon still did not see the significance the Soviets attached to trade.

During Brandt's summit meeting in the Crimea, trade issues had played a vital role. Both Brezhnev and Brandt agreed that the trade volume was still too small. Brandt picked up on Kosygin's earlier suggestion of a trade commission and explained that the FRG was now prepared to form such a commission.[157] Brezhnev, in turn, outlined even more possibilities in the oil and gas sector, floating the possibility of ordering a German-made high-tech manufacturing plant to produce plastics.[158] Brezhnev's other ideas on expanding the trade volume with the FRG included radio electronics, machine tooling, and the construction of a nuclear power plant. He also baited Brandt with the possibility of allowing German companies the privilege of being the first foreign companies to exploit Soviet natural resources.[159]

Anti-American rhetoric was plentiful during this meeting. Brezhnev suggested, without prompting, that he would not like the FRG to develop relations with the Soviet Union at the expense of its relations with other states, especially the U.S. He assured Brandt that "we had and have no such conniving plans."[160] Yet at the same time he differentiated between the role of France and Great Britain on one hand, and that of the U.S. on the other. Brezhnev suggested that his main criterion for good and promising relations was the level of independence with which a country pursued its own goals.[161] Ironically, he attributed the lack of political and economic interaction between the FRG and the Soviet Union during the 1960s to the fact that "until recently the FRG was in a position vis-à-vis the East in its foreign policy that didn't allow it to make fundamental decisions." Conveniently forgetting that it had been the Soviet Union that had isolated the FRG and not vice versa, Brezhnev continued to portray the Soviet Union as Germany's new friend, one that would enable the FRG "to assume a place in the world that corresponds with its economic and technological prowess, so that the FRG could utilize its influence for the security and cooperation in Europe."[162] In a blatant stab at the U.S., he continued, "we know that there are powers that want to benefit from the tensions between the FRG and the Soviet Union."[163]

Brezhnev then continued his policy of playing up the generous friend card toward the subjugated Germany.

> Deviating from my prepared notes, I would like to say that the Americans have really entrenched themselves in Europe since the war, especially in the FRG. … I have no clear intelligence, how far the Americans have penetrated the economy of the FRG, but it is without doubt, that they did and continue to try. You have to make up your mind on what you want to read into this fact. I do not know if the FRG likes this situation but I could imagine that your people and party wonder how to free themselves from this oppression. I only want to say that you do not need such supervision, for example in economic and technological areas. I am sure that the FRG could be much more successful when deciding political, economic, and other questions independently. In the U.S. they understand this all too well. That is why they pursue a certain policy or swear loyalty to the allies and portray the Communists as the bad guys. And the people believe that these are now our protectors, the democrats, and the others are the bitches, the communists. I am convinced that it is the other way around and that history will prove me right. I remember very well the images of fraternization between Russians and Germans during World War I.[164]

Unfortunately, the translator's protocol documenting this digression does not reflect whether Brandt in any way argued for or against these statements. While it is doubtful that Brandt actually believed this biased recollection of the past, the fact remains that Brezhnev had in fact offered Germany an active and leading role in a future Europe that would be marked by security and cooperation. While Brezhnev provided only a vague glimpse of what this new Europe would look like, he was very clear about its prerequisite: Germany would have to behave in a more independent manner vis-à-vis the United States. Having the FRG embedded in a European Economic Community made a more assertive Germany a foreign policy possibility.

Needing the ratification of the Eastern Treaties as much as Brandt, Brezhnev became personally involved in the process. On the day before the vote, Brezhnev invited the president of the Bundesrat, Heinz Kühn, for a conversation that lasted considerably longer than originally scheduled. Brezhnev asked Kühn to convey to Brandt that both he and many people within the Soviet Union had personal sympathy for Brandt. Repeatedly, Brezhnev and Gromyko "sometimes in the same words" intimated that the treaty was well balanced and that one could not expect the impossible from the Soviet Union.[165] "No German government will find a person to talk to about changing the treaty, should the Bundestag refuse it."[166]

Brezhnev, using the stick as well as the carrot, threatened: "A rejection of the treaties would be negative for the Federal Republic, negative for Europe, and negative for international politics as a whole." He then reverted to a more conciliatory approach, asking Kühn, "What else can we do?"[167] Brezhnev was so eager to see the Eastern Treaties approved that he even leaned on the GDR to appear publicly supportive of the Brandt government in the crucial weeks prior to the vote in Parliament. Consequently, the GDR implemented a "Brandt-Schutzwoche," taking great care to prevent any inter-German controversy that could harm Brandt politically.[168]

The Soviet back-channel contact to Brandt, Vyacheslav Kevorkov, also had a conversation with Egon Bahr in which Bahr remarked flippantly that the Brandt government did not have the kind of money necessary to bribe members of the Bundestag, and thus "such means [of gaining a majority in the Bundestag for the ratification of the Eastern treaties] have little interest to us."[169] In response to this conversation Kosygin approved a plot to deliver over a million marks to Bahr in West Berlin for the express purpose of bribing members of the Bundestag.[170] Bahr ultimately declined the offer, but this extreme measure demonstrates how much the Soviet Union was willing to meddle with internal German politics in order to achieve the ratification of the Eastern Treaties.

One strategy that Bahr would have liked to see come to fruition to help him battle the opponents of the Eastern Treaties went too far for the Soviets: upon learning that former chancellor and CDU icon Konrad Adenauer himself had floated a version of a new *Ostpolitik* in the 1950s, Bahr urged his Soviet contact, Kevorkov, to have the transcript of this interchange publicized.[171] Gromyko, upon reviewing the document, refused to release it as it was immediately categorized as a confidential conversation. His concern was rooted in a feared loss of international credibility should such a document come to light.[172]

Thanks to this intense level of Soviet support, the eagerness of West German industry, and a German public that had gradually abandoned its perception of the Soviet Union as an enemy, Brandt's *Ostpolitik* cleared this final hurdle. The razor-thin majority in the German parliament approved Brandt's leadership and his *Ostpolitik* on 27 April 1972, and with it assured the ratification of the Eastern Treaties on 17 May 1972. With the Soviets, the Western allies, and even the majority of the West German public in (sometimes tacit) support, the recognition of the status quo—the first step in the plan to overcome it—had been achieved. While this first step toward recognition had been difficult enough, the second step, a period of political change in the East, would prove even more taxing. Regardless, *Ostpolitik* had worked. Having overcome international skepticism and domestic opposition, Brandt had wrestled West Germany into accepting the realities of postwar Europe.

Through economic diplomacy, Brandt had managed to open a line of communication with the Soviet Union and demonstrated the strength of the FRG: economics. Increased cooperation with the East had normalized relations with the Soviet Union and the Eastern bloc and thereby "normalized" the image of the communist states in the political culture of West Germany. For some, these accomplishments outweighed the political repercussions that had to be faced. For others, the recognition of postwar borders, the trade deals that heavily favored the Soviet Union, and the threat to unhinge Western cohesion were too high a price to pay for the normalization of relations with the East.

However, the underlying conflict continued to revolve around how to defeat communism. The liberal argument, as advocated by the Brandt government, held that technology transfer and economic help for an enemy state could have a positive outcome, as the penetrating effects of trade and the necessary personal interactions would ultimately undermine the enemy regime and cause a positive dividend in the form of freedom and democracy. This was certainly Brandt's line of reasoning; by 1972 Kissinger appeared to have seen some value in this approach as well. Nixon, however, embraced a more conservative interpretation, viewing economic interchanges with enemy states as dangerous and only to be pursued with caution; trade deals had to be weighed carefully so as not to fundamentally aid the enemy's economic infrastructure, social stability, or military readiness. Certainly there were members of the CDU/CSU who held similar views and voiced them publicly. However, the shift in perception of the Soviet Union from an enemy state to a less threatening and more normal one—a shift brought about mostly through politics and economic diplomacy—rendered the conservative argument increasingly less applicable in the eyes of the West German public. This change would be *Ostpolitik's* lasting legacy and at the same time would function as a wedge for the transatlantic alliance. The United States had not undergone such a process and would soon shift to an even more conservative stance.

Following the successful completion of the Four Power Agreement and the ratification of the Eastern Treaties, Brandt's *Ostpolitik* appeared more successful than ever. German business involvement in the Soviet Union was at an unprecedented level, the West Berlin issue had apparently been resolved, and a military threat from the East seemed unlikely at best. The signing of the Eastern Treaties and Berlin Accords gave Brandt's initiatives unprecedented support within West Germany and the U.S. alike, seemingly turning the structure of the Western alliance on its head. The leader of the Western world, Richard Nixon, appeared to tread in the footsteps of Brandt and Pompidou rather than directing Western détente.

Traditional political interpretation holds that U.S. détente and German *Ostpolitik* were complementary, if not similar. As Gottfried Niedhardt argues, "the structural interdependence of American détente and German *Ostpolitik*" gave credence to Kissinger's statement that "your success will be our success."[173] Yet despite Kissinger's words, Brandt's success must have stung. Embracing historian Jeremi Suri's characterization of Henry Kissinger, he was "above all, a revolutionary" who sought to "redefine the use of force in international affairs" in the context of "competitive leverage."[174] In the fall of 1972, more so than at any other time, Brandt's policies appeared to have succeeded in bringing about a true revolution—without the use of force and without U.S. leadership.

Neither the style nor the structure of *Ostpolitik* appealed to the White House, and neither Nixon nor Kissinger was content to follow their allies on the road to Moscow. Nor did they approve of the qualitative level of interactions between their Western European allies and the Soviet Union. With the Vietnam conflict largely marginalized, the Soviet-American summit of May 1972 allowed the leaders of the Western and Eastern blocs to lay the groundwork for their own reconciliation, turning détente into their own superpower détente.

4

THE ORIGINS OF NATO's ENERGY DILEMMA (1972–1974)

The summer of 1972 was the heyday of Brandt's *Ostpolitik,* when he appeared to have achieved what he promised to do in his inaugural address: strike the perfect balance between reaching out to the East and retaining Western support. For the remainder of Brandt's tenure, though, it would be Nixon's détente strategies that determined East-West relations. Brezhnev recognized the revisionist element in *Ostpolitik,* especially as it undermined the status quo within the Eastern alliance. To Brandt, recognizing the status quo was not the same as being resigned to it; rather, *Ostpolitik* was a means to a peaceful change.[1] Nixon's offer of superpower détente promised much more stability and adherence to traditional alliance structures and the status quo. The following chapter deals with the Soviet downscaling of *Ostpolitik,* attempts and failures to reach this sought-after superpower détente, and the emergence of subsequent rifts within NATO.

Superpower Détente

The milestone in Nixon's détente policy with the Soviet Union was the year 1972 and the summit meeting in Moscow. In time for the November elections, Nixon's visit with Brezhnev demonstrated to the rest of the world that America's handicap—Vietnam—had been overcome and that the United States was now in a strong position to shape international relations again.

To get to that point, the Nixon/Kissinger team used the "China card" against the Soviet Union. Reconciliation with China had been a foreign policy success, putting Moscow on the defensive, escalating Soviet military costs while lowering those of the United States, and forcing the Soviets to be more cooperative and conciliatory toward Washington. Nixon also believed that improving relations with China would have the net effect of helping to settle the war in Vietnam.[2] Through various oblique channels, the Nixon White House established contact with the communist regime in China, intent on exploring the possibility of a summit meeting. On 10 May, Kissinger handed Washington's formal response to Pakistani ambassador Hilaly for delivery to Beijing. In the reply, Nixon accepted the invitation to visit Beijing.

Kissinger's secret diplomacy during his trip to Beijing did not produce normalization in relations with China for several years to come, but it resulted in immediate dividends in regard to the Soviet Union. The addition of China to what had been a bilateral U.S.-Soviet confrontation complicated Soviet strategic calculations. The Soviet ambassador to Washington, Anatoly Dobrynin, found himself in a difficult situation and was now eager to set a date for a Nixon-Brezhnev summit. As a result the *New York Times* was able to report "a change in atmosphere," a so-called turning point in the Soviet position on the previously stalled Strategic Arms Limitation Talks, opening the way for the Nixon-Brezhnev summit meeting the following year.[3] Whether it was owed to the effective playing of the China card or the need for a resolution on West Berlin, this change in atmosphere represented the first moment since Nixon's inaugural address when he could truly transition from an era of confrontation to an era of negotiation.[4]

Nixon's visit to Moscow in May 1972, coupled with the signing of the agreement on strategic arms, started the superpower détente that he had had envisioned since his inauguration. With the Vietnam issue largely resolved and his allies heavily engaged in fostering new ties with the Soviet Union, it was time for Nixon to realize his version of détente. Such a version of superpower détente was institutionalized with the Agreement of Basic Principles of Relations in 1972, which had little impact on core Soviet military capabilities but represented the United States' explicit acknowledgement of the Soviet Union's superpower status and its implicit parity with the U.S. Although this received relatively little attention in the United States Brezhnev was ecstatic, and the document was proudly interpreted as a "critically important principle." To raise public awareness of the "principle of parity and equal security" contained in the document, the Soviets launched a major propaganda campaign.[5] For the U.S., détente had set in. Enthusiastic newspapers proclaimed "The New Equilibrium," and Nixon declared to Congress that his diplomatic ties had "begun to free us from perpetual confrontation."[6]

In an ironic role reversal, it was now the Western Europeans' turn to worry that the Western alliance did not have a coordinated détente policy. This reversal expressed itself in regard to the Soviet-German negotiations on the Eastern Treaties: it was now the U.S. administration that had withheld documents for several months from its NATO allies, only to present them as a fait accompli. European voices in NATO thus referred to the summit as a "deception" that showed disregard for the alliance.[7]

Brezhnev must have been pleased with this fringe benefit. The Soviet Union only stood to gain from this political shift from "selective European détente" to "superpower détente." The only area that still dampened Soviet enthusiasm in dealing with the United States was, again, East-West trade. In the Soviet-American Agreement of Basic Principles of Relations, signed by the two heads of state in May 1972, economic ties were considered "an important element in the strengthening of their bilateral relations and thus [we] will actively promote such ties."[8] In Soviet eyes, however, this fell disappointingly short of a clear agreement on trade and the granting of Most Favored Nation status.

Nevertheless, hopes were high. In terms of exports to the United States, the Soviet Union would sell its energy resources, as one of the few Soviet commodities marketable in the West. The two proposed avenues of export, the North Star and the Yakutsk natural gas projects, required heavy investments. Estimated at $4 billion and $2.5 billion respectively, they involved the liquefaction of large quantities of natural gas that would in turn be shipped to the United States. Political concerns in the U.S. over Soviet energy imports had diminished by 1972, partially because of growing concerns over OPEC and the political instability of the Middle East. An additional wrinkle was the heavy lobbying undertaken by energy and energy equipment companies in Congress.[9]

The U.S.-Soviet summit meeting thus drastically changed the White House's perception of and approach to East-West trade. Kissinger embraced trade and advocated economic interaction that provided an element of stability to the political equation.[10] Nixon even lobbied personally for such economic interactions, encouraging "American firms to work out concrete proposals on these projects and [he] will give serious and sympathetic consideration to proposals that are in the interests of both sides."[11] The longer-lasting advantage the Soviets would reap from a trade deal, however, would be the influx of high-end steel and equipment needed to develop the problematic Soviet permafrost gas fields. To this day Russia lacks the production capability for steel pipes of sufficiently high quality to withstand the harsh conditions of the Soviet tundra. Even the Soviet Politburo was aware of the fact that without Western help, the development of permafrost oil and gas fields could occur at best sometime in the next century.[12]

The economic advantages of détente offered Brezhnev the necessary momentum for his détente policies in the Politburo. As Zubok illustrates convincingly, it was the personal meeting between Nixon and Brezhnev that caused the latter to support détente unequivocally. For Brezhnev's political success and domestic support, however, détente had to be accompanied by economic growth.[13] With all the elements in place to follow the European example in a substantial increase of East-West trade, there remained the stumbling block of the Soviet MFN status. If Soviet natural gas was to arrive on the U.S. mainland at a competitive price, the Soviet Union could not afford the 20 percent surcharge under the current tariff scale. Furthermore, the perpetual crux when dealing with the Soviets—financing—had to be arranged. The Nixon administration therefore pushed for a change in MFN status in Congress, as well as an expansion of the financing of the Export-Import (EXIM) Bank from 20 to 30 billion dollars, enabling the bank to cover the considerable sums involved in both of these deals.

For the Soviet leadership, Nixon apparently held the keys to the kingdom in regard to the future of East-West trade and the political successes associated with détente. Not only had Nixon's visit lent credibility to détente, but—much more importantly—it meant the U.S. recognized the Soviet Union as an equal and tacitly accepted the Soviet occupation of Eastern Europe. In order to reap the successes of détente, then, the U.S. had stepped into the breach as the most important Western market for the Soviet Union and thereby morphed from a political stumbling block for German-Soviet trade into the preferred partner.

Economically and politically West Germany had little left to offer, given that its industry had already invested a great deal of capital in the Soviet economy and was eager for smooth East-West relations in order to avoid any disruptive effects.[14] West German exports were mostly heavy machinery—such as the large-diameter steel press by Mannesmann Corp—which required considerable domestic investment. Yet despite selling a product that was in high demand in the Soviet Union, West Germany, as a second rate power, had little leverage in countering Soviet trade or negotiation practices, be they political or economic.

Systemic Shifts in the Soviet Union

By 1973, priorities in the Soviet Union were clearly shifting. A cursory examination of the Soviet *Westpolitik* ledger after only three years of détente negotiations reveals an impressive diplomatic record by mid 1973: an agreement on the "inviolability" of all existing European borders signed in Moscow in 1970, a series of sizable energy contracts with the Germans, and the Americans' promise in 1972 to loosen trade restrictions.

At the same time, however, the tenuous governmental consensus revolving around East-West détente began to show signs of strain. At the center of opposition stood the Soviet International Department, whose conservative minister of defense, Andrei Grechko, bluntly expressed reservations about détente in an address to a party gathering in April of 1972. Since American capitalists "constantly aim, year after year, to increase their war power toward world domination," he argued, "our country [the USSR] needs to accept the necessity of defense measures, reinforce our global policy of strengthening defense capabilities, increase the war potential of our armaments and their war preparedness."[15]

More revealing of Brezhnev's emerging attitude is one American historian's account of the private assurances he made to a group of party members in April of 1973. Apparently sensitive to conservative opposition in regard to Soviet diplomacy, Brezhnev stressed the expediency of détente, justifying it as a period of national strengthening until the Soviets might gain enough strength to challenge the "imperialists" more vigorously. An observer summarized the sense of Brezhnev's argument: "it is appropriate to recall the words of Marx in one of his letters, that in politics you may conclude alliances with the Devil himself if you are certain you can cheat the Devil."[16]

The Soviet variant of the U.S. government's shift in institutional power came with Brezhnev's decision in May 1973 to elevate Gromyko, Defense Minister Grechko, and KGB Chairman Yuri Andropov to full membership in the Politburo. Grechko, as the commander of the Soviet troops that had crushed the East German workers' rebellion of 1953 and the architect of the 1968 invasion of Czechoslovakia, was no friend of an intensive cooperation between East and West. While Gromyko and Andropov must be seen as allies in the pursuit of détente, Grechko strengthened the conservative voices in the Politburo. In this sense, there certainly was a shift to a more conservative Soviet foreign policy.

Brezhnev had numerous reasons for altering a governing body that had otherwise been remarkably stable during his era, though only two of these reasons are important here. One was the desire to consolidate his power, which since the fall of Khrushchev had been rising to its peak in 1973. He achieved this by integrating the heads of the three major government agencies into the Politburo's collective decision-making apparatus. Brezhnev clearly hoped that the consensus the Politburo traditionally engendered would both reduce the influence of individual governmental departments and enhance his role as political arbitrator.

A second, somewhat paradoxical reason was that given his uncertainty about the future of détente, he wished to widen the variety of policy opinions he could stress in formulating his future foreign policy.[17]

Over the long term, the most important consequence of this change was the legitimization of a policy-making role for the defense establishment in the areas of foreign policy, from which it had hitherto been nominally excluded. Grechko's International Department, which to this point in the Brezhnev period been a decidedly junior partner to Gromyko's Foreign Ministry, increased its voice and influence with the probable patronage of Brezhnev. This emboldened formerly quiet conservatives in the government to insert harsher notes among the leaders' prepared statements.[18] This would gradually shift Soviet diplomacy in the direction of a more aggressive stance toward the West.

Ironically, Bahr did not find this Politburo shift by any means troublesome—indeed, he congratulated Gromyko on his election to the Politburo a month later.[19] Bahr did not interpret this as a categorical shift against détente, but rather as a reprioritizing of potential partners within the Western alliance. In his view, the Soviet relationship with United States simply had gained greater priority with some in the Soviet Union.

> There exists, so to say, a "pro-American faction" in Moscow that argues that the relationship between the U.S.A. and the Soviet Union has absolute priority. The issue is by and large the question of Most-Favored-Nation status. The Russians need it; the decision should be made before the adjournment of the Senate for the summer. After that, the visit of the General Secretary [Brezhnev] to the U.S. is planned for June.[20]

Judging from the continued efforts of the East to undermine the ties between West Berlin and the FRG during the remainder of the 1970s, it seems safe to argue that a conservative shift in Soviet foreign policy accounts for some of the cooling observed in relations between the FRG and the Soviet Union. If we presume, however, that the Soviet Union used Brandt's *Ostpolitik* to force the United States into implementing its own sweeping policy of détente, Nixon's visit to Moscow was the culmination of Soviet strategy to get a superpower détente in place. Once this had been achieved, the Soviets could discard *Ostpolitik* as a superfluous strategy, thus rendering the role of the FRG less important, which makes Bahr's assessment of a shift in Soviet priorities quite accurate. This interpretation gives credence to the idea that the Soviet Union simply used Germany to get to the U.S.

A report regarding the central committee's view on this matter, provided by Bahr's secret back-channel contact, Ledlev, further strengthens this argument. It should have cautioned Bahr about the primacy of superpower détente over Soviet relations with Germany. The fact that Brezhnev quoted Lenin in his report on economic relations clearly indicates that they were using trade as a temporary measure to advance socialism, not to build a path to permanent cooperation.

> The Nixon visit was a turning point. For the first time he accepted the principles of coexistence and the borders of the Socialist world. The political fight against America will be continued because in many areas they are the enemy. Economic ties will continue to be developed. The already concluded treaty of about 10 billion dollars was just the beginning. ...
> The General Secretary [Brezhnev] spoke for almost an hour about the economic ties to the Western world. He cited Lenin, whose teachings had been forgotten in the meantime: Despite the differences of the systems, economic ties need to be strengthened. One can structure them in such a way that Capitalism works for the cause of Socialism. Not everyone in the Soviet Union understands this great potential.[21]

By restructuring the Politburo, Brezhnev had not just accounted for the opponents to Soviet détente but also ensured his own survival, should superpower détente fail to work out. With the question of economic benefits gaining central importance in the Soviet leadership and becoming a determining factor in its foreign policy, Soviet MFN status became a necessity.

Ostpolitik in the Crossfire

For the Western alliance, the new Soviet favoritism meant a reshuffling of the international deck. After the Nixon-Brezhnev summit in May 1972, the tables had turned for West Germany and the United States. Rather than "Smiles for Europe, frowns for Washington," now the West German Foreign Office observed that Soviet officials "strive for a friendly tone" — even on Vietnam — while they barraged West German/ West Berlin ties every way possible.[22]

With the accord from the summit, Brezhnev had achieved the two elements he had sought from détente with the West: first, a stable border in Europe that allowed the Soviet Union to focus more of its resources in the East, toward China; and secondly, the possibility of East-West trade to foster Soviet economic growth and exploit Soviet natural resources. The FRG was no longer needed to accomplish either goal: The status quo in Europe had been achieved with the ratification of the Eastern Treaties, and West Germany's joining the Non-Proliferation Treaty had prevented any chance of West Germany reemerging as a military threat. With regard to East-West trade, West German industry was so dependent on progress in East-West trade that economic ties seemed irreversible. Large investments by Western European banks and companies in long-term contracts closely tied the fate of both to the continued success of Soviet economic growth and détente policies. Now the "German card" had become a liability more than an asset.[23] A more confrontational approach toward *Ostpolitik* and West Berlin might placate some disgruntled hard-line allies.[24]

The first issue for West German officials arose in the venue of sports. On 10 June 1972, during a track meet between the delegates from the Soviet Union and FRG, the Soviets argued that the German team had to be labeled *Bundesrepublik Deutschland/West Berlin*, even though official German policy did not allow the use of the term West Berlin if the team was mixed.[25] A more serious demonstration of the Berlin issue occurred at a trade fair for machine tools in Brünn, Czechoslovakia, in September 1972. The organizers of the fair listed West Berlin as an independent country in the catalogue and during the official ceremony, despite having previously accepted the link between West Berlin and West Germany. When German Ambassador Finckenstein objected to the printing of the catalogue, he received the evasive reply that logistics prevented any changes in the printing. When he further protested the raising of the Berlin flag during the initial ceremony, however, the issue became more palpable. The Czech representative indicated that "the treatment of West Berlin firms at fairs and exhibitions in the CSSR is linked to the question of normalization between the two countries." Finckenstein interpreted this new Czech stance as a permanent problem: the CSSR would not budge on the issue and linked this policy to a directive from the Soviet embassy.[26]

The origin of these problems was the very ambivalent language of the Four Power Agreement. Essentially, it allowed West Germany and West Berlin to be linked on a case-by-case basis, depending on whether the two countries in question decided they should be or not. As one would expect, Western allies interpreted a stronger link between the two than did the East. The vagueness inherent in the Four Power Agreement stemmed from the West German side having been more concerned with reaching an agreement than hammering out ironclad language. When the CDU leaked the problems with the Four Power Agreement formulations to the press, Bahr compared the situation of West Berlin to that Lichtenstein: he explained in the interview that no one questioned Swiss representation of Lichtenstein, despite the fact that Lichtenstein is a completely sovereign nation.[27] Likewise, he argued, "[a]ccording to international law, Berlin does not belong to the Federal Republic of

Germany ... Lichtenstein is not part of Switzerland, either."[28] Despite this undoubtedly valid point, the ambiguity in the negotiations and the subsequent conflict centering on its interpretation are logical only if the Soviets took Bahr's analogy between Berlin and Lichtenstein to mean that Berlin's representation by the FRG would be a matter of negotiation at a later point in time and not automatic. After all, signing an agreement that both sides anticipate interpreting somewhat differently is common practice in high diplomacy.

In May 1973 the problem of West Berlin's status, as manifested at the Czechoslovakian trade fair, reoccurred in the Soviet Union. On this occasion the exhibits from West Berlin were—according to the Soviets—supposed to be opened by Berliner officials, and the flags of both Berlin and the Soviet Union would be raised. The Soviets insisted that FRG delegates refrain from participating in this ceremony, arguing that the military occupation forces were the sovereigns of West Berlin and that the FRG could not represent them. The FRG, of course, did not share in this interpretation, which resulted in numerous discussions and the forceful removal of Undersecretary Rowedder from the scene of the opening ceremony by Soviet security forces. Apparently Rowedder, as an official West German representative, had attempted to push the West Berlin representative and the Soviet delegate aside in order to get to the center of the ceremony. Soviet security personnel claimed that they had feared for the Soviet delegate's life and thus had him removed from the scene.[29]

They Soviets further assaulted the West Germany–West Berlin link in a book on the history of Berlin. The German embassy in Moscow noted the "intensity with which the author tries to prove that the special ties of the Berlin Accords between the FRG and West Berlin do not hinder the independence of West Berlin."[30] The author continued to outline the Soviet interpretation of the Four Power Agreement:

> From the viewpoint of sovereignty, West Berlin is a unique political organism that does not belong to any state. ... West Berliners are as residents of such an organism neither citizens of the Federal Republic nor the GDR and hold special identification papers.
>
> The Soviet position with regard to West Berlin has not changed and cannot change. The Berlin Accords do not contain decisions and do not introduce a procedure known to international law that would change the status of West Berlin.[31]

According to the Germans, the Soviet Union was narrowly focusing on the issue of sovereignty as outlined in the Four Power Agreement, conveniently ignoring the clause that said it was a moral duty to strengthen ties between West Berlin and West Germany. Yet even in view of the conflicts over Berlin, the Brandt government hoped to resolve these controversial issues. Brandt and Bahr remained confident that West Germany was no longer just a pawn caught between the United States and the Soviet Union, but an important player in international politics.

In May 1973, as Brezhnev restructured the Politburo, Kissinger, overly confident, assured Nixon that Brezhnev "should be deeply committed to a more positive relationship with the U.S."[32] He was right, of course, that Brezhnev strove for an intensification of ties with the U.S. He did not, however, recognize the area where cooperation was needed most. By limiting foreign policy to diplomatic issues, Kissinger neglected the adage that all foreign policy is also domestic policy and its corollary that domestic pressure can seriously harm international strategies. As Hanhimäki illustrates, the domestic influence of President Nixon was a crucial component in implementing foreign policy. With Watergate discrediting the president's image and political strength on an almost daily basis in the fall of 1973, domestic opposition to the president's policies grew proportionally in strength.[33]

The Jackson-Vanik amendment was the political issue that threatened to wipe out Kissinger's vision of détente with the Soviet Union. Senator Henry Jackson (D-WA) raised the issue of an exit tax the Soviets imposed in August 1972 on Jewish citizens who wished to leave the Soviet Union. In October 1972, Jackson and Representative Charles Vanik (D-OH) had introduced bills in both the House and the Senate that linked the question of Jewish emigration to improvements in trade. As James Goldgeier illustrates, the irony of Senator Henry Jackson's opposition to Kissinger was that he and Kissinger advocated the same linkage strategy. The only difference in Jackson's approach was that he linked the carrots—in this case U.S. economic incentives—with the internal behavior of the Soviet Union, while Kissinger looked exclusively at external behavior.[34]

A congressional committee traveled to the Soviet Union in December 1972, intent on exploring the possibilities of East-West trade. The members of Congress concluded that "MFN status, workable commercial relationships for United States businesses in the U.S.S.R., and acceptable conditions for approving large-scale U.S. governmental and private credit to Soviet-United States joint project" are essential elements to a growing trade relations. A rejection of MFN status for the Soviet Union might bring the potential trade to a standstill.[35]

The most problematic of these issues, to the Soviets and the Nixon White House alike, was the Jackson-Vanik amendment. As the congressional delegation observed,

Soviet officials on all levels were concerned with the attitude of the U.S. Congress on Most-Favored Nation Status for the Soviet Union. Specifically, the link between the Jackson Amendment to the East-West Trade Relations Act linking exit fees to MFN status was very much in their minds. ... In fact, the vehemence of Soviet reference suggested that the approval of MFN may be a test case or a turning point in progress not only of commercial but of Soviet–United States relations as a whole.[36]

Kissinger displayed disdain for the amendment, but fundamentally underestimated how crucial East-West trade had become for the Soviet Union. Brezhnev, eager to rid himself of the problem presented by the Jackson-Vanik amendment, stopped the practice of exit fees in April. Jackson, though, having found a topic that resonated with the American public for his potential presidential campaign, decided to take it one step further, insisting that the Soviets needed to specify a minimum number of exit visas and extend the same right to non-Jewish emigrants.[37] Clearly demonstrating how fervently the Soviets desired MFN status, Brezhnev informed Kissinger during the preparation for the summit that "all those who want to can go."[38] Kissinger, however, discarded the issue as "peripheral," thereby allowing the issue to become a public power struggle within the U.S., culminating in punitive measures that the Soviet Union could only regard as meddling in its internal affairs.

Even though Kissinger failed to view the issue with much concern, Brezhnev certainly did. He realized how critical MFN status was to his strategy of keeping hard-liners content while fostering détente. Balancing aggressive gestures toward Western Europe with expressions designed to mollify the United States, Brezhnev sought to appease the hard-liners, all the while continuing to reap the benefits of East-West trade. Brezhnev's upcoming visits to Bonn and Washington, thus, would be two very different experiences.

The Brezhnev Summits in West Germany and the U.S.

Initially, Brezhnev's proposed visits to the West appeared to pit the two Western versions of détente against each other. Upon hearing from Bahr that Brezhnev was planning to visit Germany, the Americans "reacted somewhat surprised and floated the idea through Dobrynin whether it would not be more appropriate if Brezhnev first visited America."[39] Clearly, the issue of Western leadership was at stake.

As a consequence, the German-American summit meeting of 1–2 May 1973 proved to be somewhat tense. Despite Nixon's lingering resentment over Brandt's "ambivalent support" and the implication "that [Nixon's] decisions and actions have lacked humanitarian concern," the Nixon administration felt compelled to raise numerous issues that it felt should be the subject of transatlantic cooperation.[40] Nixon outlined his views on European integration as follows: "I have strongly supported European integration and intend to continue to do so, but as I believe we both agree, European integration should also be seen as a step toward increased Atlantic cooperation."[41] Demonstrating the sorry condition of transatlantic cooperation and consultation he felt obligated to express that he "hope[d] that before any proposals are made final we will have an opportunity to express our views."[42]

More important than economic issues were the concerns about a widening rift within the alliance. Nixon bluntly asked Brandt whether he found it difficult to be confronted by France or England about choosing to put either Europe or America first. Brandt responded that he had always made it clear to the French that "in questions of security or the world currency reform he could not proceed against the U.S."[43] While this appeared to be a satisfactory answer, the qualifications—security and currency reform—left plenty of tension between Nixon's and Brandt's views of the alliance. As Brandt explained to Brezhnev only a few days later, he rejected what had become Kissinger's trademark: linking different aspects of negotiation.

> Kissinger has tried to bring military, trade, currency, and diplomatic questions all together in one form and this did not correspond with reality. ... How things would develop is not clear, but Western Europe will gain more its "own personality" as the French call it, even in relations with the U.S.A., on whom they have depended to such large extent after the Second World War.[44]

Nixon, of course, could in no way have been pleased with this desire to separate issues, as it basically negated any European concessions in return for the military protection provided by the U.S. and theoretically allowed for unilateral policies. Ironically, while driving this point home to Brandt, he excluded trade as the one aspect that could be conducted unilaterally.

> He [Nixon] accepts that there is an economic competition between a united Europe and America. This does not trouble him. For him, it is also not important if Europe purchases more oranges or tobacco. What is important, however, is that the impression is not created that the Nine [Western European Countries] are organizing against America in affairs of a certain political significance as the American defense readiness must suffer from this. ...

> Cooperation with the Soviet Union does not happen for love, but for
> bitter necessity. Western cohesion must not be impeded by provincial
> quarrels. ... The problem, thus, is how the West can avoid a disintegra-
> tion that would strengthen the enemy forces.[45]

In summary, Brandt's orientation toward placing French interests
before U.S. ones seems abundantly clear. With the Soviets still appearing to back Germany's pioneering role in world diplomacy, Brandt
felt no need to bend over backward to please the United States. In the
name of Europe, the U.S. was expected to accept developments that ran
counter to its interests.[46] By separating economic, political, and military
dialogues, West Germans hoped to create political room in which to
maneuver, even if the remainder of the globe was still mired in tensions
over the Cold War. In Bahr's assessment of the relationship between
Europe and the United States, self-confidence and trust in the new German foreign policy were central. Furthermore, his sense that Germany
no longer needed to contribute anything to the transatlantic alliance is
striking.

> Europe's weight increases proportionally as the relative importance of
> the security question declines. Over the past years, we have actively con-
> tributed in getting the two superpowers to come closer together and thus
> made them politically easier to manipulate, despite being immovable
> militarily.
>   America guarantees today the security of its allies, just as the Soviet
> Union does, without either needing their respective alliances. Both sys-
> tems are political coordination machines, while the Americans increas-
> ingly want to relieve their financial burdens. The Russians accomplish
> this with trade deals negotiated through blackmail for prices under world
> market levels in order to benefit from the occupied countries economi-
> cally. The Americans do the same through unequal currency exchange
> rates.[47]

Using such drastic language to equate the Soviet Union and the
United States demonstrates how little Bahr thought the FRG had lost
by loosening ties with the United States. Confident in the importance
of Germany and the rest of Europe in the world, he was convinced that
the United States would remain in Europe, no matter what the Europeans did. Yet Nixon need not have feared. For Brezhnev domestically,
engaging the U.S. while vilifying West Germany was a much more sensible policy than vice versa. As the West Germans had noticed but not
understood, the crises over West Berlin signaled as much.

During the German-Soviet summit meeting, the issue of West Berlin
became rather prominent. As previously outlined, the East was under-

mining the Western understanding of the Four Power Agreement, and Brandt felt compelled to raise the Berlin issue again when Brezhnev visited Bonn in May 1973. He prodded that "when dealing with issues of trade, economy, culture and sports, the basic guideline in accordance with the spirit of the agreement must be not to separate artificially. If we could agree on this, it would make life much easier."[48]

Brezhnev, however, responded with a stalling tactic. He refused to comment on the grounds that he did not remember the text in detail and would have to consult with Gromyko. In his recollection of this event to the U.S. ambassador to Germany, Brandt explained that Brezhnev never returned to the subject. Accordingly, Brandt—after issuing a final statement on the summit meeting—broke with accepted protocol and, walking up to Brezhnev, cautioned him in the presence of Gromyko that the Soviets had to accept not only the general declaration that West Germany and West Berlin were separate entities, but also the concluding remarks that the ties between the two entities need to be strengthened. Brandt bluntly explained that failure to do so would poison West German-Soviet relations. The Soviet leaders acknowledged him but did not respond to his argument.[49]

The fact that the Soviets were no longer willing to let the FRG represent West Berlin was also evident in lower-level negotiations. A working group consisting of Gromyko, Falin, and four German delegates (Bahr among them) met to work out the wording of the final declaration of the Brezhnev visit. The debate once again centered on the issue of mentioning West Berlin firms as part of West German–Soviet economic relations. Bahr commented that the term "companies from the Federal Republic of Germany" also included companies from Berlin (West). Gromyko responded: "[W]e do not know that. We do not know your contacts with companies there. We can only close our eyes." Bahr replied: "You do not have to close your eyes. We have a trade agreement that contains a Berlin clause." Gromyko concluded: "All right, then with open eyes."[50]

Yet another argument over the inclusion of West Berlin occurred in regard to the supplemental agreement for science and technology cooperation. The Soviet representative, Bondarenko, objected to the German requirement that a Berlin clause be included in this document, arguing that the FRG was trying to change the Four Power Agreement on Berlin, which stated that the treaties of the FRG *may* be extended to West Berlin; now, he claimed, the FRG wanted to make this optional regulation a binding one.

Even West German industry leaders were rebuffed by Brezhnev over suggestions for closer cooperation and modifications to the economic structure of *Osthandel*. The major issue of contention was the diversification of bilateral trade. To the German industrialists, this could only be achieved through a multifaceted interweaving of the two economies via "as many varied forms of cooperation as possible." This meant moving beyond barter deals to "a common development of industrial products and a joint distribution of these to third countries."[51] Brezhnev categorically ruled this out. No foreign investments or joint ventures with Soviet firms would be possible.[52] Abandoning the practice of barter deals was not something that could be counted on in the foreseeable future, either.[53] He even balked at increasing cooperation between Western European companies, that is, allowing German companies to conduct large-scale Soviet orders jointly with France, Japan, or other partners. This was a practice that the Germans preferred, as Soviet orders traditionally were on a scale that went beyond the customary size. Brezhnev indicated that the Soviet Union wanted to undertake manageable projects and that "he did not wish to rule out multilateral cooperation entirely … but first one had to talk bilaterally with each other."[54]

Lastly, the demand for greater diversification—in terms of both deals and orders, so that mid-sized industries could benefit—failed to materialize to some extent. Brezhnev agreed that these kinds of deals could be useful, "but [stated that] large-scale projects are more important."[55] He even chided German industry and the government for not thinking in longer terms. Attributing the German interest in mid-sized orders to a lack of courage and the lingering effects of the strained relations of the last thirty years, he publicly chastised West German industry that this was not the way to inaugurate a period of a long-term growth with large-scale projects.[56]

Brezhnev's harsh words on Berlin and economic cooperation failed to have an immediate effect within the German business community. The Soviets' unwillingness to modify their economic system in order to make its products more competitive and the subsequent rise in Soviet debt on the German market had no effect on Soviet creditworthiness.[57] By 1973, the Soviet Union had become "by far the greatest of our [German] debtors," yet the German business community was willing to continue to foster trade with the East and to consider further large-scale loans.[58]

Brezhnev came across as much more buoyant in his subsequent trip to the United States. Publicly, the meetings occurred in a very relaxed atmosphere. Owing to the fact that the two sides were unable to come to an understanding on the two most contentious issues, the Middle East crisis and Vietnam, no groundbreaking agreements were concluded during the summit. The nine agreements that were signed dealt mostly with general commitments to cooperate in matters of trade, culture, taxation, and transportation. Perhaps the most notable of these agreements was the Prevention of Nuclear War Agreement. However, even here Kissinger had managed to whittle it down to insignificance.[59] The more significant aspect of this summit was not what was actually signed, but rather the attitude with which it was conducted. Kissinger's visit to the Soviet Union in May 1973, which laid the groundwork for the summit, was marked by Brezhnev's jovial attitude, willingness to compromise, and frank remarks.[60]

The Soviet leader continued this apparently pleasant attitude during his American visit, presenting himself affably to the U.S. public with good-natured humor and conciliatory statements. His "I'm going to leave here in a very good mood" attitude managed to pleasantly surprise the American public and shatter the stereotype of ill-natured Soviet dictators.[61] Brezhnev presented himself in such a neighborly manner that some commentaries suggested America should overlook the insignificant agreements and rejoice in the spirit of cooperation that sprang from this visit.[62] Even behind the scenes, Brezhnev—content that the Soviet Union's position was now considered on par with that of the U.S.—seemed to have gone beyond mere rhetoric, as his demand for a late-night meeting in Nixon's study to fix the Middle East problem demonstrated.[63] It seems clear that Brezhnev was enthusiastic about having achieved his goal of engaging the United States as an equal. If the 1972 Moscow summit meeting had initiated this development, Brezhnev's comfort level and affability had fortified it, not in words but rather in spirit. If anything, the 1973 summit was a public demonstration that the two superpowers were willing and able to cooperate with one another.

But in one key aspect, MFN status, the visit did not live up to Brezhnev's expectations. As demonstrated above, MFN was the linchpin on which East-West trade, and ultimately the success of détente, hung. Brezhnev needed MFN and had made it clear to Kissinger that he would do most anything to get it. It was no accident that Brezhnev had pushed forward the construction of a Siberian oil pipeline from the Samotlor oilfield to Eastern Europe. Requiring that workers take on double shifts and sometimes even run two pipes parallel in the swamps of Siberia, he had been able to dedicate the pipeline on 17 June, the day before he departed for the United States.[64] Despite the demonstrations of abundant energy commodities and heavy lobbying efforts with members of Congress during his visit, MFN would remain elusive. A Watergate-embattled White House was unwilling to seize on the blossoming climate of East-West relations and push MFN through Congress. As a result, Brezhnev would leave the U.S. without MFN.

For West Germany (and France), the public demonstration of superpower détente during the summit of 1973 was a mixed blessing. On one hand, an easing of superpower tensions invariably alleviated confrontation in Europe; on the other there was the realistic fear of becoming an insignificant pawn in the European corner of the geopolitical superpower chessboard. In this context, Kissinger's ill-fated public comments on the American proposal for a "Year of Europe" must have strengthened European concerns. Having distinguished between the United States' global interests and the European allies' regional interests in an interview dated 23 April 1973, Kissinger had essentially sidelined the Europeans. The lesson of the summit meeting in Washington was a demonstration of how well the superpowers could actually get along.[65] In a show of how disjointed the American and European flanks of NATO had become, Brandt vehemently refused a reassertion of U.S. tutelage. Having interpreted Kissinger's announcement of a "Year of Europe" as such, he declared that "refurbished Atlantic relations in no case put in question West Germany's policy of reconciliation with the Communist states."[66] Despite Brandt's outspoken affirmation regarding the success of *Ostpolitik*, the repercussions of Brezhnev's visits to Germany and the U.S. had shaken *Ostpolitik* to its core.

Cementing Superpower Détente and the Middle East Crisis

If one had to pinpoint a time when the U.S. held absolute sway over the course of Western détente, it would be the summer of 1973. This was not, as it might seem, necessarily due to the skillful maneuvering of Nixon or Kissinger, but was a result of Soviet actions. The summits between the Americans and the Soviets had made it clear that Brezhnev craved and enjoyed the recent recognition of the Soviet Union as the equal of the U.S. and also saw increasing prospects for stepped-up trade with the U.S. Indeed, the large U.S. economy and its global interests were an ideal match for Soviet demands. With the Soviets clearly favoring superpower détente, the Brandt government was forced to reorient itself and seek German reunification, as its predecessors had done, under the auspices of U.S. leadership.

In a blatant attempt to have his cake and eat it too, Brezhnev wrote Brandt to warn him that anti-German rhetoric would be on display during the upcoming Warsaw Pact meeting in August 1973. In particular, he emphasized his commitment to the continuity of the policy of peace that he and Brandt had pursued, and he attributed the agreement between the U.S. and the Soviet Union on the prevention of nuclear war to that policy. He described Nixon as "a statesman, who keeps his word as a solid partner" and viewed the improvement in U.S.-Soviet relations as a "good support for the course our two countries are taking."[67] Bahr, for one, bought into Brezhnev's rhetoric. He believed Brezhnev's declaration of peaceful intent to be sincere and pointed to the fact that in his letter Brezhnev had twice used the term "turning point" (*Wende*), not realizing that for Brezhnev the turning point was actually one toward a superpower détente. Bahr concluded that "the Eastern Summit is of course used to calm the truly upset group of chickens that make up the Warsaw Pact. Most of them are no smarter than our allies: they are afraid to be sold out."[68]

But it was the Brandt government that would be sold out. The director of the Osteuropa Institut in Munich, Dr. Heinrich Vogel, brought an increased number of contacts between certain Soviet foreign policy officials and the CDU/CSU to Bahr's attention. Using the example of Prof. Michail Sergeevic Voslenskij's visit to Germany, he explained that certain Soviet foreign-policy experts viewed the issue of German reunification as a dangerous one. They were disturbed by Bahr's emphasis on reunification and hoped to find a partner in the CDU/CSU who would foster a policy that clearly delineated between the FRG and GDR.[69] More important than pursuing contacts with the German opposition, though, was the rhetorical use of a revanchist West Germany as a binding agent for the Warsaw Pact. In a speech in August 1973, Brezhnev singled out the FRG as critically important to Soviet peace policy. First, though, he accused the Brandt government of fostering a policy designed to undermine the communist order, as he stated that this phenomenon was not just apparent in the opposition.[70]

Vilifying West Germany as the raison d'etre for the Eastern military alliance apparently exceeded Brandt's tolerance for what Brezhnev had warned him was rhetoric intended for domestic consumption. Feeling compelled to respond to these accusations, Brandt used an increasingly critical tone toward Soviet policy in his reply to Brezhnev, but most of all he voiced his "disappointment over the fact that this [Four Power Agreement] is still a problem between us that can overshadow the entirety of our relations. I would really hope that it is possible to reach a point at which no questions about Berlin bother us anymore."[71] Such a point, however, would never be reached during the Brandt administration. Starting in August 1973, Czech authorities refused any contact with German administrations in Berlin who requested legal assistance. The reason was the absence of West Berlin in the corresponding agreement between West Germany and the CSSR. While the agreement previously had been interpreted to implicitly include West Berlin, now nothing short of an explicit mention of West Berlin would suffice.

The GDR continued this line of pressure. On 25 September 1973, immediately following a diplomatic victory through their admission to the Inter-Governmental Maritime Consultative Organization (IMCO), a sub-organization of the United Nations, GDR delegates protested against the FRG's 21 September 1965 statement, which extended the validity of the IMCO agreements to "Land Berlin." The East Germans argued that this was a violation of "the quadripartite agreement of September 3, 1971, that Berlin (West) is not part of the Federal Republic of Germany and should therefore not be governed by it."[72] In short, the GDR turned the short-lived West German success of the Four Power Agreement on its head by claiming that nothing short of an explicit mention of West Berlin would be considered valid in its eyes.

For the Brandt government, the question of West Berlin was truly its Achilles' heel. As a former mayor of Berlin, and having argued that his *Ostpolitik* would improve the life of West Berliners, Brandt could not afford to see the advances on the topic of West Berlin reversed. An internal document from the Brandt government suggested an immediate response in IMCO and evaluated the GDR protest as significant, as it could weaken the German position overall.

> This is the first case in which the GDR denounces the Berlin declaration of the German government on admission to a special organization of the United Nations. It must be expected that this procedure will repeat itself once the GDR joins other international organizations. This could weaken our position in the international arena in the long term simply by the fact that the circulating documents depict the inclusion of Berlin as questionable. It is therefore recommended to try in the next conversation with Undersecretary Kohl to keep the GDR from further protests of this kind.[73]

During consultations that took place the following day, the Germans' desire for a forceful response from their three Western allies was met with reluctance on the part of the British and the French. The British and French representatives agreed that only Bonn should issue a statement; meanwhile the three allies, through their silence, would give their tacit approval. Yet with only four days before the next IMCO meeting, it would not be possible to reach agreement on a statement. Only the U.S. representative countered these opinions. Understandably, the Germans considered the French and British stance to be disappointingly weak. The U.S. position was that "we must counter the GDR in the same arena that it challenged us. If this would be left only for the FRG to do, the three powers would convey the impression that it is the role of the

Federal Republic of Germany to enforce the Four Power Agreement." It was further noted that the United States would issue a declaration on its own if no joint declaration by the three powers could be agreed upon.[74] Faced with this tough American and German stance, the French and British delegates agreed to participate in a joint answer issued by all four powers during the next IMCO meeting.[75]

The wavering British and French support for the German cause on the international scene demonstrates that the United States was the only ally that offered unqualified support for German reunification. After such a clear illustration of loyalties, renewed emphasis on the relationship with the U.S. was the obvious course of action. Brezhnev's unwillingness to continue strengthening bilateral ties with Bonn, to the extent that *Ostpolitik* would be a potential tool for German reunification, drove Brandt back into the arms of the United States. With his Western European allies lukewarm regarding reunification, Brandt could not even continue to emphasize the role of the EC over transatlantic ties. In essence, both his *Ostpolitik* and his *Westpolitik* with the EC had failed. What remained was not a special, ever-increasing cooperation between Western and Eastern Europe that would create a peaceful bubble in Europe. Ultimately, returning to the fold of the United States tied the possibility of reunification to where it had been prior to his inauguration—namely, American-style détente and the remote hope of a geopolitical peace rather than a European peace.

By summer 1973 its was not only *Ostpolitik* that had suffered setbacks. Many in German government and industry had also become disillusioned with the state of German *Osthandel*. A year earlier, Otto Wolff von Amerongen had already identified the systemic problems with Eastern trade. The two major ones were the lack of diversification in the range of available Soviet products, which limited trade flow and improved the trade balance in favor of FRG exports, and the lack of Soviet willingness to allow the establishment of cooperation agreements between Soviet and German firms.[76]

In addition to the problem of increasing trade to counter the huge trade imbalance that forced the Germans to subsidize Soviet imports with German credit, the potential for Soviet exports had not been reached. Crude oil exports from the Soviet Union were lagging behind the quotas that the FRG had established for the Soviet Union and were well behind German demand (2.8 million tons delivered, versus 4.4 million tons expected). This was especially striking given that Italy and France were able to purchase considerably higher quantities of crude oil from the Soviet Union (11 million and 6 million tons, respectively). Even the German government's boost—at the Soviets' request—of the quota for heating oil from 1.5 million to 2.8 million tons failed to trigger higher crude oil exports.[77]

As a result, Soviet debt increased drastically, swiftly putting it at the top of the list of Germany's debtor countries. By late summer it was estimated that in 1973 the Soviet Union would double its debt from 1972, raising it to a staggering 3.6 billion marks.[78] With the political impetus for *Osthandel* somewhat dampened, negotiations on the major showcase deals soldiered on unsuccessfully. Trying to maximize the potential of Soviet natural resources, Brezhnev had pushed for the continuation of large-scale orders for industrial plants to be built in the Soviet Union on German credit. The next showcase would be the steel plant at Kursk, which was to be of such a magnitude that German industry balked at assuming responsibility for its construction, much less its financing. This refusal centered on the fact that the Soviets wanted to improve on the financial conditions they had been offered before. They shrewdly refused to include the financing cost in the overall price of the project and steadfastly rejected paying these financing costs until the construction was completed.[79] The Soviets also insisted on a twelve-year loan at an interest rate of 6 percent, which would mean a federal subsidy of 1.5 billion marks.[80]

German historian Oliver Bange illustrates Brandt's *Ostpolitik* as a coin labeled "German unification," with a long-term strategy of undermining the Soviet Union on one side and the creation of a security conference that would pave the way for German reunification on the other. If we accept the central premise of Bange's illustration, then Brandt's coin was worn down on both sides, given Brezhnev's refusal to adjust the nature of German-Soviet interchanges and the emergence of a superpower détente that made the CSCE secondary, at best. Sodaro's analysis of Soviet attitudes toward détente with the FRG further illustrates that Brandt's *Ostpolitik* lost appeal once the Soviets were in a position to gain the U.S. as a partner. Sodaro identifies a traditional Soviet distrust of Germany that was also pervasive among the Soviet leadership. Accordingly, they continued their military buildup, refusing to link military and political détente. Brezhnev's visit to Bonn also made clear that it was not just military and political détente that they were unwilling to link, but economic and political policies as well.[81] Undermining the Soviet system through rapprochement thus appeared fruitless.

In Brandt's vision, the establishment of an effective European security system would allow for eventual German reunification. Within a European framework of peace and stability, Germany's reunification would no longer be perceived as a threat. While this was probably acceptable to Germany's European neighbors, it ran contrary to Soviet

interests. A complete disarmament of Europe would seriously undermine control over Eastern Europe and increase the influence Germany
already exercised economically.

> While a withdrawal of troops and weaponry from the continent might
> well reduce America's role in Europe substantially, it would also emascu-
> late the Kremlin's controls over Eastern Europe. A West German govern-
> ment that could no longer be portrayed as a serious threat to the security
> of the region would only accelerate the East Europeans' desire to free
> themselves from Soviet domination. To risk potentially irresistible pres-
> sures to establish a unified and powerful German state, while at the same
> time risking the disintegration of Moscow's security buffer in Eastern
> Europe, would be to jeopardize virtually everything Leonid Brezhnev
> and his generation of Soviet leaders had fought for in World War II and
> immediately afterward.[82]

Superpower détente enabled the Soviets to continue their rule over Eastern Europe, now with tacit Western approval. This entailed a hard-line
pro–Warsaw Pact approach that vilified West Germany and facilitated
a stronger internal cohesion. At the same time, the Soviet Union would
continue to benefit from its preexisting economic ties with Germany.
Brandt's goodwill approach had done all it could.

The lack of linkage between East-West trade and benevolent Soviet
international behavior denied West Germany any lever with which to
coax a change in Soviet policies. The absence of such a link, however,
has not been a heavily debated point in the discussion on the efficacy
of *Ostpolitik*. In hindsight it seems readily apparent that negative linkage did not work with the Soviet Union. The striking failure of the 1963
pipeline embargo and Carter's grain embargo serve to underscore this
point nicely. The explanation for this failure seems equally apparent in
the "asymmetry between the political and economic stakes. … The economic stakes were only secondary. The USSR could have survived without German trade if it had to."[83] Undoubtedly, Stent is correct that the
Soviet Union would not have crumbled for lack of large-diameter steel
pipes or chemical factories. Nonetheless, Brezhnev's political commitment to East-West trade and the need for improvements in agricultural
productivity attached a certain political expediency to trade with West
Germany that had not existed in 1963. Certainly, such expediency would
not have propelled Brezhnev to accept the Western position on Berlin,
but if West Germany had held some leverage over East-West trade, it
might have given him pause before vilifying the FRG. Given the situation as it was, Brandt had to redirect West Germany's foreign policy.

With the German government increasingly less enthusiastic about
continuing to bankroll trade with the Soviet Union, the Soviet trade

delegations threatened a possible cooling of relations with the FRG over the issue of loan conditions in December 1973.[84] Without political pressure, though, German industry was not willing to go the extra mile. In an essay on trade with the Soviet Union, Amerongen was now convinced that trade with the East was a special case, something to be treated differently from trade with the West. The fundamental realization was that the Soviet Union was unwilling to modify its system of a planned economy for the sake of Western investments.[85] While he postulated the possibility that heavy Soviet indebtedness might be offset by limited Soviet purchases in 1974/75 (so as to end the five-year plan with a balanced trade volume), even with the prospect of increased Soviet oil revenues due to the Middle East crisis, the article predicted that *Osthandel* had only limited growth potential in the coming years.[86]

Amerongen also rejected Soviet demands for a further liberalization of import restrictions, as over 90 percent of all goods could already be freely imported. He accused the Soviet Union of a lack of initiative in trying to penetrate the German market. Other problems, including lack of knowledge of the German market and customer care, as well as limited Soviet attendance at trade fairs, hampered the marketability of Soviet imports. The problems faced by German exports, on the other hand, was not a question of the desirability of the goods but of a Soviet lack of hard currency, which meant that German sales to the Soviet Union always involved the question of credits.[87]

Lastly, cooperation that extended beyond a simple purchase-and-deliver system was not fostered between companies in the two countries. Apart from the question of property ownership in a communist country, cooperation in the spheres of taxes, tariffs, and the status of foreign workers was essential to the blossoming of *Osthandel*, yet the issues remained unresolved. Overall, Amerongen's assessment was, therefore, pessimistic.[88]

This publicly voiced pessimism places the start of German industry's disillusionment with *Osthandel* in the latter part of 1973 and not, as Rudolph claims, in 1975. Certainly, a 1975 CIA warning of the existence of a significant Soviet trade deficit, which Economics Minister Friderichs tried to keep under wraps, coupled with a Deutsche Bank calculation of a record Soviet deficit with Western countries totaling over $4 billion, offered more concrete reasons for investors to be wary.[89] Yet by 1973 the initial "gold rush" excitement had already worn off. It would take an upheaval in the landscape of international relations and energy trade to catapult German-Soviet trade back into the limelight. Such an upheaval, however, was not immediately in sight. Quite to the contrary, superpower seemed more real than ever before.

Yet the White House failed to seize the momentum of Brezhnev's visit to clinch an MFN deal with Congress and reassert leadership over the Western alliance. This failure would prove fateful to superpower détente. On 6 October 1973—Yom Kippur, the highest of high holy days for Jews—Egypt and Syria initiated a surprise attack on Israel. Egypt's forces swiftly crossed the Suez Canal and overran the Bar-Lev line. Syria moved into the Golan Heights and nearly reached the 1967 border with Israel. With Israel's general staff convinced of Israel's safety from future Arab attacks, neither UN Resolution 242 nor Egyptian President Sadat's peace initiative had led Israel to withdraw to the pre-1967 armistice lines. Sadat's threats of war throughout 1972 and much of 1973 to the contrary, neither the U.S. nor the Israelis were convinced that an Arab attack was a realistic possibility. Therefore they misinterpreted the buildup of armed forces along the canal as military exercises rather than preparations for an attack and were completely surprised by the turn of events.[90]

The damage to the Soviet-U.S. relationship came when the tide of war turned in favor of the Israelis on 10 October. Having regained lost ground, Israel began to advance into Syria proper, and the Soviet Union felt compelled to respond with an airlift of military supplies to Damascus and Cairo. Since the U.S. was allied with Israel, a proxy war ensued: the U.S. responded to the Soviets' actions on 12 and 13 October with massive U.S. airlifts of supplies to Israel. Israeli forces then crossed the Suez Canal and surrounded the Egyptian Third Army on 21 October.

The war started an international crisis when Egypt appealed to the Soviet Union to save its Third Army by reinforcing it with Soviet troops. Brezhnev complied, suggesting a joint operation with U.S. forces to maintain a previously negotiated cease-fire agreement based on UN resolution 338, which had already been broken. Brezhnev threatened Nixon by saying that "if you find it impossible to act jointly with us in this matter, we should be faced with the necessity to consider the question of taking appropriate steps unilaterally."[91] The U.S. countered this threat by raising the alert of its military forces to DEFCON III on 24 October, demonstrating and later communicating to Brezhnev that the U.S. would not stand for any type of unilateral Soviet action. Before the situation could escalate any further, the U.S. managed to persuade Israel to accept a second cease-fire on 25 October 1973, sparing the embattled Egyptian Third Army.

Despite the swift cease-fire, the war produced ripple effects throughout the world. If we accept Blacker's argument that for the Soviet Union détente meant lowering the possibility of a military escalation with the United States as American power declined throughout the world, then the Yom Kippur War must be seen as a disappointment in Soviet eyes.[92]

Not only did Israel retain the upper hand militarily, but Kissinger managed to impose a cease-fire agreement, essentially marginalizing the Soviet Union and leaving the U.S. as the central power broker in the region.

Potentially more damaging for the Soviets than being shut out of the Middle East peace process, however, was the reshelving of the trade act in Congress that would have granted the Soviet Union MFN status. With East-West tensions at a new high, the Nixon administration saw no prospect of getting such legislation passed. Senator Jackson had prevailed in the battle over Soviet MFN status and the Soviets realized that no close economic cooperation with the U.S. would be forthcoming. The particularly damaging aspect of this situation was that the two proposed liquefied natural gas deals would not come to fruition. The expense of liquefying the gas prior to transporting it across the Pacific left little financial maneuvering room. The addition of a significant tariff surcharge rendered Soviet prices far above market level. In essence, the possibility of a close détente on a political or economic level would be severely limited. Soviet involvement in the Arab-Israeli war had given the hawks in Congress the upper hand.

The Transatlantic Rift Emerges

If the White House and Congress were quick to escalate East-West relations to a higher level of confrontation and aggression, Western Europe was not. Almost immediately, Europeans rained criticism on U.S. policies, partly for America's unrestrained support of Israel and partly for the swift unilateralism with which the U.S. reacted—particularly its raising of the DEFCON level without consulting the European allies. This action aroused great concern, as it could have dragged Europe into a military confrontation with the East. Beneath this obvious issue of consultation, however, was the underlying question of the cohesion of an alliance in which members had differing interests and perspectives.

Kissinger, in his memoirs, shows little regard for such considerations. To him, the European allies had "an obligation to subordinate their differences"; to do otherwise "weakens the structure of common defense and the achievement of joint purposes."[93] On the other hand, if consultation was not an essential part of any alliance, then, by Kissinger's line of reasoning, NATO would devolve into a mere tool designed to implement U.S. policy. The core problem was not clashing visions of alliance, but differing interests vis-à-vis the Soviet Union, which Kissinger recognized but did not validate. Lamenting the fact that one NATO ally after another refused to allow the U.S. to use the bases in their countries for the airlift to supply Israel, he points at the underlying conflict.

> Dissociation from us in the Middle East war was thus coupled with an attempt to opt out of any possible crisis with the Soviet Union. ... they would not risk over the Middle East the web of their economic relations with the Communist world—which grew increasingly vital to them for economic reasons as the oil crisis triggered a worldwide recession.[94]

In essence, Kissinger wished to involve the European allies in a fight that they perceived, whether rightly or wrongly, as not their own. In a twisted way, the Europeans' reactions proved the validity of Kissinger's observations on the "Year of Europe": the Europeans were most concerned about, and gave priority to, their own regional interests, which in this case involved maintaining good relations with the Soviet Union. Even so, unilaterally raising the DEFCON level rendered the Europeans nothing more than pawns in the superpower game.

With major NATO partners such as Spain, Greece, Turkey, France, and Great Britain refusing to allow their bases to be used for the airlift to assist Israel, the FRG was placed in a somewhat unusual position. Not being fully sovereign, and acutely aware of the need for U.S. backing on the Berlin question, it pursued a "don't ask, don't tell" policy. Yet when it became public knowledge on 24 October that the Israeli ships docked in Bremerhafen intended to be loaded with military supplies, the Brandt government told the U.S. to halt all arms shipments to Israel from German soil.[95]

Kissinger condemned this step in his memoirs, noting that as "we were already carrying out the Federal Republic's private request, the purpose of the public statement could only be to distance Bonn from Washington for the benefit of a presumed Arab constituency in the midst of an acute crisis."[96] In the true Machiavellian fashion that had led Kissinger to ignore the lack of U.S. domestic support for détente, he ignored the Western European public outcry over the escalating conflict with the Arab nations and the Soviet Union. Instead, the White House placed the blame for the allied reactions squarely on the anti-American sentiments of European leaders.

The following day, 26 October, Nixon publicly chastised his Western European allies for their lack of support during a crisis that would have affected them even more than the United States. With Secretary of Defense James R. Schlesinger at his side, he issued the first direct criticism of the European allies since NATO's origins. Schlesinger even hinted at a partial withdrawal of U.S. forces from Germany as "the reaction of the Foreign Ministry in Germany raises some questions about whether they view enhanced readiness in the same way that we view enhanced readiness."[97] The opposing views of the Americans and the Germans are perfectly illustrated in a discussion held between Kissinger and German Ambassador von Staden that same day.

> 18. The German Ambassador said that there was a serious problem of communication which had developed in the last 14 days.
> 19. The Secretary said he recognized this aspect of the problem. He had given instructions that as negotiations for a solution in the Middle East develop, a means should be found to inform our European Allies more swiftly and completely. There was a problem here, however. It was difficult for the allies to insist on a right to private briefings when their fundamental attitude was either slightly or openly hostile.
> 20. The German Ambassador insisted that if information were provided more promptly the policy adopted by the European Allies was less likely to be divergent.
> The Secretary said this was perhaps so, unless our underlying philosophies were different.[98]

With this, Kissinger summed up the underlying dynamics and the problem that had beset the transatlantic alliance with the onset of European détente. The issue of military shipments from German soil would largely be resolved within a couple days, given the compromise that the U.S. would ship only its own military equipment on U.S. vessels, thereby giving the German government the opportunity to feign ignorance over where the shipments were destined.

Even so, European reservations regarding U.S. unilateralism remained heated, and the Brandt government had the unequivocal support of the other Western powers.[99] As Bahr reported from London, he had never seen British Prime Minister Edward Heath "so brutal or refreshingly realistic. He was bitter and critical vis-à-vis the Americans. Distance between London and Washington was the fundamental impression in my conversations."[100] This philosophical distance would continue throughout the rest of the Nixon administration and spawn many independent European foreign policy initiatives. For the Western Europeans, it was the resolution of the Middle East crisis that was of utmost importance, not the standing of the U.S. in the region. Hence, they were willing to involve the Soviets in peace talks, something that Kissinger was determined to avoid at all costs. Through his back channel, Bahr offered Brandt as a mediator and egged the Soviets on: "If the Americans talk with the Egyptians, why should the Russians not talk with the Israelis?"[101]

Some of the European allies equated the idea of more diplomatic influence as a peacemaker with more military power as well. Eager to replace U.S. military influence with the military power of Europeans, Pompidou floated the idea of a European Defense Council. This, of course, would profoundly undermine the division of issues that allowed the FRG to maneuver internationally, and Bahr strongly opposed the idea.

> There can only be security with America. After we blocked Kissinger's nonsense to provide the alliance with functions that would go significantly beyond security, we now have to stop the French danger: A European Security Council would divide the alliance. There can be only one strategy and the French have to return to it.
>
> Allowing France to pull eight countries to its position would be the beginning of the end of NATO. The American echo to a European Security Council can not only be devastating but will disassociate America from Europe. In any case it will be an Insecurity Council because if it does not have anything to say it will confuse and be a new sign of European helplessness. Why does Europe not focus on its strength: the economy and politics, instead of belaboring its weakness, its defense?[102]

While Bahr might have perceived the international situation from a pro-American perspective, the overall political climate following the Yom Kippur war benefited the Soviet Union. However much Brandt and Bahr wanted to separate military, diplomatic, and economic issues, the fact remained that they were invariably connected, if for no other reason than that the other nations linked them. The Yom Kippur War had given Brezhnev, for example, new impetus to enlarge the gulf between the U.S. and Western Europe.

The Soviet leadership saw the Middle East crisis as an opportunity for another round of divide and conquer. Bahr's back-channel contact in the Soviet Union, Ledlev, was quite excited by West Germany's public stance on the Israeli transport ship. As Bahr explained to Brandt, Ledlev was "really excited" as West German criticism of the U.S. "had provided support for General Secretary [Brezhnev] in this difficult situation. We could have gotten anything we wanted on Berlin for this."[103]

Brezhnev expressed his own enthusiasm personally, giving an impromptu dictation of his thoughts to Brandt as a way to "foster the close and trusting contact." In a frank and provocative manner, he expounded on how the U.S. "had been driven solely by their own selfish interests." Playing on existing Western European fears, he portrayed the Western alliance as nothing but a means to American ends.

> It seems that they [the Americans] only need their partners when they find it necessary for the completion of their goals. This was the way it happened in Korea and Vietnam, where they dragged their allies into the conflict. In other cases, they not only ignored the interests of others but had no problem gaining advantages at the cost of others if their interests didn't coincide with the American ones. ... Of course everyone in Washington knew that the support for Israel and the emerging confrontation

with the Arab world would trigger crude oil sanctions. But since, unlike Europe, they are much less dependent on oil, they did not pay any mind to this possibility.[104]

In a demonstration of how well he understood Brandt, Brezhnev reminisced about all the aspects of U.S. policy that had upset Brandt in the past, starting with the elevation of the DEFCON alert "without informing you." Depicting the Americans as the agitator in the war, he feigned ignorance as to "why they orchestrated this production," applauding Western European criticisms of the U.S. but cautioning that "we are still not safe from relapses."[105]

Brandt responded to this provocative propaganda piece with quite undeserved earnestness. After assuring Brezhnev that he understood his fears, he failed to rectify the provocatively one-sided account, offering instead only a lame reference to internal politics as a reason for the "hard to explain American reactions." Further expressing his view that the people involved (a clear reference to the U.S.) "had not always been angels," he drew a line of distinction between U.S. and Western European foreign policy and even cautioned that an Arab oil embargo "does not create solidarity but could even lead to a point where the Arabs trigger a change in the independent stance for which the Western European countries strive" vis-à-vis the United States. After selling out alliance cohesion for Arab oil, he asked for an increase of oil shipments from the Soviet Union.[106]

The blending of politics and trade issues became even more apparent with the onset of the energy crisis. "The gulf that the Europeans have chosen to open between themselves and the U.S.," as German Finance Minister Schmidt put it in a letter to Kissinger, made itself felt in the one-sided U.S. attempt to reestablish adequate oil deliveries from the Middle East.[107] On 4 March, following the lines of what Brandt indicated to Brezhnev, the EC members decided to pursue negotiations with the Arab countries over the oil crisis independently from the U.S. and without consultation, thereby leading to a further separation of interests and policies.[108]

The Soviets continued to pour oil onto the fire of transatlantic dissent. In an apparent shift back toward Western Europe as the most important trading partner, the Soviets played up the U.S. competition to Western Europeans while dangling prospects of increased trade before them. Soviet strategy also contained a new spin: rather than playing all Western countries against each other, Soviet leaders had apparently embraced the concept of a joint European Economic Community policy on trade and now suggested combined Western European projects as a means of viable competition to American or Japanese offers.

During Economics Minister Friderichs' visit with Kosygin, the Soviet expert on international trade touched on a vulnerable spot in U.S.-German relations. The Soviets indicated that in the new five-year plan they wished to involve the FRG even more than previously. However, Kosygin noted that as a result of the devaluation of the dollar U.S. products had become less expensive, and therefore stronger competition was now developing between the U.S. and Germany with respect to their economic relations with the Soviet Union.[109] Later on he expressed his conviction that "combining the possibilities of European countries (FRG, France, Italy, and England) provides solid ground for further efforts" in the economic sector.[110] Kosygin played the same card a week later with Bundesbank President Karl Klasen. After describing Soviet efforts not to devalue the ruble, he indicated that "U.S. equipment was much cheaper these days." He also mentioned the large dollar reserves that the FRG held, stating and reiterating the financial dependence of the U.S. on those same West German currency holdings.[111]

Kosygin also pursued this line with the German labor union leader Otto A. Friedrich. As Friedrich explained to Economics Minister Friderichs,

> especially Prime Minister Kosygin pointed out that competition in trade and services would become fiercer for the German economy thanks to the American efforts and their advantages through the dollar devaluation and lower wage increases. Even so, Kosygin expressed his confidence that the trade relations and technological cooperation with the German industry would continue to grow. ... Kosygin emphasized that even with a weakening Western economy, the Soviet economy would continue to expand as planned.[112]

The Soviet preoccupation with the strength of the German economy, as Friedrich put it, clearly indicated that the Soviets were contemplating a shift in its economic strategy.[113] Their underlying premise seems a logical reaction to the Jackson-Vanik amendment: if the U.S. could not deliver the products needed, Western European cooperation could therefore not only counter the Americans' restrictive tendencies on East-West trade but also offer sufficiently powerful production capabilities to fill large-scale Soviet orders. In addition, sowing discord among the Western allies was a desirable by-product of reviving trade.

Reviving Western European–Soviet Trade

With the U.S. no longer a viable partner for détente, Brezhnev found himself in a real dilemma. The economic weakness of the Soviet Union badly affected the Warsaw Pact. Evidence of this can be seen in a conversation held between Brezhnev and Bulgarian leader Todor Zhivkov. Zhivkov had come to Brezhnev to ask for a significant increase in the power supply to Bulgaria. Not only did he request that a second nuclear power plant be built, but he also requested a significant increase in allotment of oil exports as "no other socialist country is as poor in natural resources." Even given a conservative energy requirement estimate of 18 million tons, the Soviet Union had only promised 12.5 million tons. Low agricultural subsidies left Bulgaria in a position where they "can import some 3 million tons from the Arab countries. Even if they are ready and willing to export more oil to our country, we will not have the funds necessary to pay for these imports."[114]

The most likely source of future investment and high-tech know-how was Europe. In order to reinvigorate the stalled negotiations on Kursk, the Soviet Union was now willing to accommodate Western concerns, at least partially. Until October 1973, the Soviet strategy had been to deal with Western countries on a bilateral basis, which enabled them to play companies and governments from one country against those of another. After October, Kosygin seemed willing to entertain the notion of conglomerates of companies from different nations (the FRG, France, Italy, and Great Britain) participating in large-scale, investment-heavy projects. These projects, of course, should focus on metalworking.[115] In an interview in Brussels a month later, it became clear that this was just a temporary concession designed to revitalize trade. The Soviet ambassador Falin stated that the Soviet Union would remain dedicated to the principle of bilateral agreements, even if the EC countries transferred their authority to Brussels in 1974.[116]

Employing multinational conglomerates overcame the difficulty of the size involved in Soviet projects, but financing remained the central problem. In December 1973, after the visit of a Soviet trade delegation led by Deputy Minister for Foreign Trade Komarov, the entire Kursk project was settled—with the notable exception of the financing. Economics Minister Friederichs reminded Brandt of the great symbolic meaning of the project, warning that the FRG could not "overestimate the gravity of this project for the Soviets" and asking Brandt to let him know "if, for political reasons, you do not wish to risk failure of this project over the question of the interest rate."[117] Brandt agreed with Friederichs's assessment of the Soviet significance of the project "also in regard to our overall relations with the Soviet Union" and asked Friderichs to nail down the Soviet demands during the next meeting.[118] By the end of the Soviet trade delegation's visit on 17 December 1973, the Salzgitter/Krupp/Korf consortium had come closer to finalizing the financing. The Soviets insisted on 6.05 percent though the going market rate was much higher.[119]

Implementing a carrot-and-stick approach, in January 1974 a high-ranking Soviet trade delegation led by Deputy Prime Minister W. N. Novikov embellished the benefits of continued trade with the Soviet Union. Economics Minister Friderichs received note upon note that "the Soviet Union is willing to devote much effort to utilizing these [plentiful Soviet] natural resources, but requires help in financing these undertakings from countries that want these resources." The Soviet Union needed not only technical, but also financial assistance in utilizing its resources.[120]

> If the FRG wants to have electrical power or natural gas from us it must help us construct and finance the power plants, pipelines, and equipment. Also, the FRG could become a good partner in the area of machine tooling. It would, for example be possible that its companies produce half-finished goods in our country since production here would be cheaper.[121]

Brandt was quick to acquiesce to the Soviets' demands during his meeting with Novikov. He stated that the financing of the Kursk project was "somewhat unusual" but felt that "if the Soviet side would be flexible, the German one would not be a problem, either, and that one could come up with a positive result in time for the deadline."[122] However, Brandt's willingness to bankroll yet another Soviet project at discounted interest rates was blocked in the cabinet by Finance Minister Schmidt and Economics Minister Friderichs, for whom these concessions went too far.[123]

After his unsuccessful negotiations in Germany, Novikov returned home and decided to employ the stick. In a conversation with West German ambassador Balser, he reiterated the Soviets' financing demands. Novikov spoke of the frustrated mood, and the chairman of the Soviet EXIM bank, Ivanov, threatened that the FRG did not realize the implications of unfavorable German export credits "for German-Soviet economic relations and a continuation of *Ostpolitik*." Should the German side persit in their ideas about credit conditions, "the project [Kursk] will fail just as the proposed Daimler-Benz involvement in the Kama [River] project had failed."[124]

Despite the Soviets' rhetoric, the German consortium remained reserved about the prospect of a deal. By the beginning of February 1974, the Kursk project had been postponed indefinitely because the German consortium was not able to envision a way to accommodate the financing the Soviets demanded.[125] Ambassador Falin approached Economics Minister Friderichs to express his dismay about the German consortium's rejection of the Soviets' offer to continue negotiations. He pushed hard for a continuation of talks.[126] Yet only direct intervention by Bahr and a supporting letter from Brandt helped save one of the largest projects ever offered to German industry.[127] It is interesting to note that the dynamics had changed somewhat. For the first time since 1969 the Soviets failed to get satisfactory financing, but they still agreed to the deal. After Bahr personally intervened with Brezhnev, the Soviet side agreed to pay for the first stage of the project in cash (2.5 billion marks out of 6 billion for the entire project) and thus brought the process forward again.[128] The remaining stages of the project would encounter difficulties as well. A mixture of COCOM restrictions, Soviet administrative difficulties, and the inclusion of Eastern European contractors left the West German consortium with a severely truncated role, one that was focused mostly on the provision of high-tech parts.[129]

The increase in oil prices significantly benefited the Soviet Union in its negotiations with the FRG. It stands to reason that the Soviet Union would have been hard pressed to finance a huge project like Kursk without the extra hard-currency inflow. Even so, the Soviets soon demanded that the second stage of the Kursk project be financed via German credits. The reason behind this may have been the shortage of oil the Soviet Union was actually able to export to Western European countries. Already unable to meet its import quota for crude oil to West Germany in 1972, the Soviet Union saw its export capacity reduced even further as it had to supply its Eastern European allies with oil that they could no longer afford themselves on the world market. While Soviet natural resources were plentiful, exploiting them — given the difficult terrain in which they were located — was another matter entirely.

Soviet interest in cooperating with German industry also revolved around nuclear issues. Here, Soviet plans were twofold. They wanted the Germans to build a sizable nuclear power plant, and they also wished to sell their uranium ore to fuel West German reactors. As early as the German-Soviet summit of 1973, Brezhnev repeatedly and forcefully pushed for both of these projects.[130] Uranium deliveries were a politically sensitive issue, as the U.S. had up to this point been the sole provider of uranium for German nuclear power plants. During Brezhnev's visit, however, the Brandt government expressed no objection to a one-time delivery of uranium. The Soviet Union, meanwhile, wished to break into the U.S. monopoly on uranium supplies through low-cost, long-term offers. Because the U.S. government would "react indignantly over close ties of the German industry with the Soviet Union in this sensitive area," the German negotiation approach was "generally open but without any firm commitments."[131] It would take a few more years for uranium to become another Soviet fuel supplying West German energy needs.

The construction of a nuclear power plant was actually an alluring potential project for the Germans. In 1972, the Economics Ministry had expressed concern over the long-term supply of electricity to West Berlin.[132] When Novikov met with Brandt in January 1974, he suggested supplying Berlin with electricity as part of the payment for the construction costs of the plant.[133] The Soviet delegates had very clear ideas about the plant.

> The Soviets expect a complete offer by the end of February and have clear intentions to make a deal with the KWU [Kraftwerk Union AG, Mühlheim Ruhr] if the simultaneously conducted financing negotiations turn out satisfactorily for the Soviets. Here, the entire deals would be conducted on the basis of compensation (electricity). Herr Kuljow frequently mentioned the political goodwill of the federal government.[134]

Even more striking than assuring a stable supply of electricity to West Berlin was the Soviets' outspokenness in their desire to have this deal come to fruition. Deputy Chair of the State Committee Kuljow used an unusual diplomatic tactic—visiting the German embassy in Moscow—to arrange for a meeting with Undersecretary Bahr. He reminded Bahr that the German companies should submit their bids for constructing a nuclear power plant at the agreed time (28 February) and promised that the Soviet Union would respond in an expeditious manner. Kuljow did not fail to mention that Finland and Italy tended to operate much more quickly than West Germany and that the Soviet Union would be forced to look elsewhere should the Germans fail to quickly complete the deal and agree to a loan at 6.7 percent (Bahr had offered 10 percent).[135]

Although all the economic components were in place, the political implications eventually ruined the deal. The Germans felt that it was necessary to gain COCOM approval for the export of nuclear power technology, and the U.S. attitude regarding this subject proved difficult to reconcile with Soviet policy. The U.S. government had indicated that it would agree to the COCOM exception only if the Soviets accepted International Atomic Energy Organization (IAEO) visits and safety checks. The U.S. government felt it would be unable to justify the proposed COCOM exception to the American public without adequate IAEO safety checks.[136] The Germans pointed to the fact that the Soviets had continuously refused to be bound by IAEO safeguards and had previously rejected any deal that committed them to such regulations.[137] As a consequence, the deal failed because neither superpower was willing to budge. The conflict over the reactor deal is an excellent illustration of the intermediate position in which the FRG found itself again and again following the Yom Kippur War.

With U.S. companies unable to finance and implement the pioneering work on the new gas fields that were developed, German companies took up the slack. The project of foremost interest was the completion of the Iranian gas deal of October 1974. After Brandt settled on a pipeline route that ran through the Soviet Union as opposed to Greece and Turkey, negotiations faltered on the proposed role the Soviets should play in this deal. The Germans wished to buy the gas directly from the Iranians, treating the Soviet Union as nothing more than a transit country. The Soviets, however, preferred to act as an intermediary, thereby assuming a more influential role. In January 1974, however, Brandt used the word "triangle," implying an equal part for the Soviet Union in front of Soviet officials, much to the concern of the German ambassador. So far, the term triangle had been strictly avoided, as it seemed counterproductive to the Germans' negotiating stance.[138] Yet it seemed the tide had turned in favor of the Soviet Union, and the deal was concluded in October 1974.

The deal never resulted in any transportation of natural gas, as after the 1979 Iranian Revolution the Iranian government broke the contract.[139] Nevertheless, this illustrates a strengthening of the Soviet position in economic matters. Neither the uranium imports, the triangular Iranian gas deal, nor the third gas pipeline deal of 1975 (in which the Germans took over the development of the gas fields earmarked for U.S. companies) triggered any warnings about too much Soviet influence on West Germany.[140] Somehow, the Soviet Union had become a normal state with which to do business, even if the hoped-for political concessions had not materialized. In this, West Germany had assumed its own foreign policy, creating a substantially different international position from that of the United States.

In summary, the period between the Soviet-U.S. summits in 1972 and 1973, though it was a period of domestic weakness for President Nixon, became a period of increased U.S. influence in inter-allied politics. With the Soviet Union trying to implement a détente that sought recognition of superpower parity with the United States, Western European partners in détente efforts became less important. The Soviet Union had used Western European powers to force the hand of the United States while at the same time binding the economies of the FRG (and other European powers) to the success of its own economy. Brandt, however, saw his *Ostpolitik* reach the limits of its possible success when Brezhnev balked at integrating the German and Soviet economies beyond an order-delivery exchange.

The inherent conflict of *Ostpolitik*—courting the Soviet Union on one hand and ultimately trying to reduce superpower conflict and influence on the other—caused *Ostpolitik* to stall. Even worse, by the summer of 1973 it was evident that the Soviet Union would not permit an increase in ties between West Berlin and West Germany, the Achilles' heel of *Ostpolitik*. By painting West Germany as a revanchist power, Brezhnev insulated himself politically against setbacks in détente.

The effects of this period on the West German–U.S. relationship were significant, if not somewhat delayed. Brandt, having compartmentalized different areas of international relations, felt confident that German security was guaranteed by the United States, regardless of his actions. In an attempt to further his ultimate plan of pan-European integration, he pursued a largely independent policy, which he always protected by cloaking it "in Europe's name." Only with Brezhnev's final rejection of any possible solution on West Berlin did the Brandt government come around, supporting superpower détente at the side of the U.S. as the only remaining road to German reunification. This led to more intensive transatlantic consultations and the opportunity for the Nixon administration to solidify its leadership on détente. With Kissinger's refusal to acknowledge domestic opposition to East-West trade, however, the Jackson-Vanik amendment blocked MFN status for the Soviet Union, and with it the Soviet opportunity to competitively market natural gas on the U.S. market.

Thus, Soviet involvement in the Yom Kippur War ended all hope for the ratification of MFN and made economic dealings with the Soviet Union difficult at best. The political ramification on the Soviet side was disillusionment with superpower détente and a return to a divide-and-conquer game with the Western European countries. Trade with Germany had stalled during 1973 because the political incentives failed to outweigh the significant disadvantages that trade with the Soviet Union entailed for West German companies. Realizing that they had to offer more incentives in order to revitalize trade, the Soviets temporarily allowed for the creation of multinational conglomerates designed to meet large-sized orders, abandoned their unrealistic financing demands, and paid hard currency for the first stage of the Kursk steel mill project.

With the West Germans put off by the Americans' use of their harbor to supply Israel's defense force and the elevation of the DEFCON level without prior consultation, the Soviets were able to use political issues to drive a wedge into the transatlantic alliance. Ultimately, though, it was the differing concepts regarding the nature of the transatlantic alliance and the divergent foreign policy interests vis-à-vis the Soviet Union that opened a rift in the alliance an cemented NATO's energy dilemma.

5

HELSINKI AND THE FALL OF DÉTENTE (1975–1982)

The conflict within the Western alliance was not immediately apparent as the transition to a new U.S. President brought a temporary reprieve. In fact, Ford (and by now Kissinger, as well) was quite open to similar agreements. Unfortunately, Senator Jackson had in the meantime succeeded in amending the 1974 trade bill by linking it to emigration controls with the Jackson-Vanik amendment. Under the trade bill signed into law by President Ford on 3 January 1975, any country that was to receive MFN status would have to allow free emigration of its citizens. As Kissinger reported during a Ford cabinet meeting on 8 January 1975 following the Vladivostok summit on 24 November 1974, "the relationship in the political field with the USSR is good while the relationship in the economic field is under question at the moment."[1] Kissinger pointed the finger at the Jackson-Vanik amendment as the culprit, with the "question in Soviets' minds …, how dependent can the USSR become on United States domestic decisions?"[2]

More than domestic U.S. decisions, though, what made the Jackson-Vanik amendment unacceptable was the Soviet tightrope act of increasing imports from the West while at the same time maintaining public faith in planned economies. This delicate balance entailed a continued emphasis on détente internationally alongside tight control of dissent domestically. Under these conditions the Jackson-Vanik amendment could not be tolerated, even if this meant forfeiting economic gains.[3] On 14 January 1975, Kissinger summarily announced to the press that the Soviet government had directed him in writing to cancel the 1972 trade agreement on the grounds that impositions on internal matters were unacceptable. The Soviet government was also angered by the Stevenson amendment, which had passed Congress in late 1974. The $300 million ceiling it placed on U.S. credits to the Soviet Union over the next four-year period would make any large scale project to export natural gas to the United States a pipe dream.[4] This rejection was accompanied by increased anti-American rhetoric in the Soviet press.[5] Kissinger showed little consternation about the failed trade deal and predicted that it would not have "implications beyond those communicated."[6]

The next day, President Ford chided Congress for interfering with the president's powers during his first State of the Union speech, citing the failed trade deal with the Soviet Union as the prime example. "Legislative restrictions, intended for the best motives and purposes, can have the opposite result, as we have seen most recently in our trade relations with the Soviet Union."[7] Ford's complaint should have pleased the Soviets: because of Watergate and Vietnam, U.S. presidents faced a "credibility gap" and the U.S. Congress, suspicious and leery of presidential powers, sought to constrain the U.S. military and intelligence agencies abroad. The different branches of the U.S. government turned on each other, allowing the Soviet Union to develop more influence in places such as Angola.[8]

Even so, the hard-line stance of the Jackson-Vanik amendment resonated with the American people. Henry Jackson, no doubt wrangling for the Democratic presidential nomination, reached the height of his popularity while the Jackson-Vanik amendment was in the minds of the people. His poll numbers for the presidential nomination jumped to an all-time high of 22 percent in July 1974 and again hit 22 percent in February 1975, but they dwindled throughout the rest of 1975, finally falling into the single digits.[9]

Whether one considers the popular sentiment toward East-West trade or the political dynamics, trade with the Soviet had become almost impossible to implement. This set the U.S. apart from its allies in Western Europe, where the leaders washed their hands of all responsibility, citing the benefits of East/West trade and maintaining that such trade was ultimately removed from government control as it took place in the sphere of private industry. High-tech and steel pipe exports were touted as a means of creating and maintaining job security for thousands of German workers through trade with a "normal" state. Natural gas imports were pursued under the banner of "diversification" in energy imports, resulting in low energy prices and a reliable means of making Western Europe less dependent on imports from the volatile Middle East. In this sense, any political debate over the wisdom of allowing a communist country to have access to Western high-tech goods while at the same time bolstering its energy infrastructure never became a serious debate after Brandt's 1973 reelection.

It is ironic that Willy Brandt, who had staked his entire political career on a rapprochement with the East, fell from power– at least officially – over promoting East German spy, Guenther Guillaume, to an important position in the chancellor's office. His credibility and leadership abilities compromised, Brandt resigned from office on 7 May 1974.

His successor, Helmut Schmidt, continued the course of economic co-operation, albeit while strengthening military ties with the United States. He also abandoned the "economic ties at all costs" approach that Brandt had pursued. As economics and finance minister, Schmidt had always opposed subsidizing trade with the Soviet Union, only to be overruled by Brandt. The former embraced the idea of more credits in the name of foreign policy while the latter countered that such measures were not sensible given the massive existing trade surplus with the East. Here German industry had been a powerful ally for the former chancellor. Fearing for their export markets, the German Chamber of Commerce (DIHT) and the machine-building industry federation (VDMA) both argued for equal export subsidies among Western countries, thereby allowing West German firms to continue enjoying export credits.[10]

There was also a qualitative difference between Brandt's and Schmidt's conception of the Soviet Union. In a 1976 interview conducted with both statesmen, they were asked about the Soviet Union as a potential threat to West Germany. While Brandt remained convinced of the peaceful and cooperative nature of the current Soviet regime, Schmidt perceived the Soviet Union more as an aggressive state.

> We do not have to question Brezhnev's explanations at the 25th party congress, that ideologically and socially, there cannot be a peaceful co-existence, which means that the leadership of the Soviet Union has not given up on its ultimate goal of a communist world order. We have no need to avoid such a confrontation as long as the inner strength of the Western democracies and their credibility in unified defensive preparations remain.[11]

In retrospect, it may appear that Schmidt had read Brezhnev more accurately. In a speech to the East German government he reminded them that "[o]ur enemies are no communists. If we develop relations with them, then it must be clear: we must not allow any unjustified concessions for our opponents."[12] In regard to Schmidt's upcoming visit to the Soviet Union and the potential problems surrounding Western influence on domestic issues, such as dissidents and the issue of West Berlin, Brezhnev responded: "We have a communist, a socialist Humanism. ... Humanism is a beautiful word, but it has to be understood in a communist way. We, who have worked several decades in the party, will assume this communist position firmly and consistently."[13]

Despite Schmidt's misgivings, even he could not resist the structural dynamics at work. In light of the energy crisis, diversification was a major priority for Germany. Especially after Soviet trade with the U.S.

seemed to stall, Western Europe and Japan had again emerged as the major trading partners. Visiting Berlin in the fall of 1974, Brezhnev's main
interests were the CSCE, SALT, and economic cooperation. Schmidt's
recollected that Brezhnev and Kosygin as well "felt the economic development of their country to be their main task."[14] The difficulties that
the Soviet leadership faced in this regard are nicely illustrated by an
anecdote in Schmidt's memoir: as a sign of Soviet technological and
economic achievements, Brezhnev proudly presented Schmidt with a
digital watch—which stopped working after a few days.[15]

Such small setbacks notwithstanding, the existing economic ties and
the concept of the Soviet Union as the up-and-coming economic powerhouse gave Brezhnev considerable leverage as well as control over
the process. For Germany, diversification of export markets and the
development of new sources of raw materials and energy emerged as
key concerns. The German government continued to lobby for import
liberalizations, permission to set up joint economic and technical cooperation commissions, and raises in the available ceiling for export credit
guarantees.[16] Especially following the Soviet Union's development of
yet another natural gas field near Orenburg in the Ukraine, the lure of
more Soviet natural gas was strong.[17] Consequently, on 29 October 1974
a new gas pipeline agreement was reached between the FRG and the
Soviet Union for the delivery of 2.5 billion cubic meters of natural gas
annually, financed by a German bank consortium.

Soviet Dependence on Western Europe

Such dealings played well into Brezhnev's plans. As the ninth five-year
plan drew to a close in 1975, economic difficulties manifested themselves on the horizon. As Brezhnev outlined in a conversation with
other socialist leaders, the Soviet Union faced a number of different
challenges. Among them were the need for "increased productivity
of agriculture, oil, gas, and lumber, construction of the Baikal-Amur
railroad, obligations to the fraternal countries, and further improvement of the living standards of the population."[18] These were the same
three problems that had troubled the Soviet Union five years earlier:
agricultural production, energy resources, and poor living standards.
More importantly, Brezhnev admitted that "we have thought seriously
about how to make our economy more profitable. So far, unfortunately,
the return of the investment has been decreasing."[19] Indeed, Moscow
was forced to deal with a number of economic setbacks, not the least of
which was the agricultural sector.

As the ninth five-year plan drew to a close, a slowdown in virtually all sectors of the Soviet economy became apparent, indicating the need for stimulants to spur a sluggish economy. Problems continued to arise particularly in the agricultural sector, where fodder and grain supplies were insufficient. The agricultural shortages of the 1974/75 Soviet harvest added to shortages in hard-currency reserves. Additionally, the recession of 1974/75 in Western Europe disrupted all Eastern European countries' trade balances with the West. Before, Western Europe was all too willing to subscribe to "non-interference in domestic affairs" and "mutual benefits based cooperation." For the better half of the 1970s, France, West Germany, Great Britain, and Italy had undercut one another's offers to the Soviet Union for industrial machinery and high-tech products, often shouldering significant financial risk for industrial production plants or oil/gas exploration. The exportation of these production facilities guaranteed the production of products that could easily be sold on the Western markets.

Yet despite the hard-currency windfall generated by such projects as the three natural gas pipelines to West Germany (1970, 1972, 1974/75) and the production of goods salable on Western markets, the recession of 1974 reduced the related revenues considerably. Furthermore, additional grain purchases needed to be made in order to offset Soviet agricultural shortages. With the Jackson-Vanik amendment in place, there were few Soviet commodities that would realize significant cash inflow to the U.S. Grain imports thus could not be arranged on a barter basis but precipitated a large cash outflow. For Brezhnev, then, the tenth five-year plan would replace a domestically oriented economy with a more export-oriented one.[20] The focus here, however, was not on exports to the Eastern bloc but exports to Western markets. The race for *Westhandel* was on.

The failure of Soviet agriculture, paired with the Western recession of 1974/75, affected not just the Soviet Union but its Warsaw Pact allies as well, and to a greater extent. With excess Soviet energy commodities being redirected toward the West, Eastern Europe increasingly was left to fend for itself.[21] This meant acquiring oil and gas from the international markets. Ironically, just as the quest for large-scale Soviet orders had pitted one Western ally against another, now Warsaw Pact allies were trying to outmaneuver each other for lucrative *Westhandel* deals in order to cover their energy purchases and repay their debts

East Germany, for example, formerly suspicious of East-West trade, now eagerly participated in economic détente, creating a lively trade with Western Europe and West Germany by 1974. When world commodity prices rose sharply in 1974, though, East German exports rose

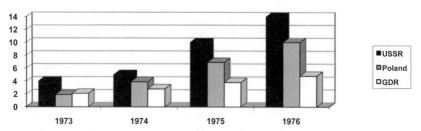

Figure 5.1 USSR/Eastern Europe: Net Hard Currency Debt, 1973–1976 as cited from Memo, William E. Odom to Zbigniew Brzezinski, Subject: Evening Report, 25 February 1977, RAC NLC-12-21-2-7-6, 2.

only moderately, deteriorating the GDR's terms of trade. Covering trade deficits with heavy borrowing, the hard-currency trade imbalance became the East German government's biggest problem in 1975.

Several long-term projects were discussed that would create hard-currency exports for the GDR. In early 1974, the East German Politburo approved the idea of allowing the FRG to build a turnkey nuclear power plant destined for the Soviet Union in East Germany. To sweeten the pot and receive hard currency inflows, the plant would in turn sell electricity to West Berlin.[22] When it became clear that West Germany was interested in the deal, two Eastern powers, the Soviet Union and the GDR, vied for the deal. Consequently, a befuddled West German government approached the Soviets over whether the nuclear power plant ought to be built in the GDR or the Soviet Union. In response, the Soviets clamped down on the internal rivalry and insisted it be located on Soviet soil.

Another project involved the "order" of a turnkey oil refinery, to be located in East Germany, to sell gasoline to West Berlin and West Germany for the explicit purpose of increasing the hard-currency reserves of the GDR.[23] Built with West German financial resources, it would sell Soviet oil to West German markets. Relying on the Soviet supply of crude oil through the "friendship pipeline," they asked for 1.5 million barrels of crude per year. Here, too, the Soviets behaved more like competitors than socialist brothers. They balked at the commitment and even withheld Iraqi oil that East Germany had purchased and arranged to transport through Soviet pipelines.[24] Once the Soviets finally did commit—to one-third of the requested amount—it was under the condition that the project be reworked to produce heating oil rather than gasoline. Here, the Soviets were already saturating the West German market, which made East Germany less of a competitor for the sought-after hard-currency inflows.[25]

Even the security angle produced more goodwill than results. Clearly, the Soviet regime was not interested in allowing Eastern European countries to move into too great a dependency on Western Europe. On the other hand, the Soviet Union was not able to absolve East Germany from its trade obligations. In a conversation between two economics experts, Politburo member Gerhard Schürer and Minister of Economics Nikolai Tikhonov, during the summit meeting in Moscow on 31 July 1974, the two lamely agreed to "closer cooperation." Tikhonov sought to reduce East Germany's reliance on West Germany but recognized that this "could not be solved within the next five year plan," nor could "the USSR replace everything that the GDR imports from the FRG."[26]

When the request for help went to the highest level, General Secretary Honecker asking Brezhnev for assistance in 1975, the Soviets were willing to stretch their bilateral trade balance in favor of the GDR significantly, but at the same time dealt a blow to the East German hard-currency trade. The Soviets had to deal with their own economic shortfalls by placing them—at least partially—on the shoulders of the Eastern Europeans. They raised prices for Soviet energy commodities while at the same time pressuring Eastern-bloc partners to invest further funds in the development of Soviet oil and gas projects. Meanwhile, the Soviets supplied only about a third of the customary grain deliveries to East Germany, forcing the GDR to obtain the remainder at world market prices with hard currency. Honecker was caught between a rock and a hard place: he could sell East German domestic products as exports to the West for hard currency but would thereby undermine the contentment of his citizens. The alternative was to provide export-worthy goods to his own constituency, raising the standard of living in the GDR and contentment but hurting his East-West trade balance further and risking a severe economic crisis over a debt that was spiraling out of control.[27] Either way, in economic terms the Soviet Union could do little to assist in stabilizing his international trade position or his political regime.

Brezhnev sought to maintain cohesion through political means instead. The old anti-German rhetoric was reheated to help unify Eastern Europe and remind the bloc of threats to their security. Nowhere could the "aggressive and revanchist" West German attitude be showcased more easily than in West Berlin. In early 1974, the Soviets orchestrated a barrage of attacks on the legal bond between Berlin and Bonn. On 21 January 1974, the CSSR protested against the inclusion of West Berlin in the Convention on the High Seas (Hohe See und Fakultativprotokoll), following up on 1 February 1974 with a protest against the inclusion of Berlin in the Protocol to Amend the Convention for the Suppression of Traffic in Women and Children (of 1921), of the Traffic in Women of Full Age (1933), and of White Slave Traffic (1904).[28] The GDR chimed in, protesting the inclusion of Berlin in the IAEO in February 1974 and the inclusion of Berlin before the General Assembly of the United Nations on 27 March 1974.[29]

The establishment of the Environmental Protection Office (Bundesumweltamtes) in West Berlin again escalated the Berlin issue, with the Soviets standing squarely behind the GDR and caricaturing a West Germany that sought to push eastward. The unilateral establishment of this German federal office resulted in harsh reactions from the Eastern bloc. In a conversation with Deputy Foreign Secretary Rush, Bahr expressed grave concerns regarding the Soviet stance on the issue and the potential crisis that might ensue. In particular, he was worried about the GDR's announcement that it was contemplating refusing transit to Berlin to employees of the Environmental Protection Office and their dependents. Furthermore, the GDR threatened potential actions if trading with the East German mark was not prohibited by the West German government, giving the government of the GDR a pretext to implement controls on transit traffic. Bahr saw all of this as being instigated by a Soviet policy designed to counter the creation of the Environmental Protection Office in West Berlin.[30] Clearly, any independent German foreign policy initiative that the Brandt government had hoped might result from the signing of the Four Power Agreement was thoroughly undermined by this development.

Soon afterward Brezhnev warned against an interpretation of the Four Power Agreement that established close links between the FRG and West Berlin. To avoid misunderstandings, he advised that "one must view the Four Power Agreement as a balancing of interests of all sides and not try to pry more from the agreement than it contains."[31] For the Soviets, the issue would become even more charged. On 28 February 1974, the Soviet ambassador Falin protested against the existence of the Environmental Protection Office in Berlin and even demanded the removal of the Federal District Court (Bundesverwaltungsgericht) from Berlin. He furthermore protested against the fact that Berlin residents were able to vote for the West German president, even though this had already been the case for several years.[32] The Soviets obviously were not going to leave West Berlin to the FRG without a fight, despite having a Four Power Agreement.

In a meeting with Brezhnev, Bahr expressed his grave frustrations with the Soviet stance. He explained that in Chancellor Brandt's opinion, nothing had harmed his government as much as the stagnation of *Ost-politik*. ... The goal of my visit is not only trade but, equally important, to explore if the questions surrounding Berlin can be solved between us. For this, I will stay as long as it is sensible. These questions are like small stones in a shoe. If you do not get rid of them, they start to hurt and you cannot walk any more, despite still having a long way ahead of us. It is not sensible but a sign of failure if the same topics will be discussed at a chancellor's visit that have already been discussed last year in Bonn.[33]

Yet Soviet attempts to strike the FRG in its Achilles' heel would continue throughout the 1970s. In April, the Soviets attempted to exert pressure on Austria in order to change its use of "Land Berlin" in its treaties with the FRG. Austrian ambassador Willfried Gredler indicated his "disappointment about the firm German line" in response to Austrian probing on whether any change would be feasible. Clearly, the Austrian government wished to avoid ending up in the crossfire of a battle that was not its own. In response to German insistence on keeping the formulation "Land Berlin" in the treaties, Gredler suggested that a note of support in this regard be issued by the Western allies.[34] Having received such a note, the Austrians toed the German line for another year.

The Soviets renewed the pressure on Austria in meetings that took place on 12–13 June 1975 with Soviet ambassador Bondarenko, who complained about the inclusion of Berlin in treaties that had nothing to do with Berlin at all (such as the agreement allowing both the FRG and Austria to use the Salzburg airport). However, much stronger was his criticism of the formulation "Land Berlin." Despite assurances that the Western powers condoned this formulation, the Austrian ambassador Michael Steiner viewed the matter with "grave concern."[35] The matter escalated further when the Soviets accused the Austrians of violating their constitution (Staatsvertrag), in which Austria committed itself to accept any agreement by the allied powers that served to reestablish peace for Germany. The Soviets asserted that "Land Berlin" violated the Four Power Agreement, as no such term was used in the agreement. The West German side placed a strong emphasis on the term "established procedures" in the agreement, which guaranteed the continued use of language that had previously been established.[36] A year later, in December 1976, they finally found a semantic compromise that pleased both sides. The Austrian government intended to reuse the phrase "Land Berlin" as the FRG had insisted, but wanted to include a form, yet unspecified, that would indicate that this referred to Berlin.[37]

Beyond the vilifying of West Germany, it was the Conference on Security and Cooperation in Europe that was to bring economic salvation.

Turning the economic reality on its head, Brezhnev touted East-West trade as a boon to socialist solidarity. In a flippant remark on the benefits of East-West trade in connection with the Conference on Security and Cooperation, Brezhnev commented that "when we deliver our oil and gas from the heartland to the western regions, we will be able to throw in an additional cistern to each fraternal country."[38] Since cooperation with the West was beneficial, then, "our entire commonwealth should work skillfully and with great energy to bring this conference to completion successfully."[39]

The Blessing and the Curse

Once the U.S. had, via the Jackson-Vanik amendment, sidelined itself as a potential lender and economic partner (apart from grain exports), the Soviet Union needed the Western Europeans as willing trading partners. With Western Europe thus rising to a new level of importance for the Soviet Union, the formalizing of peaceful relations through the CSCE was of prime importance to Brezhnev. He had long advocated such a conference, even attempting to initiate it, and now the fall of superpower détente rendered it an absolute necessity. A CIA assessment of Brezhnev's motivations also pointed to another goal in Brezhnev's drive for the CSCE—the establishment of a "permanent organizational machinery through which the USSR could become more directly involved in Western European affairs, economically and politically."[40]

Both these goals made sense for Brezhnev, as he had staked the success of his foreign policy on peaceful coexistence and the usage of East-West trade as a means of strengthening the Soviet economy during the 24th Party Congress in 1971. In this sense a conclusion of the CSCE would be his own personal success. This, however, meant placating the fears of an aggressive Soviet Union even more effectively by reaching an understanding on the CSCE.[41] This, in turn, meant committing again to the purposes and principles of the Charter of the UN and the Declaration of Human rights in Basket III. The Soviet Union finally did agree to include human rights protections in the Helsinki Final Act, signed on 1 August 1975.

In the West, the CSCE was interpreted as a success for the Western alliance. Kissinger gloated on the CSCE successes, once again blind to the structural divergence of trade.

> All the new things in the document [Final CSCE Charter] are in our favor—peaceful change, human contacts, maneuver notification. At the Conference, it was the President who dominated the Conference and it

was the West which was on the offensive. It was not Brezhnev who took a triumphal tour through Eastern Europe — it was the President.[42]

Kissinger correctly interpreted the CSCE as less than a triumph for Brezhnev. Nevertheless, it certainly was not a defeat for the Soviet leader, either. In a sense, it was a sequitur to his former policies, preserving the Eastern alliance as well as détente. With an economic crisis looming in Eastern Europe and the Soviet Union unable to supply its allies with the necessary commodities, East-West trade had to continue. In this sense, the CSCE represented a success for Brezhnev.

A Soviet commitment to human rights had to be dealt with very carefully. After all, East-West trade itself already posed a threat to domestic stability. Nonetheless, this did not seem an overly negative point for the Soviet leadership, as it would still be the Soviet leadership that would "enforce" those principles of human rights.[43] Brezhnev, then, thought it an acceptable risk to sign off on the words of the human rights declaration while maintaining a hard-line stance in spirit. In the end, Brezhenv got his wish: the Conference on Security and Cooperation in Europe was signed on 1 August 1975 with a somewhat troubling Basket III on human rights but more importantly with Basket II on agreements to increase economic cooperation and trade.

Yet even the CSCE was not to bring immediate relief to the debt-ridden Warsaw Pact states. East Germany's solution to the economic problems turned out to be the same as that of the Soviet Union. In 1976, as a temporary fix, Honecker and Brezhnev diverted more consumer products from domestic markets to exports and also sold gold and other strategic reserves in order to keep the spiraling debt in check.[44] In addition, the Soviet Union also increased its sales of arms.[45] Ultimately, though, these were just stopgap measures; it was the continued engagement in East-West trade with more access to Western markets that these leaders hoped would result in long-term balanced trade positions. In other words, it was the continued policies of détente and East-West trade that would bring economic stability and prosperity—if the subversive Western influences could be held at bay and the more pronounced internal dissent be suppressed for two or three more five-year plans.

For that time period, or until economic recovery was at hand, this new level of pan-European cooperation and an increasing dependency on Western Europe had to be balanced with a tougher stance on Germany. For the sake of Eastern cohesion, now more than ever, West Germany had to serve as the villain, a revisionist power posed to strike at any minute. For West Germany, this spirit led to a less than satisfactory outcome of the CSCE negotiations in regard to West Berlin. Despite numerous attempts, the FRG was unable to anchor legal ties between West Germany and West Berlin in the framework of the CSCE. The FRG had strongly pushed for an inclusion of Berlin but had faced strong Eastern objections. Finally, it had had to content itself with the general application of the conference's results in all of Europe, thus implicitly including West Berlin. Just as in the Four Power Agreement of 1971, this would leave much room for interpretation, which proved an ominous sign for future West German–Soviet relations.

West Germany as the Villain

As Brezhnev explained to a group of Eastern European heads of state, Schmidt was all right, but "influential forces in the FRG put forward demands both in regard to West Berlin as well as … to gobble up Honecker. Those revanchists are insatiable. … This is the danger, which we should always remember, and which we should always counter."[46] The balance that had to be struck, then, was one of friendship toward Western Europe while continuously keeping the unsatisfactory status quo of the German question at the forefront of international debate.

This presaged more trouble for West Berlin, and indeed, the latter half of the 1970s saw the Eastern bloc undermining West German–West Berlin ties whenever possible. The Soviet Union (6 June 1975), Hungary (2 July 1975), and the CSSR (11 July 1975) protested in Washington and London against the inclusion of West Berlin in the Non-Proliferation Treaty.[47] Rumania chimed in with the other Eastern-bloc states when it refused to agree to the inclusion of Berlin in a basic treaty between the FRG and Rumania on scientific-technological cooperation. From one day to the next, after the details had previously been worked out to everyone's satisfaction, the Rumanian side presented new suggestions that would have eliminated the inclusion of Berlin in the agreement. In the German ambassador's assessment,

> The same problems that we have been experiencing for years in negotiations with other East European states and for example prevent the conclusion of a framework agreement for scientific-technological cooperation with the Soviet Union, have now occurred with Romania for the first time. Romania has so far been the only East European country with which we have such a framework agreement that contains a satisfactory Berlin clause. The execution of this agreement seems to create difficulties here, as well.[48]

In 1976 the German government also sparred with the Soviets over the issue of Berlin in the international press. Op-ed pieces supporting the Western position called on the Soviet government to stop hindering East-West cooperation and to abide by the Four Power Agreement, especially on the international representation of West Berlin.[49] The Foreign Office entirely agreed with this article and its interpretation, and desired to gain as much exposure of this viewpoint as possible. It therefore sought to reprint it in several languages, first in the *Bulletin der Bundesregierung* and then, upon the refusal of the German Press Office due to the confrontational tone of the article, in the government-financed *German Tribune.*[50] An interesting element of this article is the SPD's and FDP's clashing viewpoints on foreign policy toward the Soviet Union.

> The article reflects a line of argument that has become more and more visible over the last months. I recall Foreign Minister Genscher's remark that as long as he is Foreign Minister, the Federal Republic will not conclude a treaty without a Berlin clause. I further point to the accompanying study which the Foreign Ministry has submitted to the Group of Four without involving other parts of the government or the Berlin Senate. This study demands a firmer stance vis-à-vis the Soviet Union from the three powers and, thus, undermines exactly like the article in the magazine *Europa-Archiv* all efforts to deescalate the Berlin controversy with the Soviet Union through limited compromise. I would not rule out that the article, the study, and certain public remarks were done with regards to the coming coalition negotiations.[51]

The "Eastern Interpretation" of the Berlin issue continued to materialize in 1977, this time manifesting itself in German relations with Yugoslavia. In a report generated by the German embassy in Belgrade, Ambassador Jesco von Puttkamer points to a gradual shift away from an acceptance of West Berlin as part of the FRG. Apart from smaller issues, such as Yugoslav officials avoiding visits to West Berlin or listing the Berlin Ensemble as being from West Berlin rather than the FRG, the contentious area was the Berlin clause in official treaties. On 12 October 1968 Yugoslavia had already agreed to a Berlin clause ("gilt auch für das Land Berlin") in the Agreement on Social Security, just as it did a year later in the Agreement on Culture of 28 July 1969. Despite this history, in the negotiations for a fourth two-year Cultural Program in 1977 the Yugoslavs balked at including a reference to Berlin, and only upon personal initiative by the Yugoslav minister of culture were the objections of the Yugoslav Foreign Ministry overridden. Any supplements to the Cultural Agreement itself failed because the Yugoslavs were no longer willing to include the Berlin clause in the agreement subsequently.

The most striking point was the agreement on double taxation, which had already been initialed in 1973. In June 1977, the Yugoslavs presented a list of desired changes, among them the removal of the Berlin clause. These negotiations also failed, as the Germans insisted on it while the Yugoslavs categorically refused.[52]

Despite continued West German difficulties with the East over the status of Berlin, there was no turning back from the course of East-West trade that West Germany was already committed to. On 19 December 1975, another $500 million credit by a German bank consortium was granted to the Soviet Union at a time when U.S. Congressional hearings expressed serious doubt over the future creditworthiness of the Soviet Union.

Ford's Lack of Direction

NATO's energy dilemma would be ignored under Ford, however. Ford did not seek to overcome Congress's restrictive stance on East-West trade, though all the while he approved of European contacts with the Eastern bloc. For the first time since Kennedy, the White House viewed East-West trade not as a political tool, but rather more in line with Western European approaches. Consequently, Ford was elated to conclude a successful economic summit in Puerto Rico with the Western Europeans. Kissinger in particular was pleased with the unity of the alliance over East-West trade, as "we just wanted to raise the issue, but we got all the countries to agree that this trade had to be looked at in more than commercial terms — rather in terms of overall relationships and in a coordinated way among us."[53]

On East-West trade, President Ford did issue two National Security Study Memorandi. One was done in February 1976, addressing among other things "the likely level of U.S. energy import dependence over the next five years," "possibilities for diversifying imports of energy," and "possibilities for the United States to encourage restraints in OPEC pricing."[54] Interestingly enough, this memorandum did not call for a strategy to address energy dependence in Western European countries. Without including Western allies or taking a view longer than five years, no fundamental addressing of the issue could take place.

Only when Democratic presidential nominee Jimmy Carter accused the Ford administration of being soft on the Soviet Union did Ford demand a more comprehensive review of East-West foreign trade. While the primary focus remained on "U.S. economic interests in Eastern Europe and the Soviet Union," it also incorporated questions of economic diplomacy such as "How, and to what degree, could economic relations between the industrialized Western nations and Eastern nations be used to pursue non-economic policy interests?" It also implied a concern regarding economic leverage employed by the Eastern European countries. "How, and to what degree, could the Eastern Europeans and the Soviet Union collectively or separately use economic relations with the industrialized nations to achieve economic or non-economic objectives inimical to the interests of the U.S. and the West?"[55] Even in this lengthy memorandum, the possibility that the interests of the U.S. and those of "the West" did not overlap was not addressed.

In his last State of the Union address, Ford outlined his belief that the Atlantic rift of earlier years was gone.

> Our alliances with major partners, the great industrial democracies of Western Europe, Japan, and Canada, have never been more solid. Consultations on mutual security, defense, and East-West relations have grown closer. Collaboration has branched out into new fields such as energy, economic policy, and relations with the Third World. We have used many avenues for cooperation, including summit meetings held among major allied countries. The friendship of the democracies is deeper, warmer, and more effective than at any time in 30 years.[56]

This, however, just glossed over the deep structural divide that existed between economic interests and perceptions of the Soviet Union on the two sides of the Atlantic. During the Ford presidency, the Western Europeans could cite White House support for East-West trade and blend their alliance politics into their trade interests. Opposition to the White House Congress, however, was voiced by Congress and the American public. This transatlantic rift would break open during the Carter and Reagan presidencies. First and foremost, the embargo policies of these two administrations would clash with European interests in East-West trade. Second, the shift in European perceptions of the nature of the Soviet Union would create differences on how to treat questions of human rights, an issue central to Carter's presidency.

The three major crises depicted in the last part of this chapter illustrate how far the transatlantic rift had already progressed at the turn of the 1970s. Under Ford, the conflict did not arise—but it certainly did under Carter and Reagan. The three crises demonstrate Western European actions against U.S. foreign policy initiatives vis-à-vis the Soviet Union. While the crisis was fought out in the political arena, it was mostly economic interests that were at stake for the Europeans. "European détente" had become more economically powerful than ever before.

Jimmy Carter's Human Rights Campaign

Even prior to his inaugural address, Carter's background was viewed with suspicion by Europeans. Gleefully conjuring up the image of a political nobody, a peanut farming minister whose own mother was surprised by his candidacy for U.S. president, the German press pounced on the political inexperience and atypical background of Jimmy Carter.[57] In contrast to the situation in Western Europe, however, where realpolitik dominated the field of international relations, Carter's projected honesty and high moral standards for international relations gave the American public, still dealing with the Vietnam fiasco, a long-needed concept to rally behind.[58] As Nixon promised to "undo" Johnson's foreign policy mistakes, Carter now promised a decisively anti-Kissingeresque foreign policy: "We ought to be a beacon for nations who search for peace and who search for freedom, who search for individual liberty, who search for basic human rights. We haven't been lately. We can be once again."[59] More specifically, he focused on the communist regimes, arguing that U.S. foreign policy should be used as a lever to advance human rights in the communist East. Pointing to the Helsinki Accords as a legal basis, he assured a concerned American public that Soviet dissidents "will be very much on my mind when I negotiate with the Soviet Union."[60]

Once elected, he stayed the course. After opening with a quote from Micah on goodness and justice in his inaugural address, he elaborated on human rights as one of only two major foreign policy goals. He argued that "we can never be indifferent to the fate of freedom elsewhere," implying a respect for societies cherishing human rights and promising confrontational policies toward those that did not.[61] In response, Western European newspapers accustomed to realpolitik failed to recognize this ideological approach as the pillar of U.S. foreign policy, labeling Carter as an "unknown quantity," an "enigma" who said little about "genuine priorities." One paper, demonstrating wishful thinking, predicted that Carter, now in Washington, would continue the foreign policy of Kissinger, whose political style he had so criticized during his election campaign.[62]

Yet Carter's tenure established a marked shift in U.S.-Soviet relations. Apart from military deescalation, Carter established a cooler tone with Moscow in regard to trade and détente in general. As in the cases of his predecessors, the administration under Jimmy Carter was deeply divided over the merits of East-West trade. Indeed, by the onset of his tenure in 1977, the trade volume had already dwindled significantly.[63] With a shrinking U.S.-Soviet trade volume, national security adviser Zbigniew Brzezinski and Energy Secretary James Schlesinger saw little hope of moderating Soviet behavior through trade and pushed for more restrictive export controls, while State and Commerce pushed for increased liberalization.

Carter had no strong aversion to East-West trade, though ultimately, his emphasis on human rights presented one more hurdle to its possible resurgence. He demonstrated his convictions publicly by inviting the well-known Soviet dissident Vladimir Bukovsky to the White House, and he continued to highlight the violation of the Helsinki Accords by the Soviet Union. Of special significance is also the public nature in which Carter put forth his concerns regarding human rights.[64] With the Carter White House, human rights had become a near precondition for détente and East-West trade.[65]

Such a precondition to trade was nearly as troubling to Brezhnev as the Jackson-Vanik amendment. Allowing Soviet dissidents to speak freely undermined the carefully managed balance between allowing East-West trade while curtailing Western influence. For Carter it appeared to be a simple human rights issue; for Brezhnev, a Western government sought to undermine his regime. It is therefore easy to appreciate Brezhnev viewing Carter's foreign policy as "psychological warfare."[66] Upon Carter's initial contact and the broaching of the issue of trade and human rights, Brezhnev could not but vehemently reject the U.S. infringement in domestic affairs. "Without this, without rejection of attempts to somehow or other link trade with questions relating to the domestic competence of governments, not only will economic contacts suffer, but overall relations between our countries will also suffer a blow."[67] When the issue was again raised by a U.S. delegation to Moscow by bringing up the question of Soviet dissident Aleksandr Ginzburg, the Soviets condemned this attempt at "freeing a criminal" in the strongest terms.[68]

Undercutting Brezhnev's tightrope walk between economic openness and political control effectively undermined U.S.-Soviet relations over moral principles. By infusing morality in U.S. foreign policy, Carter sought to reclaim the high ground in international relations and the leadership within the Western alliance. In regard to domestic politics, such an emphasis might initially have made sense, particularly since there was little to lose: U.S.-Soviet trade had remained stagnant, and few political concessions seemed apparent. Internationally, however, Carter's humanitarian quests triggered as much resentment as his famous "malaise speech" would with the American public. Unlike U.S.-Soviet trade, Western European–Soviet trade had blossomed. East-West trade was firmly entrenched, even dominating key industrial sectors such as the steel industry and machine tooling. Risking severe disruptions in these sectors, the closure of several banks that had extended loans to Soviet projects, and a whole slew other unpredictable consequences over human rights for Soviet dissidents did not seem worth the risk.

When it became clear that Carter would, as promised in his campaign, use human rights as a pillar of his foreign policy, the Western European press became extremely critical. Within the first few months of his tenure, the German press came to loathe Carter and his "crusade for human rights," describing the inaugural speech of "lay preacher" Carter as an "empty and pathetic ... Sunday sermon." His "political crusade" as" moral counselor for the entire world" heavily undermined relations between the U.S. and half a dozen countries.[69] Carter especially hurt the policy of détente, which before his tenure "both in East and West had sheer indefinite future perspectives."

The press depicted a self-righteous Carter who arrived at his conclusions in spur-of-the-moment decisions. Using his evangelical morality to determine foreign policy, Carter was botching East-West relations. Carter's attention to human rights and his communication with Soviet dissidents undermined "the 'absolute submission of the masses under one power' (Lenin), which is after all the basic law of the Soviet state."[70] Therefore, in the Soviet Union Carter's initiative would only serve to increase repression of dissidents, "with whom the Soviets had dealt rather well in the past."[71] Altogether, "he weakens the position of his détente partner Brezhnev, who accepted human rights and information exchange in Helsinki mainly for the sake of détente and the economic aid."[72] Finally, the article closed with a summarizing citation from the London *Sunday Telegraph:* "In Europe suspicions grow that Carter might be as foolish as he sounds. This is a amoral world and many things point to the fact that Carter is too good for it."[73]

The West German government and especially its chancellor, Helmut Schmidt, had problems with the new president from the very beginning. Schmidt had openly praised incumbent President Ford during the 1976 election campaign but said nothing about Democratic candidate Carter. Thus already on a rocky road, the two statesmen soon thereafter clashed over the possibility of West German exports of nuclear technology to Brazil as well as strategies to stimulate the world economy.[74] Most importantly, though, Schmidt had hoped to use Carter's presumed interest in détente to overcome West German Foreign Minister Hans-Dietrich Genscher's stalling on a beginning a "second phase"' of *Ostpolitik*.[75] While the SPD had continuously sought to push the achievements of the early 1970s further, its coalition partner, the FDP, was not ready for sustentative changes in West Germany's relations with the Soviet Union. An endorsement of renewed détente efforts by a U.S. president would certainly push Genscher and his party in the right direction. This hope, however, would not be realized, as Carter's human rights policy did anything but foster a second détente. For a frustrated Schmidt, Carter's attempts to modify the internal structure of the Soviet Union were illusionary. "The Kremlin possesses supremacy over a number of other states and over countless millions of humans and the Kremlin can tighten the ideological, police, and military controls, if it feels this to be appropriate."[76] And tighten it did.

For Brezhnev, Carter's human rights agenda appeared as an aggressive gesture. The precarious balance that Brezhnev had previously struck allowed more Western economic influence to build up the Soviet economic infrastructure while at the same time any Western ideas and concepts that might permeate Soviet society were heavily scrutinized. Allowing Soviet dissidents to articulate their opinions freely, even if that would have created goodwill with the West, could undermine this strategy. Thus, following the election of Carter, trade with the Soviet Union had again become politically sensitive.

Yet Western Europeans pursued their trade interests all the same, whereupon Carter's concern over human rights became a stumbling block in alliance relations. Schmidt felt it necessary to caution Carter not to jeopardize "gains already achieved or [turn] the meeting into a confrontation" before the follow-up meeting to the Helsinki Accords in Belgrade. Nonetheless, Carter insisted that "we should not forego the opportunity to insist on a careful review of the implementation of the Helsinki accords."[77] By the time of the German-American summit in July 1977, Western Europe had had enough. Helmut Schmidt was spoiling for a confrontation on Carter's human rights policy. Schmidt had commented negatively on Carter's policy before, and the personal dislike between the two men certainly may have played a role, but by July Schmidt intended to be more direct, making it clear that West Germany could not support Washington's hard-line policy against Moscow as it would jeopardize German *Ostpolitik*.[78]

Schmidt was not alone: he carried messages of concern and protest from West and East alike. British Prime Minister James Callaghan asked Schmidt to convey his objections to Carter, and French President Valery Giscard d'Estaing criticized Carter's human rights policy as ill-conceived, arguing he had broken the "code of conduct of détente" and even threatening to cancel a trip to Washington should Carter continue his verbal attacks against Moscow.[79] Brezhnev also complained in Bonn about Carter and his human rights agenda, and *Pravda* labeled Carter an "enemy of détente," hoping that Schmidt could effect a change.[80]

Bonn's main concern was not necessarily the efficacy of human rights issues, per se. Rather, in deteriorating U.S.-Soviet relations Schmidt saw less "maneuvering space for Germany's détente policy," a policy that had made the inter-German wall more translucent, allowing several million people to visit friends and relatives in the other Germany as well as repatriating several thousand ethnic Germans from the East.[81] Furthermore, Schmidt feared that Carter's dual-track policy of trying to negotiate a SALT agreement while at the same time criticizing the Soviet Union over human rights violations would be ineffective. Without continued arms reductions, however, détente would ring hollow. In this sense, Schmidt felt obligated to fight for the achievements gained as a result of the détente policies of the last seven years, which Carter's moralistic policies threatened to undo.

Before the confrontational meeting could occur, however, Carter shifted his positions. During an interview on 25 June 1977, Carter appeared shocked over Soviet opposition to his human rights campaign and maintained that he had never singled them out. This interview was, however, the first instance where he acknowledged that the Russians might have taken his attacks personally.[82] A personal exchange of letters between Carter and Brezhnev also appeared to have taken place, which hinted at the possibility of a summit meeting.[83]

By the time Schmidt appeared at the White House, Carter had already made a turnabout. He bestowed compliments on the German guests, calling Helmut Schmidt his "friend," and ignored previous stabs made at the Carter White House by the German allies.[84] Especially after Carter promised to tone down his human rights rhetoric, alliance relations relaxed. Thus projecting harmony at the follow-up meeting to the Helsinki Conference in Belgrade, with Carter forbearing to use the conference as a pulpit for his human rights agenda in the East, the German press termed the friendly and hopeful atmosphere "a small miracle."[85] Even beyond the conference, Carter did tone down his human rights rhetoric and avoided inviting more Soviet dissidents to the White House. Taking it one step further, he announced before an American audience that the Soviet Union was unlikely to adopt Western-style human rights in the foreseeable future, but that despite this, the Soviet Union and the United States "share many overlapping interests. Our job is to explore those interests and use them to enlarge the areas of cooperation between us on a basis of equality and mutual respect."[86]

Whether because of the protest by the allies or his recognition that the Soviets were indeed put off by his accusations and would not cooperate on SALT in the current climate, by September 1977 Carter had embraced the need for East-West trade as a tool for improving U.S.-Soviet relations. In talks with Soviet Foreign Minister Gromyko Carter demonstrated a clear sense of pragmatics by seeing the Soviet need for trade as a by-product of détente. Whereas in his February letter to Brezhnev he had referred to the Jackson-Vanik amendment—the main obstacle to U.S.-Soviet trade—as a given, he now wanted to "to ameliorate this source of tension and misunderstanding" and asked Gromyko to help him convince Senator Jackson to repeal the law.[87] Gromyko confirmed this new approach: "You correctly pointed out the importance of trade-economic relations. It is also true that they are essential for the development of political relations."[88] Carter even concluded by requesting a visit by Soviet Trade Minister Patolichev.

Yet even the more "Kissingeresque" stance of ignoring human rights in favor of diplomacy and trade failed to improve Carter's image as a statesman in Europe. In the context of President Carter wising up to the ways of Washington, his change was not viewed as something positive. Instead, the "disaster" with Moscow was attributed to "the President's strong sense of his own infallibility." "Mr. Carter examines problems with great thoroughness. He understands them, and when he has reflected on them, he produces a solution. It then becomes extremely difficult for him to grasp how anyone can disagree with so obviously correct a solution that he has produced after such long labour."[89]

Despite his erstwhile shift toward pragmatism, Carter eventually resumed his hard-line position, further underscoring the inconsistency of U.S. leadership. Whether it was a lack of progress on the SALT negotiations, the convictions of more Soviet dissidents, or a renewed confidence in his sense of morality, the "miracle" of a softer Carter did not last long: he had reverted to a confrontational stance with the Soviet Union by December 1977. In the biannual report to Congress on the compliance of the signatory nations relation to the Helsinki Accords, the Carter administration pointed out continued human rights violations within the Eastern bloc.[90]

In 1978, consequently, Schmidt's open criticism and expression of personal dislike of Carter ("a 'Jimmy' will not come across my lips") had reached new heights. His disdain created serious concerns within the German political establishment over a possible permanent severing of transatlantic relations.[91] Of particular concern between the two statesmen were the human-rights "polemics" that upset the pragmatist Schmidt. Schmidt even put his objections in writing, and he continued to complain about Carter in public.[92] Once he even suggested to a news magazine reporter that he might just as well read Cologne's train schedule to Carter, since he didn't listen anyway.

And Carter did not listen. During the Belgrade Conference in March 1978, the Soviet Union increasingly came under fire for violating the Human Rights Agenda of the Conference on Security and Cooperation in Europe. Historian Svetlana Savranskaya convincingly argues that it was the international pressure at that conference that spurred the Soviet leadership's decision to move from monitoring and harassing to full-scale arrests and incarcerations.[93] Whether, as she claims, a direct link between dissident activities in the 1970s and in the early 1990s can be established is beyond the scope of this book. However, it was certainly another crisis for the Western alliance.

Despite Schmidt's frustration with Carter, and Carter's continued criticism of the Soviet Union, the German-American relationship settled on a course of somber detachment. On Schmidt's visit to the Carter White House on 5 June, the German magazine *Der Spiegel* commented with relief that "They didn't kill each other." While the return visit by Carter "had more show than substance," it nevertheless formalized a relationship.[94] Breaking protocol, the German chancellor personally welcomed Carter as he deplaned Air Force One and even invited him to his private home in Hamburg. The entire visit reeked of symbolism and allowed only two hours of personal discussion between the statesmen.[95]

Given this resignation to a more formal relationship—one in which Schmidt would not just call up the U.S. president to give his opinion, as he had done with Ford—Carter's political antics mattered less. America's position in the world was still accepted, but Carter's leadership was not. For this reason the European press took scant notice of Carter's most hard-line foreign policy speech to date. In a commencement speech on 7 June 1978 at his alma mater, the U.S. Naval Academy in Annapolis, he attempted to demonstrate a consistent line in his foreign policy with the Soviet Union. Here, he emphasized that "the abuse of basic human rights in their own country, in violation of the agreement which was reached at Helsinki, has earned them the condemnation of people everywhere who love freedom." He further recalled the bloody suppression of the revolt in Hungary and, in the harshest terms his administration had used to date, offered the Soviet Union a choice between "confrontation or cooperation," assuring his audience that the U.S. was prepared for either.[96]

On the other hand, in July he conducted his own tightrope walk, trying to befriend the Soviet Union at arms negotiations. Carter issued a statement of "deep concern" over the arrest of Mr. Viktoras Pyatkus, a member of the Lithuanian Helsinki group, meanwhile preferring to seek the release of Anatoly Shcharansky and Alexander Ginzburg through secret channels. At the same time he also decided to proceed with a new round of negotiations with Moscow on reducing overseas arms sales.[97] When the Soviets arrested the last leader of the Helsinki group, Carter became more careful in his wording. Rejecting the idea that he was waging a personal vendetta against the Soviet Union, he went out of his way to explain that he did not wish to interfere in internal affairs and wanted to continue U.S.-Soviet trade and SALT negotiations.[98] He also assured the Soviet Union that there would be no more U.S. reprisals over Soviet human rights violations.[99]

It comes as no small surprise that Soviet Ambassador to the United States Anatoly F. Dobrynin could not deliver a clear-cut explanation of Carter's policies to his superiors. He contended that a minimum level of détente was assured, even with Carter, because of the interest of "influential political and business circles" as well as the common people. As he explained, "in the minds of the unsophisticated residents of this country, détente is associated with a simple thesis: détente mitigates the threat of confrontation with the Soviet Union, and thus, of nuclear war with it."[100] Carter valued U.S.-Soviet relations for its strategic-military aspects. Beyond that, however, the White House was willing to allow relations to deteriorate over "the notorious policy of 'defense of human rights' or 'dissidents.'"[101]

Brezhnev himself recognized a "serious deterioration and exacerbation of the situation," pinpointing the Carter administration as the primary source of the problem. To Brezhnev, Carter was consciously "intent upon struggling for his election to a new term as President of the USA under the banner of anti-Soviet policy and a return to the 'cold war.'"[102] As the Soviet Union was dependent on the continued economic and strategic benefits of détente, he concluded that "[w]e must fight actively and persistently for peace and détente. We must do all that is possible in order to hinder the policy, which is fraught with the threat of a new world war."[103]

Besides being a strategic imperative, it clearly became an economic one in 1979. Production of the Soviet export cash cows, oil and natural gas, could not keep pace with increasing domestic needs as well as the demands made by other socialist countries. Unlike the situation during most of the 1970s, the Soviet Union's excess energy production leveled off in 1979 and did not increase significantly in the 1980s. Such an increase would have been necessary to facilitate growth in East-West trade. By March 1979, the Soviet Union had to announce that its Finnish and Swedish importers could expect a 30 percent reduction in supplies from the Soviet Union.[104] Kosygin also had to tell his European allies to expect little in terms of Soviet oil. His assessment was that despite vast oil reserves in Siberia, drilling and transport costs would make them unexploitable.[105] Furthermore, the agricultural sector had suffered yet another bad harvest, suggesting a need to import 35 million tons of grain, leading the CIA to describe the Soviet situation as an "economic crisis in industry, energy, and agriculture."[106]

With the United States out of the picture as far as détente was concerned, the logical choice for the Soviets was to reemphasize relations with Western Europe. In several segments of Western European society, the military threat of the Soviet Union was viewed as negligible.[107] Brezhnev played to this sentiment by pleasing Western Europe when in October 1979 he announced the withdrawal of 20,000 Soviet troops and 1,000 tanks from East Germany as a preliminary gesture and then doubled the numbers in November. Naturally, West Germans were very pleased with this announcement, while Carter dismissed it as a ploy to weaken the Western alliance.[108]

European frustrations with Carter's leadership had manifested themselves strongly in European public opinion and in turn benefited the Soviet Union. In a 1979 survey, the United States Information Agency found that "most Europeans believe the Continent's economy will do better by being more independent of the US."[109] In every Western European country polled, except for the FRG, the overwhelming majority spoke in favor of an independent course for the European Community—independent from both the United States and the Soviet Union. Only in the FRG did working more closely with the U.S. outweigh an independent course, 42 percent to 32 percent. Interestingly enough, the FRG also had the highest percentage of people expressing the desire for an emphasis on more cooperation with the Soviet Union (7 percent).[110]

A CIA long-term assessment of "Changing Power Relations Among OECD States," i.e., Western Europe and Japan, came to a similar conclusion in regard to the decline of American influence. Without mentioning Carter in person, it clearly implies disillusionment with his leadership style.

> The problem is not one of increased enmity or even—as yet—of basic divergences in interests between the United States and its allies. The change entails, instead, a diminution of American decisionmaking power and influence with its allies resulting from lack of trust in US responsiveness and policymaking skill, as well as from a perceived decline in relative American politicial, economic, and military power.[111]

In what reads as a defeat for the Carter administration, the CIA report cites Western European questioning of "the wisdom of various American intitiatives" in the two areas Carter had outlined in his inaugural address: arms reduction and human rights. While the Europeans recognized the potential harm of these policies, they also saw them as an opportunity to create distance between themselves and the United States. The report cites West Germany as a prime example:

In part, the change in the West German attitude can be attributed to the presence in office of Chancellor Helmut Schmidt—supremely confident of his own abilities, disdainful of many others, and able to work in close cooperation with French President Valery Giscard d'Estaing. It is unlikely, however, that West Germany will return to its previous docility when Schmidt leaves the Chancellorship; it simply took someone of his personality, ability—and generation—to make the breakthrough.[112]

The most pointed summary of Western European attitudes toward a flailing U.S. leadership was that "they welcome the opportunity to advance their own interests as they see fit" while being "reluctant to incur the attendant economic costs" of leadership.[113]

The Afghanistan Crisis and Carter's Embargo

The Europeans were not the only ones uncomfortable with Carter's rhetoric. The gradual worsening of relations with the Soviet Union led the Soviet Politburo to shift its view of Afghan resistance from one of a regional challenge to one of aggressive U.S. intervention in a neighboring country.[114] In the mind of the Soviet leaders, such agitation demanded a strong response. Yet it was the West that felt threatened by a full-scale military invasion of Afghanistan. Once Radio Kabul announced the replacement of President Hafizullah Amin with Soviet crony Babrak Karmal on 28 December 1979, the West needed to act. The day following the Soviet coup, Carter condemned the invasion as "a grave threat to peace" and consulted with the allies on what to do.[115]

Despite the public bow to the allies, the decision was made within the White House. Here, advisors scrambled to develop suggestions for an appropriate response, which Carter wished to deliver during the State of the Union Address on 4 January 1980. In an attempt to avoid military escalation, economic sanctions—specifically, a grain embargo—seemed to be the most efficient way to send a message to the Soviet Union. Yet opinions ranged widely, with Chief Domestic Policy Advisor Stuart Eizenstat cautioning Carter against a grain embargo. Pointing out that a grain embargo had never before been used as a political weapon, even against Iran, Eizenstat argued that a such a measure would also be devastating on political and economic grounds. For one, this would mean breaking a campaign promise to Midwestern farmers not to levy a grain embargo except for national security purposes. For another, it would set a devastating precedent for agricultural products, the biggest U.S. export commodity. Apart from the Soviet Union looking for other long-term suppliers of grain, it would upset the domestic grain markets and force the U.S. to break existing contracts.[116]

White House Staff Director Alonzo L. McDonald, clearly concerned about the effects over time of a grain embargo, also tried to soften Carter's stance by suggesting only a ninety-day embargo designed to gain time to reassess the long-term consequences of such actions. Warning that a permanent rupture of relations could take a decade or more to restore, he viewed commercial relations as "our main hope for a peaceful coexistence," as "social and cultural [relations] cannot do the job, and we have no prospect of bridging our political system."[117] Driving home the pitfalls of implementing a permanent embargo, as he clearly feared Carter would do that day, McDonald suggested a lack of political support, as critics would question "whether this was indeed an act of 'a calm, thoughtful leader,'" since "attacking Afghanistan, a country few of our citizens can spell, is not the same in their minds as attacking Pearl Harbor."[118]

Nonetheless, with a presidential election campaign looming and the fiasco of the Iranian hostage crisis at hand, Carter felt he had to pursue a tough stance. On 3 January, he asked Congress to hold off on ratifying the SALT Treaty until the crisis could be resolved. The next day, in his State of the Union speech, he labeled the Soviet invasion of Afghanistan "a radical and aggressive new step" for which he felt "the Soviet Union must pay a concrete price." This price would be an economic one, he announced: Soviet ships were to be blocked from fishing in U.S. waters, and exports of high-tech equipment and agricultural products would be cut. Fortunately for Carter, Congress had just tightened the 1969 Export Administration Act a month before. The new version of the bill granted the Defense Department increased authority in withholding dual-use items, i.e., items that could have military or civilian applications.[119] Tightening the export controls on the American side, therefore, would be relatively easy.

In admitting, however, that it would require "allies and friends to join with us in restraining their own trade with the Soviets and not to replace our own embargoed items," Carter had already pointed out the weak spot in his plan. Given the short time frame before the State of the Union speech, allied consent could not be secured. Not surprisingly France, in keeping with its foreign policy traditions, opposed Carter's approach of punitive measures against the Soviet Union. As France's Foreign Minister M. Jean Francois-Poncet put it: "Before drawing pessimistic consequences, France considers it better to pursue a dialogue with the Soviet Union to stress its responsibility."[120]

Even without France's participation—France being an insignificant exporter of grains—Carter's gut reaction on the efficacy of a grain embargo still was an effective one. A CIA assessment on 15 January summarized the Soviet state of agriculture in 1979 as "one of the worst years on record."

> An official of the Ministry of the Food Industry confirmed that at least some premature slaughter of cattle and pigs would be necessary. To keep slaughtering to a minimum, the Soviets had purchased close to 40 million tons of grain, soybeans, and soybean meal for delivery between July 1979 and June 1980. ... Freezing temperatures since late October, however, have probably damaged fall-sown grain for harvest next summer, particularly in the Southern Ukraine and North Caucasus. Low soil moisture has caused poor germination in much of this area. ... Growth in farm output will be further hindered by a 25 percent reduction in fertilizer deliveries.[121]

Such a catastrophic year seemed the ideal time to implement embargo effectively. The U.S. was the leading supplier of grains, and dropping its exports to the 8.5 million–ton minimum ensured in international agreements would leave the Soviet Union devastated. As can be seen in Table 5.1, even if the other suppliers had doubled their grain exports, the Soviet Union would still have fallen short by 8 million metric tons. Nonetheless, allied cooperation was key in assuring that the embargo would not be circumvented.

With cooperation such a crucial component and concerns already being voiced by the allies, Carter sent out letters on 11 January to France, Great Britain, Italy, Germany, and Canada, reiterating his message of

Table 5.1 Soviet Grain Imports by Producing Country, 1972–1980

	1972/73	1973/74	1974/75	1975/76	1976/77	1977/78	1978/79	1979/80 pre-embargo	1979/80 post-embargo
U.S.	14.1	4.5	3.2	14.9	6.1	14.6	15.3	25.9	8.5
Canada	4.8	0.5	1.0	4.2	1.6	2.7	1.7	2.6	4.0
Australia	1.0	0.1	0.8	2.3	0.4	0.2	0.6	3.1	3.0
Argentina	0.2	0.3	1.7	1.4	0.2	3.2	1.6	3.0	5.3
EC	1.6	0.1	0	0.8	0	0.2	0.2	0.6	0.7
Other	0.8	0.2	0.9	1.9	0	1.5	0.2	0.8	3.5
Total	22.5	5.7	7.7	25.6	8.4	22.5	19.6	36.0	25.0

Source: Soviet Import of Grains 1972–1980; USSR Imports of Grain by Soviets 1972/73–1979/80, October/September Years (million Metric Tons), as in Memo, Lynn Daft to Stu Eizenstat, "The Soviet Grain Suspension," 25 March 1980, Folder: "Soviet Grain Embargo, 2/25/1980 to 9/80," CF O/A #743, Box 2 of 3, 1.

Soviet aggression from his State of the Union speech and reminding them of the importance of their commitment to the embargo. "Failure on our part to respond adequately to the Soviet action in Afghanistan can only encourage the Soviets to take similar moves elsewhere."[122] Anticipating Brezhnev's move to separate Western Europe from U.S. interests, Carter cautioned that

> we have already noted a predictable tendency in the Soviet Union's prop- aganda to try to divide the United States and Western Europe over the matter of Afghanistan. Indeed, I think we can expect the Soviets to launch a "Peace Offensive" in Europe in the near future. Moscow will undoubt- edly hope that by offering various inducements to Western European Countries, they can secure a "Business-As-Usual" approach by these countries, a tacit agreement to let concern about the Soviet Occupation of Afghanistan fade away. I know that you will be particularly sensitive to this Soviet objective and will work with me and our colleagues from the other Western European countries to ensure that this Soviet aim is not realized.[123]

The Soviet approach to counteract the threat of shortages in so vital an area as agriculture was twofold: it called for "a firm line in inter- national affairs in opposition to the Carter Administration's provoca- tive steps," and it sought to "intensify our influence on the positions of various NATO allies of the USA, particularly on France and the FRG, to the greatest possible extent using our interests in the differences that have been revealed between them and the USA in their approach to the choice of measures used in response to the actions of the Soviet Union in Afghanistan."[124] This divide-and-conquer strategy appealed to statesmen who had learned over the past three years that Carter was an unreliable leader who willingly sacrificed international relations and détente policy for his personal quests and morality.

Schmidt's response to Carter's admonitions about toeing the line was, consequently, lukewarm. Instead of fully committing to the embargo, he emphasized the need for direct continued consultation with the So- viets, feeling that "it is not sufficient for the dialogue to be reduced to signals that are given and received indirectly or via the public."[125] As Schmidt indicates in his memoirs, he would have been willing to go along with an actual trade embargo (and boycott of the Olympic Games), but Carter's lack of consultation and broader vision to resolve the Afghanistan crisis led him to refuse to follow the Americans' lead.[126] As Carter attempted to remain in frequent contact with Schmidt during the crisis, the emphasis must have been more on the lack of a broader vision or, most likely, the lack of a vision that was suitable to European interests. The failure of Carter's more "Wilsonian" foreign policy of spreading American idealism must have been glaring.

Ironically, even in regard to human rights the grain embargo backfired. In 1980 the Soviet Union decided to crack down hard on internal dissent. The banishment of Dr. Sakharov to Gorki left the final member of the "Helsinki Group" exiled or imprisoned. With the U.S. having done everything it felt could be done to punish the Soviet Union, and France and the FRG holding fast to their relationships with the East, Brezhnev had little to fear from the West.[127] As for the anticipated disruption in the Soviet economy, the results were mixed. There seemed to exist a consensus that in the Soviet Union the grain suspension had in fact caused shortages and the depletion of hard-currency funds used to purchase grains at top dollar elsewhere. One could also argue that the embargo strained relations within the Eastern bloc as the Soviet Union pressured Hungary for more exports and withheld its own grain shipments to Poland and the GDR.[128] Major effects such as widespread food shortages or seeing Soviet farmers butcher their animals had not materialized as expected.

What had begun to decrease, however, was the Western allies' willingness to continue with the embargo. Secretary of Agriculture Bergland noted that the U.S. had managed to withhold 7 million tons of grains from the Soviet Union, but "cooperation of allies is waning and will further erode by this summer."[129] Tighter control of U.S. grain exports as an alternative would be "unworkable, unwise, and likely to have no significant effect on the USSR."[130] Only high-level talks could achieve further cooperation.

Carter picked up the cue in a letter to Schmidt. After listing all the contributions the United States had already made to showing the Soviet Union that "business as usual" could no longer continue after the invasion of Afghanistan, he demanded concrete German action "in its extensive economic relationship with the USSR which would complement United States measures." He asked for a severe restriction of the federal export loan guarantees that were a necessity for any large-scale contract with the Soviet Union. Furthermore, Carter indicated his desire for tighter export control through COCOM, the control committee that had largely been rendered ineffective by the flood of exceptions and dual-use exports. According to Carter, COCOM, which in recent years had moved away from controlling commercial products to dealing strictly with militarily sensitive exports, "should be expanded to include technology critical to the modernization and expansion of the Soviet Industrial Base." This included the halting of major projects such as a smelter and steel plant ordered from the U.S. companies ALCOA and ARMCO, respectively. Carter "hoped" that Western or Japanese companies would not take over the projects American companies had been prevented from fulfilling.[131]

Carter's call for sanctions on grains had little impact on Western European–Soviet relations, but his call to limit industrial trade had greater potential for upset. Not willing to undermine painfully established East-West relations, Europeans would acquiesce to embargo only goods with immediate strategic significance. Basic trade, such as steel plants, chemical factories, or aluminum production plants must not be affected, as this would disrupt the core of Western European–Soviet cooperation.[132] Carter's next step in pressuring his allies, the summit meeting in Venice on 22–23 June, 1980, backfired as well. Confiding in Schmidt that he hoped for a commitment to "confirm that there will be no business as usual with the USSR until Soviet Troops withdraw from Afghanistan" and "underline our commitment to restrict through CO-COM the transfer of High Technology to the Soviet Union," he rearticulated the very same requirements he had put to the allies in March. Again the Europeans rejected Carter's demands, complaining about his unpredictable changes in decision making and attributing to him a "conniving and backhanded" foreign policy in which the allies were "being nagged and incorporated as America's '51st state.'"[133]

Concerned about being caught in the middle between an ideological Carter bent on punishing the Soviets over Afghanistan, and a Brezhnev backed into a corner by an unfortunate move into Afghanistan, the Europeans sought a revitalization of the diplomatic dialogue. First Giscard d'Estaing and then Schmidt visited with Brezhnev, hoping to rectify Carter's confrontational diplomacy. In a triumph for European diplomacy, Brezhnev finally agreed to take up talks again while the German press repeatedly quoted Carter's helpless response to the initiative, "and what are we doing now?"[134]

In the intense climate of the 1980 election campaign, nothing took place with regard to the embargo. Given a choice between following a weakened and unreliable Carter in a "Wilsonian foreign policy" or pursuing their own political and economic interest in a European embrace of realpolitik, the American allies opted for the latter. For all intents and purposes, the embargo was dead even before President Reagan lifted it on 24 April 1981. By October 1980, there was a clear recognition that Western European compliance with high-tech export controls was being either ignored or circumvented by using a noncommunist country as a middleman.[135] With export control "really a 'West-West problem'" and Western Europe and Japan able to produce commercial high technology comparable to that made in the U.S., COCOM had become "more a monitoring mechanism than control mechanism."[136]

Reagan's Push for Alliance Solidarity

With President Reagan now in the White House it was not just the grain embargo that had outlived its usefulness: the entire idea of détente was discarded. As Reagan quipped, "détente is something that a farmer has with his turkey until Thanksgiving Day." This applied on the political level as well as the economic one. During his 1976 bid for the presidency he had joined Carter in criticizing the cooperative nature of East-West trade. In regard to trade with the Soviet Union, this meant a renewed focus on the efficacy of trade in terms of strengthening or weakening the Soviet Union. For the Europeans, however, this meant yet another shift in U.S. foreign economic policy that could severely impact European stability and prosperity.

Ironically, despite having campaigned against Carter's grain embargo, Reagan did not immediately discard the embargo. With an administration as divided as his predecessors' had been, Reagan initially sided with Secretary of State Alexander Haig, leaving the embargo in place lest its removal be perceived as weakness in light of the tensions in Poland. Bowing to domestic expediency, however, Reagan lifted the embargo on 24 April 1981.[137]

Energy trade would again be the key issue dividing Europe and the U.S., as European dependency on Soviet energy imports precipitated a much softer foreign policy toward the East. Congress was aware of the dilemma of Western Europe as a net importer of fossil fuels. In one of the few suggestions on energy policy to include the NATO allies, Senator Charles Percy (R-IL) proposed during a subcommittee hearing on energy on 14 October 1981 that American coal reserves be utilized in order to meet their energy demands. He qualified this solution by indicating that "up to now experts on both sides of the Atlantic have agreed that American railroads and ports, without major expansion, would have difficulty satisfying European energy needs."[138] Senator William Cohen (D-ME) then summed up the tone of the meeting succinctly by saying that the United States did not "have a coherent Western policy in dealing with the Soviet Union—not on trade items, certainly not on energy items." In an almost clairvoyant statement, he predicted that "the Soviet Union will be in a position ... of having drawn them [Western Europeans] into a sphere of influence where they cannot afford to be antagonistic or in any way participate in embargoes, boycotts, or expressions of disapproval of Soviet conduct wherever that may take place."[139]

Cohen's fears came to fruition with the establishment of martial law in Poland on 13 December 1981. Following calls by the Reagan administration for solidarity within the Western alliance and an export ban on oil and gas technology and equipment on 29 December 1981, only muted Western European commitments were heard. At this point the structural asymmetries between Western Europe and the United States essentially brought about a closing of Western European ranks over this one-sided ban. In Schmidt's memories of the crisis, he even quoted French Foreign Minister Claude Cheysson to outline his position on Polish martial law: "[Why] should we punish ourselves with sanctions just because there are developments in Eastern Europe that one cannot accept ... I have not heard that [the Americans have] reconsidered their agreement for the sale of 15 million tons of grain to the Soviet Union."[140]

This rift did not come to the forefront in Schmidt's visit with Reagan on 4 January, yet it influenced the decision on who was to blame for the Polish situation. While the U.S., which had no politically sensitive ties with the Soviet Union at that point, placed the blame squarely on Moscow's shoulders, the German position viewed it strictly as an internal Polish matter.[141] Certainly, U.S. criticism of Europe's lack of forceful actions had already been reported in the newspapers, and the issue of the new pipeline had been brought up.[142] By the time Schmidt left the United States, neither side had pushed the economic issues, but both sides had positioned themselves for the coming conflict. Secretary of State Alexander Haig announced that while the situation in Poland did not justify a grain embargo, as it would "impose a burden on one segment of American society," the Reagan administration continued to view the gas pipeline project "with great skepticism." Schmidt, on the other hand, indicated that no one had broached the pipeline issue with him and that he felt a grain embargo to be the single most effective means by which to sanction the Soviet Union.[143]

Following a short Franco-German summit on 14 January 1982, the Schmidt administration announced that it would allow German companies to undercut the effects of U.S. sanctions on the Soviet Union.[144] The following NATO meeting accomplished little but vague commitments to "identify" and "examine" potential trade sanctions. Chancellor Schmidt's response to in interview with William Safire is very telling in this regard. Upon the statement that the pipeline deal was very important, Schmidt replied: "No it is not. You [the U.S.] have not given us a single gallon of oil, and you can't do it, or of gas. You cannot do it.

So we have to diversify."[145] Yet he had to shift his stance when Reagan intensified the embargo by also prohibiting reexport of U.S.-made components. The West German A.E.G-Kanis factory, a builder of gas pipeline turbines, faced the problem that some parts were U.S.-made and therefore could not be exported.[146] Schmidt opposed this policy before the German Bundestag, saying, "This action implies an extraterritorial extension of U.S. jurisdiction which in the circumstances is contrary to the principles of international law, unacceptable to the community and unlikely to be recognized in the courts of the EEC."[147]

Certainly, an infringement on the perceived sovereignty of the FRG was not the only reason for the rebuke. German business was now heavily invested in the Soviet Union and had created a significant lobby. As recently as 21 July 1981, Ruhrgas had contracted to buy 10.5 billion cubic meters of Soviet natural gas starting in 1984, and Schmidt and Brezhnev had signed a 25-year economic cooperation agreement. Krupp Corp had agreed to build a polyester fiber plant and deliver cranes to the Soviet Union. On 1 January 1982, only two days after Reagan's call for a boycott, Mannesmann Corp. signed a new pipe order with the Soviets, and the German government quietly disclosed on 11 March that it had approved $517 million of federal loan guarantees to cover the sale to the Soviets. The ensuing public debate demonstrated the structural differences in trade between the U.S. and West Germany. A failure of the now well-entrenched *Osthandel* would cost West Germany 200,000 jobs, the potential failure of German banks that had financed the pipeline projects, and the very lives of major companies such as A.E.G.-Kanis (a maker of gas compressors).[148]

The Japanese found themselves in a position similar to that of the Western Europeans, albeit under less American scrutiny. The Sakhalin Oil Project, signed on 28 January 1975, appeared very similar to the gas pipeline deal. It saw the Japanese funding, exploring, and developing Soviet oil resources on the island of Sakhalin in exchange for a significant discount on half of the pumped oil for the span of a decade. With such considerable interests at stake, the Japanese were more than happy to provide 1,000 Komatsu tractors to the Soviet Union after the boycott prevented Caterpillar from delivering the ones ordered from them.[149]

Politically, West Germany attempted to engage in some face-saving measures. Under pressure from the Reagan administration, the West Germans postponed the regular meetings of the joint commission for economic affairs with the Soviets for nine months. However, once the commission was back in place, it served only to reinvigorate German-Soviet policies with a proposal to build the Yamal pipeline to Western Europe. On 13 July 1982 a West German bank consortium signed an agreement to grant $1.6 billion in credits to the Soviets for the construction of the 3,500-mile Yamal pipeline, with the German government guaranteeing 85 percent of the financing over eight years at 7.8 percent.[150]

The issue here revolved around whether the Soviet Union would ever consider turning off the supply of natural gas to Western Europe, as it had done with energy exports to Yugoslavia in 1948, Israel in 1956, Albania in 1956 and 1961, and China in 1962. Neither side could claim moral authority in this crisis, as each simply wanted to enact the block on exportable products that would cause the least pain to its respective economy. The combination of being able to purchase grain as well as sell natural gas, however, provided the Soviet Union with invaluable economic resources. By redirecting Soviet resources away from grain production and toward the production of gas, the Soviet Union could save $1.6 billion for every million metric tons of grain purchased.[151] This gave the Soviet Union the necessary purchasing power, as well as the political clout, to water down import restrictions. Now the Soviet Union was able to produce miniature ball bearings for intercontinental missiles with American help, employ U.S. computers in its air-defense system, and develop chemical and biological weapons with the help of Western firms providing equipment and expertise.[152]

If these figures are applied to the Soviet hard-currency earnings from energy exports, which amounted to $0.4 billion (18.3 percent of total exports) in 1970 and $14.7 billion (62.3 percent of the total) in 1980, it becomes clear how dangerous this cycle was.[153] The Soviet Union had relatively few other products of interest on the world market. Consequently, Soviet gas export deals did significantly aid the Soviet Union, enabling it to utilize its most important natural resource. The disagreement that escalated over the construction of this pipeline demonstrated just how deep the rift between the U.S. and Western Europe had become.

Ultimately, the Reagan administration had to cave in and allow the Western Europeans to pursue their national interests and further diversify their energy exports. Yet even after the fall of the Soviet Union, economic diplomacy remained a driving factor in relations with Russia (Figures 5.2 and 5.3).

In summary, it is abundantly clear that Carter's foreign policies initiated a substantial shift in East-West relations. His two-track approach of continuing to negotiate with the Soviets on arms reduction while at the same time criticizing them for human rights violations under the Helsinki Accords generated a severe disruption in U.S.-Soviet relations. With economic ties limited by the Jackson-Vanik amendment, American

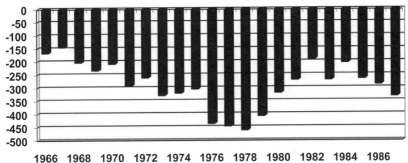

Figure 5.2 U.S. Energy Trade Deficit, 1966–1988, taken from Statistical Yearbook, Department of International Economic and Social Affairs. Statistical Office, United Nations, New York, 1969–1987.

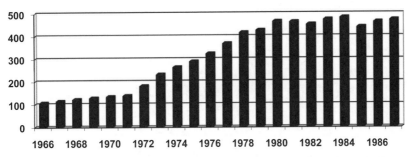

Figure 5.3 Soviet Energy Trade Surplus, 1966–1988, taken from Statistical Yearbook, Department of International Economic and Social Affairs. Statistical Office, United Nations, New York, 1969–1987.

interest in relations with the Soviet Union beyond a military détente were not a powerful force in moderating Carter's policies. Western European governments, most of all Helmut Schmidt's, had serious political and economic stakes in a continued détente with the Soviet Union. Pushing human-rights initiatives as foreign policy seemed naïve and impractical to them, unaccustomed as they were to ideological approaches in foreign relations. Carter was heavily criticized in the European press and government circles alike, and even after a short period of subdued rhetoric during the fall of 1977 he was unable to shake his image as an unreliable preacher-ideologue. While the Western alliance had weathered other crises in transatlantic differences, the Soviet invasion of Afghanistan brought the rift to the forefront.

Carter's punitive grain embargo paired with tighter high-tech export controls seemed the perfect approach to make the Soviet Union regret the invasion. However, by 1980, when he needed the Western allies to support his efforts by maintaining the embargo and accepting substantial cuts in their exports, none of them was willing to support Carter's foreign policy quest by curtailing their own exports. Fed up with Carter's admonitions and preaching about their duties, the allies rejected his leadership in this crisis. Carter's high road in foreign relations had led to a failed embargo and a divided alliance.

6

Conclusion
A Permanent Energy Dilemma for the West?

Willy Brandt resigned as German chancellor on 6 May 1974, ostensibly over the Guillaume spy affair. Nixon's relief over Brandt's replacement with the more pro-Western Chancellor Helmut Schmidt was in fact short-lived. Almost three months to the day, on 9 August 1974, Richard M. Nixon resigned from his presidency. His resignation was as scandalous as Brandt's, one outcome of the looming impeachment process. In a strange sense of serendipity both men's lives paralleled in that they were born the same year, assumed the leadership of their respective countries in the same year, and now had resigned in disgrace the same year. Yet, despite both of them also seeking the same political goal, détente with the East, their tenures in office saw clashing strategies and implementations—clashes that left the Western alliance with an energy dilemma from which it has never fully recovered.

The genesis of this parting of ways began several years before the pivotal 1970s, namely during the Berlin Wall crisis of 1961. It was during the early 1960s that Brandt's ideology underwent a drastic evolution. While he began as a decidedly pro-Western politician, the more his vision of *Ostpolitik* took shape, the more he drifted toward a more independent German foreign policy aimed at reconciliation with the East. Brandt and his assistant Bahr firmly believed that different aspects of international relations—political, economic, military, financial, etc.— had to be separated in order to create enough political and economic space to maneuver in. Thus, Brandt's assertive and increasingly independent policy is more apparent and more easily observed in the area of economic diplomacy than in other areas, such as military security.

Despite NATO's sometimes tumultuous history, the United States remained the guarantor of military security for Western Europe and especially for the FRG. America's power was a necessary factor that allowed Brandt to negotiate with the Soviet Union without having to bend to Soviet threats. The willingness, however, of former German administrations to accommodate American financial or political wishes in an unquestioning fashion in exchange for this military protection, ended with the Brandt administration. American unwillingness to defend West Germany's interests in East Germany, and the subsequent disillusionment that resulted from the rejection of inter-alliance nuclear sharing programs, made Brandt recognize that the U.S. military presence was one of self-interest. The belief that the U.S. could not and would not abandon its umbrella of geopolitical responsibility, of which Germany was a key component, enabled Brandt to pursue an independent policy course without fearing a loss of security.

The move to a new *Ostpolitik* first occurred on a conceptual level. Without the prospect of Western strength forcefully establishing German reunification, the Soviet Union became the gatekeeper to a unified Germany and Europe. By virtue of trade and necessity, relations with the Soviet Union had to shift from the aggressive opposition of the 1950s to peaceful cooperation. The Eastern European states also began to take on a larger regional significance, as they were the other states through which the interim goal of security and cooperation in Europe would be realized. Reaching the envisioned united Europe necessitated a change in strategy, away from a basis of military strength and confrontation and toward a careful balance through which the risk of nuclear war could be largely avoided. Close pan-European cultural, economic, and political cooperation should eventually make German unification a reality, either on a federal level or within a European framework. With such a design, *Ostpolitik* offered a much more intense cooperation with the East and advocated much more profound change than most other Western states sought.

East-West trade, alongside numerous political concessions, served to lure the Soviets into a high-level dialogue. Trade also constituted the first visible area in which Brandt's *Ostpolitik* succeeded. The 1962 pipeline embargo had spawned worsened West German–Soviet relations, and a "policy of Western strength" had failed entirely to bring the Soviets back to the negotiation table. Yet by 1969, Brezhnev had resolved to embrace East-West trade as a tool to fire up the sluggish Soviet economy, especially the agricultural sector. The continued need for Western grain imports and the plateauing of the Soviet standard of living made this ideologically questionable policy a necessity. Even though Western trade and know-how would strengthen the floundering Soviet economy, Brandt was eager to meet Brezhnev's need with offers of open markets and large-scale loans.

The signing of the gas pipeline deal in February 1970, then, marks that first success for Brandt while also exemplifying the differing versions of détente Nixon and Brandt entered into with the Soviet Union. Brandt initiated and actively fostered a trade deal that was full of benefits for the Soviets even though the commodity in question, natural gas, was not even needed at the time. All these economic and political sacrifices were made in order to reinvigorate the diplomatic process. For Nixon and his National Security Advisor and later Secretary of State Henry Kissinger, this level of cooperation went too far because it implied the potential for high-tech technology transfer and the loss of political "leverage."

Continued Soviet interest in East-West energy trade was evident, not just in the two follow-up deals in 1972 and 1975 but even more so in the promptness with which the first natural gas pipeline deal was concluded in the early days of Brandt's chancellorship. To the Soviets, hard-currency revenues and the subsequent influx of Western technologies and know-how were not simple sidelines to power politics and grand strategy: a booming Soviet economy, albeit with Western technology, was central to the credibility of socialism, the contentment of the Soviet people, and ultimately to the political fate of Brezhnev himself. However obscure the threat of a reunified Germany may appear in hindsight, economic concessions helped vindicate Soviet détente policies toward West Germany in the face of hard-liners in the Politburo. Undoubtedly, other factors played prominently in the foreign-policy making process as well, often overshadowing simple economic need. Such vacillations in economic diplomacy are to be expected when one understands international diplomacy to be an interplay of various, often contradictory, factors. In 1970 and 1971, however, ever increasing East-West trade and intense economic diplomacy were a crucial factor in the development of détente and served Brandt and Brezhnev alike: *Ostpolitik* and *Osthandel* went hand in hand.

More than just a loss-leader, *Osthandel* became the platform on which *Ostpolitik* could be implemented and the medium through which the German public lost its fear of the Soviet Union. The gas pipeline deal of 1970 in particular fomented a burgeoning excitement about the potential of trade with the Soviet Union. These developments allowed German industrialists to consider a multitude of projects based on their prestige value rather than economic merit. This excitement soon morphed into a gold rush mentality. The situation continued to build on itself as reports of the vast economic potential and virtually unlimited natural resources of the Soviet Union flooded back into the FRG, heightening the atmosphere of excitement still further.

From the inaugural gas pipeline deal in 1970 to the massive Kursk steel mill project in 1974, Brandt was instrumental in facilitating these deals through deft political maneuvering, such as granting federal loan guarantees, personally encouraging German business leaders, alleviating German security concerns, intervening with Soviet officials, and negotiating for a German-Soviet trade agreement. West German industry's emerging economic dependency on continued cooperation with the Soviet Union—both for payments and for jobs—created a willing and forceful advocate in the German political culture, which came into a life of its own. Eventually, West German political parties of all stripes had an intrinsic and self-serving motive to foster and maintain a good relationship with the Soviet Union.

Soviet interest in strengthening East-West trade, the fact of German industry's eagerness, and a German public that gradually shed the paradigm of the Soviet Union as an enemy all meant that in 1972 Brandt had reached the high-water mark of his *Ostpolitik*. In spite of only a razor-thin majority in the German parliament, he was able to engineer a victory and ultimately gain approval for his leadership and *Ostpolitik*. His victory was complete with the ratification of the Eastern Treaties on 17 May 1972. Having conquered these political hurdles, political and economic interaction with the Soviet Union could assume a higher priority and reach previously unheard-of levels.

This ever-increasing cooperation between Western Europe and the Eastern bloc triggered shifts in NATO that threatened to undermine the cohesion of the Western alliance. Nixon, as the supposed leader of the Western alliance, was grudgingly following a political path that he neither led nor controlled. One is reminded of the French revolutionary Alexandre Ledru-Rollin's adage: "There go my people. I must follow them, for I am their leader." Once the Four Power Agreement on Berlin had been concluded, *Ostpolitik* reflected a primacy of European over American interests. Claiming the need for stronger European integration, the U.S. was excluded from political consultations, information on East-West trade, and the EC preferential tariff zone.

By the summer of 1972, however, Brezhnev was implicitly offering Nixon an opportunity to regain leadership over Western détente. After the Moscow summit the U.S. stood to become a dominant partner in East-West trade. In deference to the hard-liners in the Politburo and the Eastern alliance cohesion, Brezhnev sought to distance himself from close cooperation with West Germany in favor of a policy of superpower détente. Not only did Brandt's *Ostpolitik* imply a reduction of superpower influence in Europe, but by 1972 West German industry was so firmly entrenched and invested in the future of the Soviet economy that East-West trade with the FRG maintained its momentum without political impetus to drive it forward. By prodding Poland into making public criticisms about the two Germanys and their revanchist policies, Brezhnev skillfully maintained Soviet legitimacy in Eastern Europe and ensured that *Ostpolitik* remained within certain politically acceptable parameters.

Failing to understand the role of economic diplomacy in détente policies is to fail understanding one key to the downfall of Kissingerian foreign policy. Nixon, like many of his twentieth-century predecessors, had had little use for East-West trade, as it contained significant ideological undertones. While he campaigned on the idea of an "era of negotiation," he continued to operate under a Cold War ideology that rejected intense cooperation with the Soviet Union unless it offered clear economic or political gains for the U.S. The gas pipeline deals and subsequent examples of East-West European trade did the very opposite, providing Western technology to the Soviet Union, accessing previously untapped Eastern energy resources, and improving the Soviet economy as a whole. Nixon's gut responses on those matters of East-West trade remained negative and might have triggered a more pronounced effort for coordination in allied economic dealings with the Soviet Union had Kissinger not sidelined such discussions. As a practitioner of high diplomacy, Kissinger was blind to economic diplomacy and its dangers, often glossing over Nixon's concerns. Allied trade policies became an issue only if they undermined U.S. "leverage" in political negotiations.

During the Moscow summit of 1972, however, superpower détente stood to serve both U.S. and Soviet interests. Political discrepancies over Vietnam had diminished and technology transfer to the East had become an apparently mute issue as Western European allies seemed poised to sell Western technology to the East anyway. Beyond that, Nixon had found a new appreciation of trade within American politics and had subsequently embraced a strongly mercantilist position that called for an increase in international exports. For the Soviets, in the atmosphere of superpower détente and its inherent recognition of Soviet parity with the U.S., Western acceptance of the status quo in Europe was more attractive than the implicitly revanchist goals of Brandt's *Ostpolitik*. In addition, establishing close economic ties with a Western power more capable of meeting the large-scale orders generated by the vast Soviet economy seemed appealing in its own right. At the end of the summit, then, an ambitious program for increased U.S.-Soviet trade accompanied the political ideas of a superpower détente.

To the same extent that superpower détente seemed more likely the Soviet Union began to attack Brandt's Achilles' heel: the ties between West Berlin and West Germany. Utilizing the convenient vagueness of the Four Power Agreement with regards to West Berlin–West Germany ties, the Soviet Union and its Eastern European satellite states publicly vilified West Germany and stoked public fears of West Germany as a revanchist power. Constant attacks on West Germany's potential links with West Berlin underscored this message. After Brezhnev summarily rejected any concessions on the Berlin issue at the German-Soviet summit in 1973, Brandt was forced to, again, look to the U.S. for leadership in the pursuit of a détente that would protect West German interests.

Kissinger's inability to recognize and exploit the significance of trade in the mind of the Soviet Union, however, spoiled Nixon's unique opportunity to shape détente in his own image. In light of the Watergate scandal, an increasingly assertive Congress and the politicization of the Jackson-Vanik amendment, the issue of East-West trade went on the back burner. Failing White House intervention, though, U.S. Congress refused Most Favored Nation status to the Soviet Union, effectively curtailing any possibilities at selling the Soviet Union's most marketable commodity, natural gas, at competitive prices on U.S. markets. At an unscheduled night meeting during the 1973 summit, Brezhnev implored a befuddled Nixon to act before it was too late, but the White House failed to cement political opportunity through economic diplomacy.

Kissinger did not push Congress for MFN status for the Soviet Union, and the voices sympathetic to East-West trade fell silent over the ensuing Yom-Kippur War. Brezhnev, touting the completion of another pipeline on his visit to the U.S., sought to impress with Soviet economic potential. But although Kissinger may have spoken German, it quite obviously was not the language of the German industrialists who had so aptly built up East-West trade during the past two years. The resulting failure to comprehend Brezhnev's economic interests helped bring down Kissinger's intricate web of high diplomacy. Early in 1974, with the passage of the Jackson-Vanik amendment, the U.S. Congress permanently sidelined the U.S. in matters of East-West trade. Brezhnev could not acquiesce to the interference in domestic affairs entailed by the amendment, as this Western influence would threaten the delicate balance between allowing Western economic influx while containing political dissent. Soviet energy exports would remain directed at Western Europe, not the United States.

Beginning in 1974, then, German-Soviet economic ties and the resulting rise in positive German public perceptions of the Soviet Union—and the lack of the same in the U.S.—precipitated a permanent positive disposition toward the Soviet Union, which left the U.S. at odds with its ally long after West German criticism over American involvement in the Yom Kippur War had been forgotten. This West German paradigm shift, facilitated in large part by Brandt's new *Ostpolitik*, was neither matched nor checked by a White House that had been blind sighted by East-West economic diplomacy. Through East-West trade, European NATO partners had acquired structural interests very different from those of the United States. With the long-term sale of their energy commodities in Western Europe, the Soviets had established ties of a nature that did not exist with the U.S. It was these ties that made it increasingly harder to reach consensus within NATO on how to deal with the Soviet Union in times of crises. NATO's energy problem was born.

The two most striking illustrations of the transatlantic rift between Western Europe and the United States are Carter's 1980 trade embargo and the 1982 Euro-pipeline debate that took place on Reagan's watch. Here, the two sides' ideological positions were so contradictory that the Western Europeans simply refused to follow along with U.S. foreign policy initiatives, as they stood to harm Western European interests. Europeans felt that sabotaging East-West trade over the Afghanistan invasion, as the U.S. demanded, required Europeans to pay the sole price for Western punitive measures vis-à-vis the Soviet Union. Such assertions were by no means groundless. After all, even Carter's grain embargo allowed for the continuation of U.S. grain sales under already-negotiated treaties, thus minimizing the damage to the U.S. agricultural sector.

NATO's energy dilemma ultimately allowed the Soviets to have their cake and eat it, too. As neither Nixon nor Brandt had modified their mutually exclusive détente designs, the U.S. and West Germany were unable to agree on a coherent policy toward the Soviet Union within NATO. Each side simply continued to pursue its national interests, and the Soviets were able to enlarge their energy infrastructure while still realizing significant grain imports from the West. If we accept a 1982 NSC report on the benefits to the Soviet economy, then the Soviet Union realized a significant economic benefit from détente. By importing U.S. grains cheaper than they could be produced domestically, the Soviets not only saved money but also managed to redirect production towards the development of natural gas production capabilities and the resulting hard-currency inflows. By saving on the grain imports and increasing the exports, the Soviet economy realized a net gain of approximately $50 billion. The infusion of Western financing and know-how alone helped the Soviet Union increase its hard-currency revenues from $444 million in 1970 (18.3 percent of all hard-currency revenues) to $14.7 billion in 1980 (62.3 percent of all hard-currency revenues).[1] As the Soviet Union had few additional export-worthy commodities, the transatlantic disagreements were certainly counterproductive with respect to the West's cause of Cold War economic competition.

Did such economic policies help end the Cold War? When it comes to agency in ending the Cold War, it would be presumptuous to offer a definitive answer based on a study of economic diplomacy alone, in which other factors, such as human rights activism or the intricacies of the military buildup and arms negotiations, could only be touched on briefly. However, this study demonstrates that the Soviet Union reaped significant economic advantages and political leverage in West Germany from *Osthandel* and the inter-alliance controversy over détente. At a time when the Soviet economy was already showing signs of potential failure, Western disunity often enabled Brezhnev to play one ally against another. For the better part of the 1970s the Soviets also seemed to have quite ably balanced the influx of Western ideas and technology with continued political control.

On the other hand, the very trade that bolstered the Brezhnev regime shifted Eastern-bloc thinking from a focus on ideological cohesion to a competition for market resources. Trade, like few other areas in international relations, strikingly demonstrates the difficulty of alliance cohesion when divergent interests are at stake. As early as 1968, the Soviet Union was forced to rein in Czechoslovakia, reminding it that ideological adherence took priority over economic ties with the West. This concern also applied to Ulbricht's East Germany, as increased East-West German communications resurrected fears of a united Germany and threatened to severely disrupt the cohesive spirit within the Warsaw Pact. Replacing Ulbricht with the more docile and malleable Honecker granted Brezhnev a temporary reprieve.

Brezhnev, however, continued to be forced into balancing the liberalizing effects of East-West trade with the stability, legitimacy, and integrity of his own state. As the Soviet Union continued to struggle with chronic weakness in its agricultural sector for the remainder of the 1970s, it was forced to sell its energy commodity surplus to the West for much-needed hard currency. With Soviet energy commodities redirected to the West, the Warsaw Pact faced its own "energy dilemma" as the supply to Eastern Europe had to be curtailed. Shortages in Eastern Europe, then, led to a bizarre rivalry among the Warsaw Pact countries over lucrative East-West trade deals, which often undermined Soviet economic interests by trying to resell imported Soviet oil and raw materials to Western Europe. This crisis intensified even further when it became clear that one outcome of East-West trade in the early 1970s was the accumulation of large-scale debts by the Eastern European states. "Brotherly" competition for hard-currency sales and an ever-increasing focus on Western ideas and marketability stoked unrest in the socialist camp.

The Conference on Security and Cooperation in Europe, one of Brezhnev's pet projects, formalized this cooperation. The reduction in tensions and increased economic cooperation between Eastern and Western Europe, again, stood to benefit inter-European cooperation. However, the inclusion of the human rights agenda in the document increased domestic unrest in the East and gave Eastern European dissidents a forum and legitimacy. In this sense, it seems quite clear that détente fostered Eastern European frustrations with planned market economies and, by implication, political dissent. Undermining the Eastern alliance and creating more political maneuverability for Eastern European states vis-à-vis the Soviet Union had a decisive economic impact. More and more evidence is emerging that highlights the role of human rights groups in toppling the repressive regimes of Eastern Europe. These groups were assisted and encouraged by Western contacts and received a basis for their legal standing through the Helsinki Charter on Human Rights. If this is the case, the economic diplomacy of *Ostpolitik* definitely facilitated such a development.

In case of the Soviet Union proper, however, the evidence is not so clear. The time lag of a decade between protest movements in Poland and those in the Soviet Union might indicate a different efficacy of détente policies in Eastern Europe and the Soviet Union. The Brezhnev regime appears to have adeptly mastered the tightrope act of limiting Western influence within the Soviet Union while allowing Western technology and know-how. Even here, Soviet policies successfully limited the flow of information to the West to present a skewed picture of the state of the Soviet economy to Western industrialists.[2]

Furthermore, the Soviet Union, as a country rich in natural resources and economies of scale, quickly recovered from its East-West trade deficit of the early 1970s and continued to produce significantly more energy commodities than domestic usage required. The détente policies of the 1970s thus afforded the Soviet Union long-term advantages that other Eastern European states enjoyed to only a very limited extent: the development of a large-scale distribution network and a guaranteed market for an export-worthy commodity. Considering that the activity of dissent groups like the Helsinki Watch group abated during the 1980s, it seems likely that the economic advantages of détente outweighed the disadvantages of political instability for the Soviet Union. This would suggest that a different agency—the Soviet people's frustration over their government's inability to furnish consumer goods—was at play in toppling the Soviet regime in 1991. This inability, of course, was linked to the redirection of economic resources toward heavy industry and the renewed superpower arms race.

The austere solution to the question of agency in ending the Cold War, then, might be that *Ostpolitik* and liberalizing economic policies ended the Cold War in Europe, while it was the superpower arms race that drove the Soviet Union into ruin. To be sure, such a straightforward formulation of "European solution to European problem" vs. "Superpower solution to Superpower problem" appears overly simplistic for so complicated a process. It certainly suggests topics for further research, such as the impact of the Eastern European revolutions on the Soviet citizenry as well as the impact European détente policies had on the election of Mikhail Gorbachev as general secretary. The contribution of this book in regard to this question, however, is to argue for a differentiation of agency between the Soviet Union and Eastern European states where economic agency is concerned. This is most useful in the case of *Ostpolitik*, as one can clearly state that Brandt's policies and economic diplomacy were successful in facilitating a destabilization of the communist regimes in Eastern Europe and in bringing about the European cooperation necessary to reunite Germany.

As for NATO, however, the diverging détente policies left a lasting structural rift. While the most pronounced upheavals within the alliance occurred in the years following Nixon's and Brandt's tenures, the long-term effects of this structural divide over energy and East-West trade has transcended the Cold War. The diversification and turmoil in the Soviet energy sector during the Yeltsin years rendered the politicization of energy exports impracticable: NATO's energy dilemma seemed overcome.

This changed, though, only three years into Russian President Vladimir Putin's presidency. The re-nationalization of Russia's energy sector had brought back NATO's energy dilemma. Russia's harsh treatment in its annual gas-price row with the former Soviet republics illuminates a resurgent Russia, willing to use its economic resources for political purposes.

As can be seen with the Ukraine, North Stream and most recently with the battle over the energy resources in the Caucasus, Europeans seek a closer association and economic ties with Russia, while the U.S. is willing to risk good relations with Russia over geopolitical interests. The most striking example, of course, is that of NATO's failure to achieve a coherent approach to admitting Georgia and the Ukraine as well as to produce a significant response to the Russian invasion of Georgia. While both, the U.S. and its European NATO partners are interested in creating a safe and secure supply of energy commodities, they have—to date—not found enough common ground to create meaningful policies within this multinational framework.

Flexibility has been considered one of the greatest strengths of NATO. Even in case of a physical attack, the language describing the proper response of the remaining allies is notoriously vague. If NATO thus needs to recognize the self-interest of most of its member states in order to be an efficient alliance, the structural differences over energy dependency on both sides of the Atlantic might well mean that Europe and the U.S. cannot respond in any meaningful fashion to Russia's increasingly authoritarian foreign policy. As it stands, the détente policies of the 1970s created structural determinants that have come to fruition. Certainly, nuclear missiles are far sexier than steel pipes—but not nearly as long lasting.

 **NOTES**

Prelude

1. *Osthandel* literally means "trade with the East" and has been used as a set term to connote trade between Eastern Europe and the Soviet Union.
2. Gregor Schöllgen, *Willy Brandt: Die Biographie* (Berlin: Propyläen, 2001), 157; Raymond L. Garthoff, *Détente and Confrontation: American-Soviet Relations from Nixon to Reagan* (Washington, D.C.: Brookings Institution, 1985).
3. Mary E. Sarotte, *Dealing with the Devil: East Germany, Détente, and Ostpolitik, 1969–1973* (Chapel Hill: University of North Carolina Press, 2001), 29 and 58; Peter Bender, *Neue Ostpolitik: Vom Mauerbau bis zum Moskauer Vertrag* (Munich: Deutscher Taschenbuch Verlag, 1986).
4. Jeremi Suri, *Power and Protest: Global Revolution and the Rise of Détente* (Cambridge, MA: Harvard University Press, 2003), 258.
5. Carole Fink and Bernd Schaefer, eds., *Ostpolitik 1969–1974: European and Global Responses* (Cambridge: German Historical Institute and Cambridge University Press, 2009), 5.
6. Most recently, Bange and Niedhardt described this as Bahr and Brandt's "Grand Design." See Oliver Bange, "An Intricate Web: *Ostpolitik*, the European Security System and German Reunification" in Oliver Bange and Gottfried Niedhart, eds., *Helsinki 1975 and the Transformation of Europe* (New York: Berghahn Books, 2008), 24–30. Another recent work that places the bulk of the success of *Ostpolitik* with the vision and agency of Brandt and Bahr is Julia Von Dannenberg's *The Foundations of Ostpolitik: The Making of the Moscow Treaty between West Germany and the USSR* (Oxford University Press: Oxford, 2008).
7. Stephen Kotkin, *Armageddon Averted: The Soviet Collapse 1970–2000* (New York: Oxford University Press, 2001).
8. John Lewis Gaddis, *The Cold War: A New History* (New York: Penguin Press, 2005), 190f, 217.
9. Angela Stent, *From Embargo to Ostpolitik: The Political Economy of West German–Soviet Relations, 1955–1980* (London: Cambridge University Press, 1981). For U.S. economic policy see for example Diane B. Kunz, *Butter and Guns: America's Cold War Economic Diplomacy* (New York: The Free Press, 1997); Philip J. Funigiello, *American-Soviet Trade in the Cold War* (Chapel Hill: University of North Carolina Press, 1988).
10. Stent, *From Embargo to Ostpolitik*, 251–252.
11. For an interesting discussion on the difficulty of attributing German industry interests in an economic empire after 1945, see Volker Berghahn's introduction to Volker Berghahn, ed., *Quest for Economic Empire: European*

Strategies of German Big Business in the Twentieth Century (Providence, RI: Berghahn Books, 1996) and Gerald D. Feldman's review *in Central European History* 29, no. 4 (1996): 599–601.

12. For detailed coverage of Willy Brandt's "Grand Design" strategy, which included bilateral rapprochement, a European security system, and ultimately a unified Germany, see Bange and Niedhart, *Helsinki 1975*.

13. For the most detailed, albeit somewhat slanted, account of Putin's energy policies, see Marshall I. Goldman, *Petrostate: Putin, Power, and the New Russia* (New York: Oxford University Press, 2008). Also, Adam N. Stulberg, *Well-Oiled Diplomacy: Strategic Manipulation and Russia's Energy Statecraft in Eurasia* (New York: State University of New York Press, 2008).

Chapter 1

1. Dulles's suggestions are mentioned in Konrad Adenauer, *Erinnerungen* (Frankfurt a. M.: Fischer Bücherei, 1967), 466–467. All translations of German primary sources (published or unpublished) were done by the author. The SPD changed its position at the Bad Godesberg party congress in 1959.

2. Robert Mark Spaulding, *Osthandel and Ostpolitik: German Foreign Trade Policies in Eastern Europe from Bismarck to Adenauer* (Providence, RI: Berghahn Books, 1997), 444–453.

3. On 6 June 1962 Adenauer suggested that the Soviet Union and the FRG should deescalate aggression for ten years in order to build up normalized relations. See Wjatscheslaw Keworkow, *Der geheime Kanal: Moskau, der KGB und die Bonner Ostpolitik* (Berlin: Rowohlt, 1995), 103–106.

4. "Osthandel," *Der Spiegel* (39/1959), 23 September 1959, 14–15.

5. Erich Böhme and Klaus Wirtgen, eds., *Willy Brandt: Die Spiegel-Gespräche 1959–1992* (Stuttgart: Deutsche Verlags-Anstalt, 1993), 38.

6. Ibid., 37, 39.

7. Ibid., 27.

8. Ibid.

9. "Brandt Is Grateful: Thanks Both U.S. Candidates for Berlin Statements," *New York Times,* 26 October 1960, 31.

10. Stephen Ambrose, *Nixon,* vol 1, *The Education of a Politician 1913–1962* (New York: Simon and Schuster, 1987), 536.

11. "Brandt Is Critical: West Berlin Major Is Cool to Kennedy-Soviet Note," *New York Times,* 12 November 1960, 3.

12. "News Summary and Index: International," *New York Times,* 10 May 1961, 47.

13. "BRANDT: Mein Freund Willy," *Der Spiegel* (13/1961), 22 March 1961, 17–18.

14. Egon Bahr, *Zu meiner Zeit* (Munich: Karl Blessing Verlag, 1996), 131.

15. President Kennedy, De Gaulle, and Prime Minister Harold Macmillan all spent the crisis vacationing at their respective retreats.

16. Bahr, *Zu meiner Zeit,* 134. See also Manfred Gortemaker, *Geschichte der Bundesrepublik Deutschland von der Gründung bis zur Gegenwart* (Munich: Beck, 1999), 364. Much has been made of recent scholarship by Wolfgang Schmidt, who sees the "conceptual foundation" of Brandt's new *Ostpolitik* as rooted not in the Berlin crisis but rather in ideas that originated in the early 1950s. This argument is one over semantics and is primarily rooted in a political motivation to ascribe visionary attributes to the man who was once ranked fourth in a survey on "the greatest Germans of all time." Ultimately, Schmidt concedes that "only the 13th of August 1961 made the failure of the old formulas [on Western strength] apparent to everyone and underscored the necessity of a new approach to the politics over Germany." Whether Brandt already had general visions of peace and a united Europe in the 1950s matters little, as even Schmidt allows for Brandt's disillusionment with the United States over Kennedy's soft stance on Berlin.

17. Diethelm Prowe, "Der Brief Kennedys an Brandt vom 18. August 1961: Eine zentrale Quelle zur Berliner Mauer und der Entstehung der Brandtschen Ostpolitik," *Vierteljahrshefte für Zeitgeschichte* 33, no. 2 (1985): 373–383, 377. Merseburger sees Kennedy's note as "friendly but cold." See Peter Merseburger, *Willy Brandt 1913–1992: Visionär und Realist* (Stuttgart and Munich: Deutsche Verlags-Anstalt, 2002), 402.

18. Bahr, *Zu meiner Zeit*, 136.

19. Willy Brandt, *People and Politics: The Years 1960–1975* (Boston: Little & Brown, 1978), 20.

20. Brandt began to understand the tacit agreement between the superpowers to respect the spheres of influence established at Yalta. See Brant, *People and Politics,* 29–30.

21. Brandt in the Berlin Senate on 13 August 1961, quoted in Boris Meissner, ed., *Moskau Bonn: Die Beziehungen zwischen der Sowjetunion und der Bundesrepublik Deutschland. 1955–1973. Dokumentation,* vol. 2 (Cologne: Verlag Wissenschaft & Politik, 1975), 861.

22. Brandt on 18 August 1961, quoted in Horst Günther Link, *Quellen zu den deutsch-sowjetischen Beziehungen: 1945–1991* (Darmstadt: Wissenschaftliche Buchgesellschaft, 1999), 120–121.

23. Funigiello, *American-Soviet Trade in the Cold War,* 216–217.

24. Memorandum From Secretary of Commerce Hodges to Secretary of State Rusk and Secretary of Defense McNamara, U.S. Department of State, Washington, 18 September 1961. *FRUS, 1961–1963, Volume IX: Foreign Economic Policy,* #302.

25. The following categories were taken from Funigiello, *American-Soviet Trade in the Cold War,* 217.

26. Reference to the decision is made in Letter from Secretary of Commerce Hodges to the Under Secretary of State (Ball), Washington, 14 February 1962. *FRUS, 1961–1963, Volume IX: Foreign Economic Policy,* #306.

27. Public Papers of the President of the United States, *John F. Kennedy, 1963* (Washington, D.C.: United States Government Printing Office, 1964), 3.

28. See Letter From Secretary of State Rusk to Secretary of Commerce Hodges, Washington, 5 September 1962 and Letter From Secretary of Commerce

Hodges to Secretary of State Rusk, Washington, 12 September 1962, *FRUS 1961–1963, Volume IX: Foreign Economic Policy*, #317–318.

29. Memorandum of Conversation Washington, 14 March 1961, Subject: "CO-COM List Review," *FRUS, 1961–1963, Volume IX: Foreign Economic Policy*, #297.

30. "AUSLAND: *Osthandel*," *Der Spiegel*, 18 April 1962, 18.

31. Memorandum From the Department of State Executive Secretary (Brubeck) to the President's Special Assistant for National Security Affairs (Bundy), Washington, 4 December 1962, *FRUS, 1961–1963, Volume IX: Foreign Economic Policy*, #319.

32. Memorandum From President Kennedy to the Export Control Review Board, Washington, 16 May 1963, *FRUS, 1961–1963, Volume IX: Foreign Economic Policy*, #322.

33. Memorandum From the Export Control Review Board to President Kennedy, Washington, 15 August 1963, *FRUS, 1961–1963, Volume IX: Foreign Economic Policy*, #327.

34. Memorandum From President Kennedy to the Export Control Review Board, Washington, 19 September 1963, *FRUS, 1961–1963, Volume IX: Foreign Economic Policy*, #329.

35. "OSTHANDEL: Ball gestoppt," *Der Spiegel*, 27 November 1963, 65.

36. Ibid.

37. "OSTHANDEL: In Treue fest," *Der Spiegel*, 26 February 1964, 54–55.

38. "OSTHANDEL: Rohrkrepierer," *Der Spiegel*, 9 January 1963, 17.

39. Vermerk über den Besuch der Fa. Salzgitter Industriebau bei Herrn Min Dir Dr. Reinhardt. Betr.: Lieferung einer Raffinerie an die Sowjetunion, Bonn, 30. Nov 1963, Bundesarchiv Koblenz [BAK] 102 [=Bundeswirtschaftsministerium] /69034.

40. Staatssekretär Dr. Neef to Bundesminister für Wirtschaft, Kurt Schmücker, Bonn, 15. Feb 1964, betr: Großraffinerie für die Sowjetunion, BAK 102/69034.

41. Chancellor Ludwig Erhard to Bundesminister für Wirtschaft, Kurt Schmücker, Bonn, 13. Feb 1964, BAK 102/69034.

42. Vermerk von Dr. Schubert, betr: Großraffinerie-Projekt Sowjetunion. Besprechung beim Herrn Minister am 20. Februar 1964, BAK 102/69034.

43. Vermerk von Dr. Kautzor-Schröder. Betr: Unterstützung von Ostblockgeschäften durch Übernahme von Bundesbürgschaften, Bonn, 20. Jun 1964, BAK 102/69034.

44. Chancellor Erhard to BMWi Schmücker, Bonn, 30. Jul 1964, BAK 102/69034.

45. The chairman of the Eastern Trade Commission of the German Economy [Ostausschuß der deutschen Wirtschaft], Otto Wolff von Amerogen, pleaded with Erhard that only an extension of the current five-year credits would be competitive in dealings with the Soviet Union, and the Deutsche Bank stated that any longer-term loan would be impossible for the German banks to grant without Hermes coverage. For a discussion of this, see Salzgitter Industriebau Aktenvermerk. Salzgitter, 23. Aug 1965 von Dr. Leithe, betr.: Deutsches Konsortium UdSSR Petrochemie, BAK 102/69034.

46. Salzgitter Industriebau to BMWi Schmücker, betr: Deutsches Konsortium für Projektierung und Lieferung eines Petrochemiekomplexes an die UdSSR, Salzgitter, 19. Feb 1965, BAK 102/69034.

47. Ibid.

48. Dr. G. Keiser, BMWi to Staatssekretär Dr. Langer, Bonn, 1. Jul 1965, betr: Petrochemie-Geschäft Russland, BAK 102/69034.

49. Vermerk von Dr. Matthias Schmitt, 6.7.1965, betr: Besprechung bei Aussenminister Dr. Schröder, BAK 102/69034.

50. Memorandum From the President's Special Assistant for National Security Affairs (Bundy) to President Johnson, Washington, 11 March 1964, *FRUS, 1964–1968, Volume IX: International Development and Economic Defense Policy*, Commodities, #151.

51. Memorandum From the President's Special Assistant for National Security Affairs (Bundy) to President Johnson, Washington, 11 March 1964, *FRUS, 1964–1968, Volume IX: International Development and Economic Defense Policy*; Commodities, #153.

52. Funigiello, *American-Soviet Trade in the Cold War*, 154–156

53. Summary of Record of the 527th Meeting of the National Security Council, Washington, 16 April 1964, *FRUS, 1964–1968, Volume IX: International Development and Economic Defense Policy*, Commodities, #154.

54. Letter From Secretary of Commerce Hodges to President Johnson, Washington, 25 June 1964, *FRUS, 1964–1968, Volume IX: International Development and Economic Defense Policy*, Commodities, #159.

55. Memorandum From the President's Special Assistant for National Security Affairs (Bundy) to the President's Deputy Special Assistant for National Security Affairs (Bator), Washington, 25 June 1964, *FRUS, 1964–1968, Volume IX: International Development and Economic Defense Policy*, Commodities, #158.

56. "Brandt Urges Trade as German Unifier," *New York Times*, 16 April 1965, 6.

57. Report of Meeting, Washington, 19 August 1964, *FRUS, 1964–1968, Volume IX: International Development and Economic Defense Policy*, Commodities, #160.

58. Letter From the Chairman of the Board of Radio Corporation of America (Sarnoff) to President Johnson, New York, 5 March 1965, *FRUS, 1964–1968, Volume IX: International Development and Economic Defense Policy*, Commodities, #166.

59. Memorandum from the Deputy Director of Central Intelligence (Carter) to Secretary of Commerce Connor, Washington, 10 March 1965, *FRUS, 1964–1968, Volume IX: International Development and Economic Defense Policy*, Commodities, #168.

60. "OSTHANDEL," *Der Spiegel*, 28 July 1965, 12.

61. Letter From the Chairman of the President's Special Committee on Trade With East European Nations and the Soviet Union (Miller) to President Johnson. Washington, 3 May 1965, *FRUS, 1964–1968, Volume IX: International Development and Economic Defense Policy*, Commodities, #172.

62. Memorandum From the President's Special Assistant for National Security Affairs (Bundy) to Holders of NSAM Nos. 324 and 333, Washington,

27 July 1965, *FRUS, 1964–1968, Volume IX: International Development and Economic Defense Policy,* Commodities, #176.

63. Memorandum of Conversation, Washington, 20 January 1967, *FRUS, 1964–1968, Volume IX: International Development and Economic Defense Policy,* Commodities, #185.

64. "PATENT," *Der Spiegel,* 3 February 1965, 7–8.

65. Airgram from the Embassy in the United Kingdom to the Department of State, London, 9 December 1966, *FRUS, 1964–1968, Volume IX: International Development and Economic Defense Policy,* Commodities, #184.

66. Willy Brandt, *Ordeal of Coexistence* (Cambridge, MA: Harvard University Press, 1963), 63.

67. The *Passagierscheinabkommen* allowed West Berliners to visit East German friends and families for the holidays in the early 1960s.

68. Ernst-Otto Czempiel, "Auf der Suche nach neuen Wegen: Die deutsch-amerikanischen Beziehungen 1961–1969," in *Die USA und die Deutsche Frage: 1945–1990,* ed. Wolfgang-Uwe Friedrich (Frankfurt a. M.: Campus Verlag, 1991), 177–178.

69. Czempiel, "Auf der Suche," 179.

70. Telegram From the Department of State to the Embassy in Germany, Washington, 15 April 1965, U.S. Department of State, *FRUS, 1964–1968, Volume XV: Germany and Berlin,* #101.

71. Ibid.

72. Thomas A. Schwartz, *Lyndon Johnson and Europe: In the Shadow of Vietnam* (Cambridge, MA: Harvard University Press, 2003), 52–53, 59.

73. Ibid., 231–232.

74. Reiner Marcowitz, *Option für Paris? Unionsparteien, SPD und Charles de Gaulle 1958 bis 1969* (Munich: Oldenbourg Verlag, 1996), 255. Here Brandt is portrayed as using de Gaulle's initiatives toward the East as a model for his own visions.

75. He stood by his convictions despite heavy party opposition, which saw his "Why just de Gaulle?" remark as a break with the Atlanticist stance of the SPD. Ibid., 228–232.

76. Brandt, *A Peace Policy for Europe,* 35–36.

77. Czempiel sees the U.S. policy toward Germany as very rough and dominating. Brandt's suggestion, therefore, must have upset the status quo. Czempiel, "Auf der Suche," 177–178. Also see Brandt, *Frieden,* 36.

78. See also Marcowitz, *Option für Paris?* 231.

79. For example, see Michael Stuermer, "*Deutschlandpolitik, Ostpolitik* and the Western Alliance: German Perspectives on Détente," in Kenneth Dyson, *European Détente: Case Studies of the Politics of East-West Relations* (New York: St. Martin's Press, 1986), 135.

80. Memo, President's Assistant for National Security Affairs (Kissinger) to President Nixon, "Brandt's Eastern Policy," 16 February 1970, folder: "Europe-General Thru May 70," Box 667, NSCF, Country Files - Europe, NPMS, NA, 3.

81. Bahr, *Zu meiner Zeit,* 172. Also, interview of the author with Egon Bahr on 6 June 2005. The implicit threat to West German security came up in a con-

versation with John McCloy. Brandt apparently stated directly that he did not believe the U.S. would withdraw its troops, no matter what the West German foreign policy was.

82. Bahr, *Zu meiner Zeit*, 205.

83. Ibid., 201.

84. Speech by Foreign Minister Brandt before the Rhein-Ruhr Club, 11 January 1968, quoted in Peter Maerz, ed. *Dokumente zu Deutschland: 1944–1994* (Munich: Olzog Verlag, 1996), 166. See also Marcowitz, *Option für Paris?* 266. Cziempel viewed Brandt, not Chancellor Kiesinger, as the driving force in the *Ostpolitik* pursued under the grand coalition. Czempiel, "Auf der Suche," 176. Timothy Garton Ash, on the other hand, sees Kiesinger as the initiator of *Ostpolitik* under the great coalition. See Timothy Garton Ash, *In Europe's Name: Germany and the Divided Continent* (New York: Random House, 1993), 55.

85. Figure 1.4: Poll of West German Perception of Threat from the Soviet Union. Noelle, "Sowjetunion," 575.

86. Willy Brandt, *A Peace Policy for Europe* (New York: Holt, Rinehart and Winston, 1969), 80.

87. Quoted in Marcowitz, *Option für Paris?* 284.

88. Merseburger, *Willy Brandt*, 527.

89. Hans-Adolf Jacobsen and Tomala Mieczyslaw, *Bonn und Warschau 1945–1991: Die deutsch-polnischen Beziehungen. Analyse und Dokumentation* (Cologne: Verlag Wissenschaft & Politik, 1992), 120–121.

90. Böhme, 128.

91. Speech by Foreign Minister Brandt before the Council of Europe, 24 January 1967, quoted in Auswärtiges Amt, ed., *Außenpolitik der Bundesrepublik Deutschland: Dokumente von 1949–1994* (Cologne: Verlag Wissenschaft & Politik, 1995), 305.

92. Ibid. Brandt (and the grand coalition) truly believed in pursuing the same goals as de Gaulle in their foreign policy. See also Marcowitz, *Option für Paris?* 266.

93. Speech by Foreign Minister Brandt before the German Bundestag, 13 October 1967, in Maerz, *Dokumente zu Deutschland*, 161.

94. Marcowitz, *Option für Paris?* 267; Sarotte, *Dealing with the Devil*, 14.

95. One example of this would be the Johnson administration urging the FRG to play down conflicts with East Germany over new restrictions on land travel to and from West Berlin, so as not to imperil American hopes of improving relations with Moscow. "News Summary and Index," *New York Times*, 16 June 1968, 71.

Chapter 2

1. Address by Richard M. Nixon to the Bohemian Club, 29 July 1967, *FRUS 1969–1972*, Volume I, #2.

2. Ibid.

3. Ibid., 7.

4. Robert B. Semple, Jr., "Nixon Says He Has Eased Views on Communist Bloc," *Special to The New York Times,* 7 August 1968, 1.

5. Harold Gal, "Czech Crisis Impels Nixon to Reconsider Views on Communism," *Special to The New York Times,* 25 August 1968, 73.

6. Address by Richard M. Nixon to the Bohemian Club, 29 July 1967, *FRUS 1969–1972,* Volume I, #2.

7. Ibid.

8. Ibid.

9. Ibid.

10. "Statement on the Forthcoming Visit to Western Europe," 6 February 1969, Public Papers of the Presidents of the United States: *Richard Nixon, 1969* (Washington, D.C: Government Printing Office, 1970), #35.

11. Ronald E. Powaski, *The Entangling Alliance: The United States and European Security 1950–1993* (Westport, CT: Greenwood Press, 1994), 83–84.

12. Stephen E. Ambrose, *Nixon,* vol. 2: *The Triumph of a Politician, 1962–1972* (New York: Simon & Schuster, 1987), 414–417.

13. "Remarks on Departure from West Berlin," 27 February 1969, Public Papers: *Nixon, 1969,* #83.

14. Richard M. Nixon, *The Memoirs of Richard Nixon* (New York : Grosset & Dunlap, 1978), 371.

15. Memorandum of Conversation [MemCon] President Nixon with French President Charles de Gaulle, 28 February 1969, folder: "President's Trip Files, Memcons – Europe (Feb 23, '69 – March 2 '69)," Box 447, NSCF, Nixon Presidential Materials Staff [NPMS], National Archives [NA]. Also see "Nixon's European Success," *New York Times,* 2 March, 1969, E12.

16. "Remarks at Andrews Air Force Base on Returning from Europe," 2 March 1969, Public Papers: *Nixon, 1969,* #94.

17. See Figure 1.1. Also, Frank Costigliola, "Kennedy, the European Allies, and the Failure to Consult," *Political Science Quarterly* 110, no. 1 (Spring 1995): 105–123, 107–108.

18. Memo, n.d., folder: "Staff Memos: Sonnenfeld, Helmut," Box 834, Name Files, NSCF, NPMS, NA.

19. Memo, Henry A. Kissinger to Nixon, 5 March 1969, folder: "MemCons – Europe (Feb 23, '69 – March 2 '69)," Box 447, President's Trip Files, NSCF, NPMS, NA.

20. Transcript of Telephone Conversation, 12 March 1969, 5:40 PM, folder: "Henry Kissinger Telephone Conversation Transcripts," Box 1, Chronological File, NSCF, NPMS, NA.

21. Henry Kissinger, *The White House Years* (Boston: Little & Brown, 1979), 100.

22. David Binder, "Germans Begin Political Debate: Heinemann Remark Sets Off Pre-campaign Clash," *New York Times,* 10 March 1969, 8.

23. Ibid.

24. Sarotte, *Dealing with the Devil,* 14; Stent, *From Embargo to Ostpolitik,* 156.

25. Helene Seppain, *Contrasting US and German Attitudes to Soviet Trade, 1917–91: Politics by Economic Means* (New York: St. Martin's Press, 1992); Stent, *From Embargo to Ostpolitik;* Hans-Dieter Jacobsen, *Die Ost-West-Wirtschafts-*

beziehungen als deutsch-amerikanisches Problem (Baden-Baden: Nomos Verlag, 1986).

26. Brandt, *A Peace Policy for Europe,* 110–111.

27. Brandt, *People and Politics,* 169.

28. VC5, Dr. Steidle, to L1 Herrn MinRat Dr. Moltrecht, Bonn, 15 Feb 1968, betr: Hannover-Messe 1968, BAK 102/100025.

29. Min Dir Dr. G. Harkort, III A 1-84.42, AA, to Min Dir Dr. Schiettinger, o.V.i.A., BMWi, Bonn 13. Mar 1968, betr: Einladung des sowjetrussischen Außenhandelsministers Patolitschew zu diesjährigen Hannover-Messe, BAK 102/100025. Also, Letter MinDir Sr. Schiettinger, VC 5 -913 743, to Min Dir Dr. Harkort, AA, Bonn, 29. Mar 1968, betr: Einladung des sowjetischen Außenhandelsministers Patolitschew zur diesjährigen Hannover-Messe, BAK 102/100025.

30. Schnellbrief Min Dir Dr. Harkort, III A 1 – 84.42, to Min Dir. Dr. Schiettinger o.V.i.A., BMWi, Bonn, 9 Apr 1968, betr: Einladung des sowjetischen Außenhandelsministers Patolitschew, BAK 102/100025 and Letter from M, Dr. Moltrecht, to BMWi Schiller, Bonn, 18 Apr 1968, betr: Einladung des sowjetischen Außenhandelsministers Patolitschew, BAK 102/100025 and M, Dr. Moltrecht, to S2, Abt V, Bonn, 19 Apr 1968, betr: Einladung des sowjetischen Außenhandelsministers, BAK 102/100025.

31. Letter S2 to Staatssekretär Dr. von Dohnanyi, Bonn, 23 Apr 1968, BAK 102/100025, Fernschreiben German Embassy Moscow, Sante, to AA, Ambassador Bahr, Moskau, 23.4.1968, betr: Einladung Ministers Patolitschew, BAK 102/100025, Fernschreiben German Embassy Moscow, Sante, to AA, Ambassador Bahr, Moskau, 24.4.1968, BAK 102/100025.

32. MemCon, "Niederschrift über das Gespräch zwischen Herrn Staatssekretär Dr. von Dohnanyi und Herrn Leg. Rat I Eggers," 15 January 1969, BAK 102/100025.

33. Ibid.

34. MemCon, "Gespräch des Bundesministers Brandt mit dem sowjetischen Botschafter Zarapkin," 10 January 1969: Akten zur Auswärtigen Politik der Bundesrepublik Deutschland [AAPD], 1969, #8.

35. Letter to Herrn Vogelsang, betr: AR-Sitzung am 2.2.1967 – Projekt Erdgasleitung UdSSR, Duesseldorf, 1 February 1967, M 50.414.1, Mannesman Archiv [MA], 1.

36. MemCon, "Gespräch des Staatssekretärs Duckwitz mit dem sowjetischen Botschafter Zarapkin," 8 April 1969, AAPD, #117, footnote 2.

37. Memo, "Mineralöleinfuhren aus der UdSSR," 26 April 1969, BAK 102/100025, 2.

38. MemCon, "Gespräch des Bundesministers Brandt mit dem französischen Außenminister Debre," 10 March 1969, AAPD, #94.

39. Ibid. De Gaulle's comments were made during Nixon's visit to France between 28 February and 2 March 1969. This was not an entirely correct summary of Nixon's stance. He had argued for more European self-initiative regarding Western European economic cooperation but not for an independent Western European diplomatic initiative, which could possibly undermine U.S. trade negotiations with Eastern Europe.

40. Memo, Bundesministerium für Wirtschaft [Economics Ministry] Dr. Steidle to Dr. Schomerus, "Besuch des sowjetischen Handelsrats Woltschkow bei Hernn Staatssekretaer Dr. von Dohnanyi," 20 August 1968, BAK 102/100000.

41. Angela Stent suggests that Soviet willingness to engage Western Europe had already emerged in the immediate aftermath of the invasion of Czechoslovakia. The rationale here is that the Soviet Union sought to legitimize and stabilize its influence in Eastern Europe. Stent, *From Embargo to Ostpolitik*, 156. With evidence of how difficult any West German–Soviet dialogue was in 1968, this seems improbable. It is also highly doubtful how sensible such Soviet rapprochement with a Kiesinger-led FRG would have been.

42. Stent, *From Embargo to Ostpolitik*, 156.

43. Andrey Edemskiy, "Dealing with Bonn: Leonid Brezhnev and the Soviet Response to West German Ostpolitik," in Fink and Schaefer, *Ostpolitik 1969–1974*, 15–38.

44. Memo, "Rede Breshnews auf dem Plenum des ZK der KPDSU am 2. Juli," 2 July 1969, Bundesarchiv Lichterfelde, Stiftung Archiv der Parteien und Massenorganisationen der DDR [BAL-SAMPO] DY/30/ J IV 2/2 J – 3021, 2.

45. Stent, *From Embargo to Ostpolitik*, 171.

46. In fact, Hanson goes so far as to divide Brezhnev's tenure into the two periods of 1964–1973 and 1973–1982. Philip Hanson, *The Rise and Fall of the Soviet Economy: An Economic History of the USSR from 1945* (London: Longman, 2003). For his assessment of Brezhnev's policies in agriculture, see p. 112.

47. Ibid., 113.

48. Memo, "Die neue Phase der sowjetischen Aussenpolitik und die Fortsetzung der deutsch-sowjetischen Gespraeche," 23 May 1969, Politisches Archiv des Auswaertigen Amtes [PAAA], II A 4 82.00/94.29, 1–3.

49. Memo, "Sowjetische Absichten zur Lieferung russischen Erdgases nach Westeuropa," 26 April 1969, BAK 102/100025, 1–3.

50. Ibid.

51. David Binder, "Brandt Welcomes Proposal Made by Warsaw Pact Nations for a European Security Conference," *New York Times*, 19 March 1969, 15.

52. Ibid.

53. "U.S. Is Cool to Idea," *New York Times*, 19 March 1969, 15.

54. "Address at the Commemorative Session of the North Atlantic Council," 10 April 1969, Public Papers: *Nixon, 1969*, #145.

55. See Figure 1.4: Survey of West German population on perceived Russian Threat level.

56. Willy Brandt, *Erinnerungen* (Zürich: Propyläen, 1989), 374.

57. Memo, by Economics Ministry Dr. Steidle, "Einladung Außenhandelsminister Patolitschev," 27 March 1969, BAK 102/100025; Memo, by Economics Ministry Dr. Schomerus, 2 April 1969, BAK 102/100025.

58. Memo, "Eventuelle Einladung des sowjetischen Außenministers Patolitschew," 16 April 1969, BAK 102/100025.

59. Memo, "Einladung des sowjetischen Außenhandelsministers Patolitschev," 23 April 1969, BAK 102/100025, 1.

60. MemCon,"Kurzprotokoll über das vertrauliche Gespräch zwischen Minister Schiller und dem sowjetischen Außenhandelsminister Patolitschew," 1 February 1970, BAK 102/100026, 4–5.

61. Memo, Economics Ministry to Chancellor Kiesinger, 29 April 1969, BAK 102/100021, 2.

62. Memo, Economics Ministry to Undersecretary von Dohnanyi, "Einfuhr sowjetischen Erdgases nach Bayern; hier: Vorbereitung Ihrer Reise nach Moskau," 20 May 1969, BAK 102/100021, 2.

63. Ibid.

64. Arkady N. Shevchenko, *Breaking With Moscow* (New York: Ballantine Books, 1985), 224. Shevchenko recalls KGB information on the German negotiating positions to be "surprising in the quality and quantity."

65. Memo, German Ambassador in Moscow Allardt to German Foreign Office, 26 May 1969, AAPD, #176.

66. Memo, Economics Ministry to Undersecretary von Dohnanyi, 16 May 1969, BAK 102/100021, 2.

67. Memo, German Foreign Office, Herbst, 27 June 1969: AAPD, #213.

68. Vorstandssitzung 12.8.68, Allgemeines und Marktlage, p1-2, Bd2, M12.045.15, MA; Vorstandssitzung 12.5.1969. Marktlage, p1, Bd. 2, M12.045.16, MA.

69. Memo, German Ambassador in Moscow, Allardt, to German Foreign Office, "Bau eines LKW Werkes in der UdSSR," 24 June 1970, BAK 102/100011, 3.

70. For a good example of this, see the proposed oil refinery to be built by the Salzgitter consortium and the pressure that the German industry exerted on the Erhard government. Salzgitter Industriebau: Letter, Salzgitter Corp. to Economics Ministry, Leithe, "Deutsches Konsortium UdSSR Petrochemie," 23 August 1965, BAK 102/69034.

71. Memo, German Foreign Office (Herbst), 27 June 1969: AAPD, #213.

72. Ibid.

73. Memo, German Foreign Office (Herbst) to BMWI (Döring), "Sowjetisches Erdgas," 3 July 1969, BAK 102/99987.

74. Memo, German Foreign Office (Herbst), 27 June 1969: AAPD, #213, footnote #4 and #6.

75. Letter, Foreign Minister Brandt to Economics Minister Schiller, 10 July 1969, B102/99987.

76. Letter, Economics Minister Schiller to Foreign Minister Brandt, 26 August 1969, B102/99987.

77. MemCon, German Chancellor Kiesinger with U.S. Ambassador Rush, 24 July 1969, AAPD, #241. Seppain even views Kiesinger's reluctance to embrace trade with the East as fully as Brandt did as a threat to the improvement of Soviet-German relations. Seppain, *Contrasting US and German Attitudes*, 194.

78. MemCon, German Chancellor Kiesinger with U.S. Ambassador Rush, 24 July 1969, AAPD, #241.

79. Memo, Foreign Office Undersecretary Egon Bahr, 1 August 1969: AAPD, #246, footnote #1.

80. Memo, Foreign Office Undersecretary Egon Bahr, 1 August 1969: AAPD, #246.

81. See Brandt, *A Peace Policy for Europe,* 122.

82. Shevchenko, *Breaking with Moscow,* 264.

83. Memo, Foreign Office, Undersecretary Egon Bahr, 1 August 1969: AAPD, #246, footnote 7 and 8.

84. Funigiello, *American-Soviet Trade in the Cold War,* 179.

85. Nixon, *Memoirs,* 343–344.

86. Memo, C. Fred Bergsten (NSC) to President's Assistant for National Security Affairs (Kissinger), 14 April 1969, *FRUS (1969–1976),* vol. III, #19.

87. I. M. Destler, Making Foreign Economic Policy (Washington, D.C.: Brookings Institution, 1980), 135–136.

88. Allen J. Matusow, *Nixon's Economy: Booms, Busts, Dollars, and Votes* (Lawrence: University Press of Kansas, 1998), 119.

89. Paper Prepared by the National Security Council Staff, [n.d. but between 16 April and 15 May], *FRUS (1969–1976),* vol. IV, #292.

90. Nixon, *Memoirs,* 343–344.

91. Memo, C. Fred Bergsten (NSC) to President's Assistant for National Security Affairs (Kissinger), 3 July 1969, *FRUS (1969–1976),* vol. IV, #303.

92. The effectiveness of trade embargos is still heavily debated to this day. Gary Bertsch and Michael Mastanduno see export controls as valuable tools for Western powers and COCOM as an effective institution. Gary K. Bertsch, *East-West Strategic Trade, COCOM and the Atlantic Alliance* (Totowa, NJ: Allenheld, Osmun [dist.], 1983), 24, 42. Michael Mastanduno, "The Management of Alliance Export Control Policy: American Leadership and the Politics of COCOM," in *Controlling East-West Trade and Technology Transfer: Power, Politics, and Policies,* ed. Gary K. Bertsch (Durham, NC: Duke University Press, 1988), 243–247.

93. Memo, Acting Secretary of State (Richardson) to President Nixon, 14 May 1969, *FRUS (1969–1976),* vol. IV, #295.

94. Ibid. See also Editorial Note, *FRUS (1969–1976),* vol. IV, #313.

95. National Security Decision Memorandum #15, 28 May 1969, *FRUS (1969–1976),* vol. IV, #299. Also Alan P. Dobson, *US Economic Statecraft for Survival, 1933–1991: Of Sanctions, Embargoes, and Economic Warfare* (New York: Routledge, 2002), 200.

96. Kissinger, *White House Years,* 152. See also Dobson, *US Economic Statecraft for Survival,* 99.

97. Letter, U.S. Embassy Vienna (MacArthur) to Deputy Undersecretary of State for Economic Affairs (Samuels), 4 April 1969, *FRUS (1969–1976),* vol. IV, #289.

98. Memo, President Nixon to President's Assistant for National Security Affairs (Kissinger), 2 March 1970, folder: "HAK/RN Memos 69–70," Box 341, NSCF, Subject Files, NPMS, NA.

99. Spaulding, *Osthandel and Ostpolitik,* 492.

100. William Glenn Gray, *Germany's Cold War: The Global Campaign to Isolate East Germany, 1949–1969* (Raleigh: University of North Carolina Press, 2003).

101. Nixon, *Memoirs*, 343–344.

102. "Bonn Is Shutting Cambodia Embassy," *New York Times*, 5 June 1969, 7.

103. Schwartz, *Lyndon Johnson and Europe*, 68.

104. Bahr was convinced that certain elements in the West German government pursued the acquisition of nuclear weapons, and the Soviets had legitimate concerns in this regard. Bahr, *Zu meiner Zeit*, 209.

105. MemCon, German Foreign Minister Schröder, 27 July 1965, AAPD, 1965, #275.

106. Kissinger, *White House Years*, 98.

107. Letter, President Johnson to Chairman Kosygin, January 1966, *FRUS 1964–1968*, vol. XI, #114.

108. "Brandt Said to Accept Delay," *New York Times*, 16 April 1969, 3.

109. David Binder, "Brandt Says West Germany is Ready to Discuss Border Issue With Poland," *New York Times*, 20 May 1969, 14.

110. Ralph Blumenthal, "Paris Step Fuels Discord in Bonn," *New York Times*, 10 August 1969, 2; Ralph Blumenthal, "A Vote for the Mark Is a Vote for Whom ?" *New York Times*, 28 September 1969, F1.

111. MemCon, President Nixon and Chancellor Kiesinger, 7–8 August 1969, folder: "Presidential/HAK Memcons," Box 1023, NSCF, NPMS, NA.

112. Martin J. Hillenbrand, *Fragments of Our Time: Memoirs of a Diplomat* (Athens: The University of Georgia Press, 1998), 279.

113. Ibid., 285.

114. Kissinger, *White House Years*, 100. Kissinger relates his position before October 1969.

115. Kissinger, *White House Years*, 410.

116. Memo, President's Assistant for National Security Affairs (Kissinger) to President Nixon, 29 September 1969, folder: "Germany Vol III. July 1969 – 11–69," Box 682, NSCF, Country Files - Europe, NPMS, NA.

117. Memo, President's Assistant for National Security Affairs (Kissinger) to President Nixon, "Visit by Willy Brandt's Emissary, Bahr," 20 October 1969, folder: "Germany Vol III. July 1969 – 11–69," Box 682, NSCF, Country Files - Europe, NPMS, NA. See also Brandt, *Erinnerungen*, 171.

118. Bahr, *Zu meiner Zeit*, 272.

119. Kissinger, *White House Years*, 411.

120. Ibid. Bahr was indeed concerned about U.S. troop reductions since they could jeopardize the "Western bargaining leverage with the Russians." Memo, President's Assistant for National Security Affairs (Kissinger) to President Nixon, "Visit by Willy Brandt's Emissary, Bahr," 20 October 1969, folder: "Germany Vol III. July 1969 – 11–69," Box 682, NSCF, Country Files - Europe, NPMS, NA, 1–3. See also Kurt Birrenbach, *Meine Sondermissionen: Ruckblick auf zwei Jahrzehnte bundesdeutscher Außenpolitik* (Dusseldorf: Econ Verlag, 1984), 328.

121. Memo, President's Assistant for National Security Affairs (Kissinger) to President Nixon, "Visit by Willy Brandt's Emissary, Bahr," 20 October 1969, folder: "Germany Vol III. July 1969 – 11–69," Box 682, NSCF, Country Files - Europe, NPMS, NA, 4.

122. Willy Brandt's inaugural speech, 28 October 1969, Auswärtiges Amt, *Außenpolitik der Bundesrepublik Deutschland*, 322–329.
123. Ibid.
124. Ibid.
125. Memo, Helmut Sonnenfeld to Kissinger, 29 October 1969, folder: "Germany Vol III. July 1969 – 11–69," Box 682, NSCF, Country Files - Europe, NPMS, NA. On Brandt's misgivings about Vietnam, see Brandt, *Erinnerungen*, 176.
126. Ibid.
127. Memo, President's Assistant for National Security Affairs (Kissinger) to President Nixon, "Brandt's Eastern Policy," 16 February 1970, folder: "Europe-General Thru May 70," Box 667, NSCF, Country Files - Europe, NPMS, NA, 3.
128. Roger Berthoud, "Herr Brandt's New Approach to Power: Bonn Will Stay a Loyal Ally But It May Be Less Accommodating," *New York Times*, 20 October 1969, A2.
129. Kissinger, *White House Years*, 410–411. It must be doubted whether this statement is entirely accurate, since Kissinger wrote these memoirs before 1979, hence at a time when *Ostpolitik* seemingly had been the way to solving the East-West conflict. However, if one considers Kissinger's belief that Brandt had only limited room to maneuver, and therefore little opportunity to do harm, *Ostpolitik* must indeed have been a welcome change.
130. Kissinger, *White House Years*, 416.
131. Brandt, *Erinnerungen*, 181.
132. George C. Herring, *America's Longest War: The United States and Vietnam, 1950–1975* (New York: Alfred A Knopf, 1979), 225–232.
133. Memo, "Deutsch-sowjetische Arbeitsgruppe für wirtschaftliche und industriell–technologische Kooperation," 20 November 1969, BAK 102/99989.
134. Axel Rueckert, "Ostpolitik und Ostgeschaeft," in *Dokumente: Zeitschrift für übernationale Zusammenarbeit* 27 (April 1971): 70–76, 73.
135. Memo, German Foreign Office (Reute), 6 January 1970, AAPD, #2.
136. Memo, German Foreign Office (Herbst), 26 January 1970: AAPD, #23.
137. Randall Newnham, *Deutsche Mark Diplomacy: Positive Economic Sanctions in German-Russian Relations* (University Park: Pennsylvania State University Press, 2002), 159.
138. Memo, German Foreign Office (Herbst), 26 January 1970: AAPD, #23, footnote 5. For the unusual conditions, see also Newnham, *Deutsche Mark Diplomacy*, 158.
139. Letter, Economics Ministry to Director of Bundeskanzleramtes, "Amerikanische Investitionen in Europa," 8 August 1966, BAK 102/100003.
140. MemCon, "Über ein Gespräch des Bundeskanzlers mit dem amerikanischen Finanzminister Schultz am 15. März 1973 im Bundeskanzleramt," 16 March 1973, BAK 102/111917, 1–2.
141. Memo, Brown to Kissinger, 17 December 1969, folder: "Europe-General Thru May 70," Box 667, NSCF, Country Files - Europe, NPMS, NA.
142. Memo, Kissinger to Nixon, 29 December 1969, folder: "Europe-General Thru May 70," Box 667, NSCF, Country Files - Europe, NPMS, NA.

143. Memo, Brown to Kissinger, 10 February 1970, folder: "Europe-General Thru May 70," Box 667, NSCF, Country Files - Europe, NPMS, NA; Memo, Haig to Sonnenfeld, 12 February 1970, folder: "Europe-General Thru May 70," Box 667, NSCF, Country Files - Europe, NPMS, NA.

144. Assistant Secretary of State Joseph Sisco at the panel discussion, "Re-evaluating the Nixon/Ford/Kissinger Era: Transatlantic Relations & US Foreign Policy in the 1970s and Beyond," 18 June 2003 at the Library of Congress, Washington, D.C.

145. Record of NSC Review Group Meeting, 23 January 1970, NSC Institutional Files, H–111, SRG Minutes 1970, NPMS, NA.

146. Memo, Sonnenfeld to Kissinger, 14 January 1970, folder: "Europe-General Thru May 70," Box 667, NSCF, Country Files - Europe, NPMS, NA.

147. Memo, Kissinger to President Nixon, 16 February 1970, folder: "Germany Vol IV. 12–69 – 9 Apr 70," Box 683, NSCF, Country Files - Europe, NPMS, NA.

148. Ibid.

149. Birrenbach, *Meine Sondermissionen,* 326–327.

150. Memo, Kissinger to President Nixon, 16 February 1970, folder: "Germany Vol IV. 12–69 – 9 Apr 70," Box 683, NSCF, Country Files - Europe, NPMS, NA.

151. This stands in sharp contrast to Birrenbach's assessment of Kissinger. Birrenbach, *Meine Sondermissionen,* 327. See also Clay Clemens, "Amerikanische Entspannungs- und deutsche *Ostpolitik*: 1969–1975," in *Die USA und die Deutsche Frage: 1945–1990,* ed. Wolfgang-Uwe Friedrich (Frankfurt: Campus Verlag, 1991), 195.

152. Kissinger, *White House Years,* 532–537.

153. Ibid., 530.

154. How interested Kissinger was in retaining control of the inter-German dialogue can be seen in his cheerful comment on having "harnessed the beast of détente" by making the treaties with the East dependent on U.S. participation. Ibid., 534.

155. Interview with Egon Bahr, 13 November 1997, quoted in M. E. Sarotte, "A Small Town in (East) Germany: The Erfurt Meeting of 1970 and the Dynamics of Cold War Détente," *Diplomatic History* 25, no. 1 (2001): 103.

156. Memo, Kissinger to President Nixon, "*Ostpolitik*," 10 March 1970, folder: "Germany Vol IV. 12–69 – 9 Apr 70," Box 683, NSCF, Country Files - Europe, NPMS, NA.

157. Birrenbach, *Meine Sondermissionen,* 327.

158. Memo, Sonnenfeld to Kissinger, "On Ray Cline Paper on *Ostpolitik*," 9 April 1970, folder: "Germany Vol IV. 12–69 – 9 Apr 70," Box 683, NSCF, Country Files - Europe, NPMS, NA.

159. News Summary of 20 March 1970, quoted in Ambrose, *Nixon,* vol. 2: *The Triumph of a Politician,* 386.

160. "The Two Germanys: A Beginning," *The Nation,* 6 April 1970, 17.

161. Norbert Muhlen, "Willy Brandt Turns East," *National Review,* 30 June 1970, 676–677.

162. Nixon, *Memoirs,* 343–344.

163. Airgram, U.S. Embassy Bonn to State Department, "Significance of the Soviet-FRG Natural Gas Arrangement," 17 February 1970, 3–4, folder "FSE W-Ger 9 1/1/70," Box 994, RG 59, Subject Numerical Files, 1970–1973, Economic, NA.

164. Airgram, U.S. Embassy Bonn to State Department, "Significance of the Soviet-FRG Natural Gas Arrangement," 17 February 1970, 5, folder "FSE W-Ger 9 1/1/70", Box 994, RG 59, Subject Numerical Files, 1970–1973, Economic, NA, 5.

165. Mikhail Heller and Aleksandr Nekrich, *Utopia in Power: The History of the Soviet Union from 1917 to the Present* (New York: Summit Books, 1982), 646.

166. Harry Schwartz, "Soviet Stresses Exports," *New York Times*, 16 February 1971, 44, 46.

167. Letter, Economics Minister Schiller to Chancellor Brandt, 4 February 1970, BAK 102/99988; Letter, Chancellor Brandt to Economics Minister Schiller, 12 February 1970, BAK 102/99988.

168. Memo, "Vertiefung der deutsch-sowjetischen Wirtschaftsbeziehungen," 12 March 1970, BAK 102/99988. This memo outlined plans for liberalization of trade with the Soviet Union, which could only be labeled as a general intention on part of the FRG, not a firm commitment—i.e., the Soviets could receive an improved status of total liberalization for 80 percent of goods, but any firm legal commitment would create too many domestic problems. The memo further concluded that it would not be possible at the present time to include Berlin in a trade agreement. Any exclusion of West Berlin, however, would make such agreements with other Eastern-bloc states an impossibility.

169. Memo, HAK to President Nixon, "Brandt Visit," 5 November 1969, folder "Germany Vol III. July 1969 - 11-69", Box 682, NSCF, Country Files - Europe, NPMS, NA.

170. Telegram, American Embassy Bonn to SecState WashDC, "Brandt Visit to U.S. and FRG *Ostpolitik*," 24 March 1970, folder "Chancellor Brandt Visit, April 10–11, 1970 [2 of 3]," Box 917, NSCF, VIP Visits, NPMS, NA.

171. Memo, Helmut Sonnenfeld to HAK, "Dates of Brandt Visit," 19 December 1969, folder "Chancellor Brandt Visit, April 10-11, 1970 [1 of 3]", Box 917, NSCF, VIP Visits, NPMS, NA.

172. Memo, Dwight Chapin forwarded to Al Haig, "Brandt Wishes More Time with the President," 31 March 1970, folder "[CF] CO 53 Germany, 1-1-70 to [11-16-70] [1969-70]," Box 6, 1969–1974, WHSF, WHCF, NPMS, NA.

173. Kissinger, *White House Years*, 424.

174. On 7 December 1970 Brandt apparently spontaneously knelt before a monument to the Warsaw Ghetto uprising.

175. Memo, Helmut Sonnenfeld to HAK, "Brandt's Inaugural Address," 29 October 1969, folder "Germany Vol III. July 1969 - 11-69," Box 682, NSCF Country Files - Europe, WHSF, NPMS, NA.

176. Speech by Chancellor Brandt at the White House Reception on 13 April 1970, BAK 102/111903.

177. Letter, Chancellor Brandt to MdB Horst Krockert, 23 January 1970, Mappe 41, Bundeskanzler, Willy Brandt Archiv [WBA], 1–2.

178. See Figure 2.3.
179. Memo, Luncheon conversation between Henry Kissinger and Egon Bahr, 8 April 1970, folder "Germany Vol IV. 12-69 - 9 Apr 70," Box 683, NSCF Country Files - Europe, WHSF, NPMS, NA.
180. MemCon, "Gespräche des Bundesministers Schmidt in Washington," 7 April 1970, AAPD, #572.
181. Memo, "Aufzeichnung des Bundeskanzlers Brandt," 11 April 1970, AAPD, #595.
182. Helmut Sonnenfeld at the panel discussion, "Re-evaluating the Nixon/ Ford/Kissinger Era: Transatlantic Relations & US Foreign Policy in the 1970s and Beyond," 18 June 2003 at the Library of Congress, Washington, D.C.
183. Kissinger, White House Years, 424.
184. CIA Directorate of Intelligence, Intelligence Report "The Prussian Heresy: Ulbricht's Evolving System," 29 June 1970, <http://www.foia.cia.gov/cpe. asp>, CEASAR Document #45, 6–7.
185. Memo, Willi Stoph, "Grundfragen der Gestaltung des oekonomischen Systems des Sozialismus in der DDR im Zeitraum 1971 bis 1975," 28 May 1970, BAL-SAMPO DY/30/ J IV 2/2 J -2994, 45–47.
186.
187. Directive, Minister fuer Aussenwirtschaft, "Direktiven fuer die handels-politische und kommerzielle Taetigkeit gegenueber der BRD," Berlin, VV, 23.2.1971, BAL-SAMPO DL/2/VA1224,3.
188. Memo, Gen Behrendt, Stellvertreter des Ministers, "Vorlage zur Stellver-treterberatung des Ministers vom 19. Juli 1971: Einschaetzung des pol-ideologischen Zustands des Kollektivs des Buero des Ministeriums fuer Aussenwirtschaft der DDR," 19 July 1971, BAL-SAMPO DL/2/VA 1223., 6.
189. Letter, Wambutt to Dr Mittag, Abteilung Grundstoffindustrie, Berlin 20.11.1972, betr: "Unterbindung weiterer Versuche zur Aufnahme perso-enlicher Kontakte durch westdeutsche Monteure im VEB Chemiefaser-werk 'Friedrich Engels', Premnitz," BAL-SAMPO DY/30-2825.1-2.
190. CIA Directorate of Intelligence, Intelligence Report "The Polish Question: East Germany," July 1971, <http://www.foia.cia.gov/cpe.asp>, ESAU Doc-ument #51, ii.
191. CIA Directorate of Intelligence, Intelligence Report "The Polish Question: East Germany," July 1971, <http://www.foia.cia.gov/cpe.asp>, ESAU Doc-ument #51, iii.
192. "POLEN-HANDEL: Gute Ernte," Der Spiegel (27/1970), 29 June 1970, 29.

Chapter 3

1. Keith Nelson, The Making of Détente: Soviet-American Relations in the Shadow of Vietnam (Baltimore: John Hopkins University Press, 1995).
2. Mikhail Heller and Aleksandr Nekrich, Utopia in Power, 647.
3. Hanson, 119.

4. Ibid., 125.

5. Edemskiy, 36.

6. Ibid., 21–28.

7. This idea was expressed time and again in the speeches and policy memo-randums that Gromyko submitted to Soviet policy makers. See, for example, Gromyko's foreign policy memorandum approved by the Politburo in 1967 in the appendix of Anatoly Dobrynin, *In Confidence: Moscow's Ambas-sador to America's Six Cold War Presidents (1962–1986)* (New York: Random House, 1995), 641.

8. For Gromyko, see *Ot Kollontai do Gorbacheva : vospominaniia diplomata, sovetnika A.A. Gromyko, pomoshchnika L.I. Brezhneva, IU.V. Andropova, K.U. Chernenko i M.S. Gorbacheva.* (Moscow: Mezhdunarodnye otnosheniia, 1994), 69. For Dobryin, see his *In Confidence*, 193.

9. Shevchenko, *Breaking with Moscow,* 226.

10. Heller and Neckrich, 646.

11. CIA CAESAR Document "Portrait of a Neo-Stalinist: Annex to CEASR XXXIX Andrey Kirilenko and the Soviet Political Succession," June 1971, <http://www.foia.cia.gov/cpe.asp>, Document #52, 74–75.

12. Ibid., 75.

13. Quoted from Ibid., 76.

14. Anatolii Andreevich Gromyko, *Andrei Gromyko: v labirintakh Kreml´ı`a: vospominani´ı`a i razmyshleni´ı`a syna* (Moscow: IPO "Avtor," 1997), 55.

15. Vladislav M. Zubok, *A Failed Empire: The Soviet Union in the Cold War from Stalin to Gorbachev* (Chapel Hill: The University of North Carolina Press, 2007), 211–214.

16. Memo, "Besuch von Minister Schiller in Moskau," 1 October 1970, BAK 102/100023.

17. Memo, "Gespräch von Herrn Minister mit dem sowjetischen Außenhan-delsminister Patolitschew am 25. September 1970 in Moskau," 30 Septem-ber 1970, BAK 102/100023, 6.

18. Letter, German Ambassador in Paris, Ruete, to German Foreign Office, "Sowjetisches LKW-Kombinat an der Kama," 21 October 1970, BAK 102/100011, 1–2.

19. Letter, German Ambassador in Moscow, Allardt, to German Foreign Office, "Bau eines LKW Werkes in der UdSSR," 24 June 1970, BAK 102/100011.

20. Ibid.

21. Memo, Undersecretary Braun, "LKW-Geschäft mit der Sowjetunion," 21 September 1970, BAK 102/100011.

22. Shevchenko, *Breaking with Moscow,* 264.

23. Memo, Dr. Henze, "Lastwagenprojekt in der UdSSR," 16 September 1970, BAK 102/100011, 2.

24. Ibid.

25. Memo, Ostausschuß der deutschen Wirtschaft to Chancellor Brandt, "Lastwagenprojekt Rußland," 7 September 1970, Nachlaß Otto Wolff von Amerongen, 72-1018-1, Rhein-Westfählisches Wirtschaftsarchiv [RWWA].

26. MemCon, Soviet Trade Minister Tarasov with German Economics Minis-ter Schiller, 30 September 1970, BAK 102/100011, 1–17.

27. Letter, German Ambassador in Paris, Ruete, to German Foreign Office, "Sowjetisches LKW-Kombinat an der Kama," 21 October 1970, BAK 102/100011, 1–2.

28. *U.S. News and World Report,* 11 May 1970, 5.

29. Speech by U.S. Secretary of Defense Laird, before the Chicago Council on Foreign Relations, as cited in Letter, German Ambassador in Washington, Pauls, to German Foreign Office, "Kritische Einstellung zu deutsch-sowjetischen Wirtschafts- und Wissenschaftsbeziehungen," 14 December 1970, BAK 102/100011, 2.

30. Memo, Dr. Lukas, "Amerikanische Haltung zum LKW Projekt an der Kama," 22 December 1970, BAK 102/100011, 1.

31. Memo, Dr. Klarenaar, "Fragestunde des deutschen Bundestages 15./ 18.12.1970," n.d., BAK 102/100011, 3.

32. Ibid.

33. Memo, "Sprechzettel für Messen und Ausstellungen 1974 - Sachstand 11 October 1973," 19 October 1973, BAK 102/100002, 3.

34. Memo, HAK to President Nixon, 23 June 1969, *FRUS (1969–1976),* vol. IV, #301. See also Dobson, *US Economic Statecraft for Survival,* 213.

35. See Editorial Note to Document #313, cited in *FRUS (1969–1976),* vol. IV, #313.

36. Memo, National Security Council Staff, Ernest Johnston, to Kissinger, 30 June 1971, *FRUS (1969–1976),* vol. IV, #336.

37. For examples see Letter, Rheinische Stahlwerke to Economics Ministry, 26 August 1965, BAK 102/100003 and Letter, Mühlheimer Rohstoffhandel GmbH to Economics Ministry, "Erteilung zusätzlicher Lizenzen für die Einfuhr von Benzin aus der UdSSR gemäß unserem Vertrag vom 2.1.1964 mit der Firma Sojuznefteexport, Moskau," 26 July 1966, BAK 102/100003; also Memo, Dr. Steidle, "Kompensationsgeschäft der Fa. Henschel-Export-GmbH mit der Sowjetunion," 17 October 1966, BAK 102/100003.

38. Memo, "Besuch des sowjetischen Handelsrats Woltschkow im Bundeswirtschaftsministerium am 5.2.1969," 11 February 1969, BAK 102/100003.

39. Letter, Dr. Lantzke to Economics Ministry Undersecretary Dr. Arndt, 18 March 1969, BAK 102/100003.

40. Telegram, German Embassy in Moscow, Stempel, to German Foreign Office, "Einfuhrerleichterungen für leichtes Heizöl und Rohbenzin," 24 March 1969, BAK 102/100003.

41. Memo, Lucas, "Maßnahmen zur Erhaltung der Preisstabilität," 13 March 1969, BAK 102/100003; Memo, Economics Ministry Undersecretary Dr. Arndt, "Erteilung von Einfuhrgenehmigungen für sowjetische Erdölerzeugnisse," 2 April 1969, BAK 102/100003.

42. Memo, Economics Ministry Undersecretary Dr. Arndt, "Erteilung von Einfuhrgenehmigungen für sowjetische Erdölerzeugnisse," 2 April 1969, BAK 102/100003.

43. Letter, Verband Deutscher Maschinenbau-Anstalten, Stäcker, to Economics Ministry, Dr. Steidle, "Erdöl und Erdölderivaten," 9 May 1969, BAK 102/100003.

44. Volkov made this clear to Mannesmann in writing and Thyssen's chairman, Mommsen, was reminded of this by the Soviet Foreign Trade Minister Patolichev. See Letter, Mannesmann Export GmbH to Undersecretary Arndt, 24 April 1969, BAK 102/100003 and Memo, Dr. Lucas, "Besuch von Herrn Wilhelm A. Kleberger," 8 May 1969, BAK 102/100003.
45. Memo, Dr. Lucas, "Wesentliches Ergebnis der Besprechung am 19. August 1969," 21 August 1969, BAK 102/100003.
46. Memo, Dr. Lantzke, "Sowjetische Wünsche auf Erhöhung der Einfuhrkontingente für Mineralölprodukte," 27 October 1972, BAK 102/100002. This memo detailed the following heating oil import quotas in million tons per year:

	1968	1969	1970	1971	1972
Basic quota	700	700	700	1,500	1,500
Additional licenses	273	850	1,250	600	600
Total	973	1,550	1,950	2,100	2,100
Used	1,145	1,340	1,870	1,941	1,483
					(Jan–Jul)

47. Telegram, American Consul Düsseldorf to U.S. Secretary of State Rogers, 9 July 1971, folder "FSE W-Ger 9 1/1/70," Box 994, RG 59, Subject Numerical Files, 1970–1973, Economic, NA.
48. Airgram, U.S. Embassy Bonn to U.S. Department of State, "FRG Natural Gas Supplies," 12 June 1972, folder "FSE W-Ger 9 1/1/70," Box 994, RG 59, Subject Numerical Files, 1970–1973, Economic, NA, 2.
49. MemCon, Chancellor Brandt with Vice President Novikov, 24 April 1972, BAK 102/100026, 3.
50. Memo, Dr. Henze, "Sowjetisches Projekt einer Lkw-Produktion an der KAMA," 24 September 1970, BAK 102/100026.
51. Memo, "Talking Points for the Visit of a Soviet Delegation to the Economics Ministry," 23 September 1970, BAK 102/100026.
52. Memo, Dr. Lucas, "Gespräch des stellvertretenden Außenhandelsministers Ossipow," 15 April 1971, BAK 102/100026.
53. Memo, Borucki, "Neuer Ausfuhrkredit für Röhrenlieferungen in die UdSSR," 14 April 1971, BAK 102/100026.
54. Airgram, American Consul Düsseldorf to Secretary of State, "German-Soviet Natural Gas-Pipeline Deal," 8 June 1972, folder "FSE W-Ger 9 1/1/70," Box 994, RG 59, Subject Numerical Files, 1970–1973, Economic, NA.
55. Telegram, German Ambassador in Washington, Pauls, to German Foreign Office, "Gespräch zwischen Bundesminister Schmidt und US-Secretary of Commerce Peterson," 26 September 1972, BAK 102/111905, 1–2.
56. F. Wilhelm Christians, *Wege nach Russland: Bankier im Spannungsfeld zwischen Ost und West* (Hamburg: Hoffmann und Campe, 1989), 50.
57. Telegram, German Embassy Moscow to German Foreign Office, "Gespräche von Bundesminister Bahr in Moskau," 2 March 1974, BAK 102/99998.
58. Telegram, German Embassy in Moscow to German Foreign Office, "Aufzeichnung des Gesprächs des Herrn Bundeskanzlers am 18. Januar 1974

mit dem Stellvertretenden Vorsitzenden des Ministerrats der UdSSR, Herrn Nowikow," 2 March 1974, BAK 102/99998, 8.

59. Memo, Foreign Minister Scheel, "Bericht über meine Dienstreise nach Togliatti vom 25. bis 30. Oktober 1970," 24 November 1970, BAK 102/100023, 2–5.

60. Ibid.

61. Ibid.

62. Report, BfA-Correspondent, Klaus Dürkoop, "Visit of the Elektrosila Plant," 28 November 1971, BAK 102/100023, 3.

63. Letter, Otto A. Friedrich to Economics Minister Schiller, "Ergebnis-Niederschrift über Orientierungsbesuch in Moskau und Leningrad 23.11-27.11.1970," BAK 102/100023, 2–4.

64. See also Karsten Rudolph, *Wirtschaftsdiplomatie im Kalten Krieg: Die Ostpolitik der westdeutschen Großindustrie 1945–1991* (Campus Verlag: Frankfurt, 2004), 297–300.

65. Letter, Dieffenbacher GmbH to MdB Baier, "Geschäfte mit der UdSSR," 26 August 1971, BAK 102/100001.

66. Letter, Egon Bahr to Chancellor Brandt, 7 March 1970, Ordner 429B, Mappe 1, Depositorium Egon Bahr, Archiv der Sozialen Demokratie [DEB], 4.

67. MemCon, Visit of Economics Minister Schiller with Prime Minister Kosygin, 26 September 1970, BAK 102/100023, 3.

68. Ibid., 5–6.

69. Ibid.

70. Ibid.

71. Telegram, German Embassy in Moscow, Sahm, to German Foreign Office, "Gespräch O. A. Friderichs mit Kossygin," 5 October 1973, BAK 102/135258.

72. Letter, Otto A. Friedrich to Economics Minister Friderichs, "Zusammenfassende Notiz über einen Besuch in Moskau vom 1. bis 5. Oktober 1973," 17 October 1973, BAK 102/135258, 2–3.

73. Christians, *Wege nach Russland*, 48–49.

74. Ibid., 49.

75. Telegram, German Ambassador in Washington, Pauls, to German Foreign Office, "Bemerkungen zur amerikanischen Außenpolitik," 21 December 1970, BAK 102/111915, 2–3.

76. Ibid.

77. Joseph C. Harsch, *Christian Science Monitor,* 21 December 1970, 23.

78. Charles Hargrove, "French Align Policies with Germans before Nixon Talks," *The London Times,* 6 December 1971, 4, column F.

79. Norbert Muhlen, "Willy Brandt Turns East," *National Review,* 30 June 1970, 34.

80. "The Brandt-Brezhnev Pact," *National Review,* 25 August 1970, 23.

81. William S. Sham, "Stalin-Hitler Pact, 1970 Model?" *National Review,* 8 September 1970, 42.

82. Joe Alex Morris, Jr., "Hammering at Recognition," *The Nation,* 25 May 1970, 614–616.

83. "A Good Beginning," *The Nation,* 31 August 1970, 131–132.

84. Paul Wahl, "Opening to the East: Brandt and the Two Germanys," *The Nation*, 1 February 1971, 142–145.
85. Telegram, German Embassy in Washington to German Foreign Office, "Der Wandel im außenpolitischen Bewußtsein der amerikanischen Öffentlichkeit seit Sommer 1970," 30 December 1970, BAK 102/111915, 3–5.
86. Ibid., 5–7.
87. Statement by the AFL-CIO Labor Union Executive Council on U.S. Strength and World Responsibility–Best Guarantee for World Peace, Bal Harbour, Fla., 19 February 1971, BAK 136 [=Bundeskanzleramt]/6220. (This statement was approved almost unanimously by the council members.)
88. Letter, German Embassy in Washington, Middelmann, to German Foreign Office, "Leitartikel des Direktors der Auslandsabteilung der amerikanischen Automobilarbeitergewerkschaft UAW, Victor Reuther," 6 April 1971, BAK 136/6220.
89. Telegram, German Ambassador in Washington, Pauls, to German Foreign Office, "Statement des Kongreßabgeordneten Philip Crane," 16 April 1971, BAK 136/6220.
90. Letter, Minister for Education and Culture, Klaus von Dohnanyi, to Chancellor Brandt, 27 November 1972, BAK 136/6921.
91. Address by former Undersecretary of State George W. Ball at the World Affairs Council of Northern California Conference, 8 May 1971, Asilomar, California, as cited in Report 180/1971, German General Consulate in San Francisco, Dr. Motz, to German Foreign Office, "Deutsche *Ostpolitik*," 13 May 1971, BAK 136/6220, 5–13.
92. Ibid.
93. Talking Points Memo, Meeting Minister Schmidt with Secretary of Commerce, Peterson, et al. in Washington, 19 September 1972, BAK 102/115022, 2.
94. Memo, Henry A. Kissinger to President Nixon, 1 September 1970, "The German-Soviet Treaty," folder: "Germany Vol VII. 1 August 70 - Nov 70," Box 684, Country Files - Europe, NSCF, NPMS, NA.
95. Ibid.
96. Memo, Henry A. Kissinger to President Nixon, 13 September 1970, folder: "Germany Vol VII. 1 August 70 - Nov 70," Box 684, Country Files - Europe, NSCF, NPMS, NA.
97. Recording of Conversation between President Nixon and Henry A. Kissinger, 29 May 1971, White House Tapes, Conversation 507-4, NPMP, NA.
98. Rainer Barzel, *Im Streit und umstritten: Anmerkungen zu Konrad Adenauer, Ludwig Erhard und den Ostverträgen* (Frankfurt a. M.: Ullstein, 1986), 172.
99. National Security Decision Memorandum 91, "United States Policy on Germany and Berlin," 6 November 1970, folder "Germany BERLIN Vol III. Jan - Apr 72," Box 691, Country Files - Europe, NSCF, WHSF, NPMS, NA, 1.
100. Ibid., 2.
101. Letter, Economics and Finance Minister Schmidt to Secretary of Commerce, Peter G. Peterson, 27 October 1972, BAK 102/115022, 2.

102. Talking Points Memo, Hanemann, Conversation Helmut Schmidt with Secretary Peterson, "Über COCOM- Fragen," 18 September 1972, BAK 102/115022, 1–3.

103. CIA Directorate of Intelligence, Intelligence Memo "Andrey Kirilenko and the Soviet Political Succession," 15 March 1971, <http://www.foia.cia.gov/cpe.asp>, CAESAR Document #51, 4.

104. Ibid., 6, 8.

105. Memo, "Stand und Fortfuehrung der deutschen Ostpolitik," 24 November 1970, PAAA, II 4 A 82, 1–3.

106. Information Nr. 18/70 fuer die Mitglieder und Kandidaten des Politbueros des ZK, Herr Ott, Abteilung Internationale Verbindungen, betr "Zur Wiederaufnahme der chinesich-amerikanischen 'Botschaftergespraeche amd 20. Januar 1970 in Warschau (Information der Botschaft der DDR in der Volksrepublik China),'" 19 March 1970, BAL-SAMPO DY/30/J IV 2/2J-2886, 4–5.

107. Ibid., 5–6.

108. Information Nr. 18/70 fuer die Mitglieder und Kandidaten des Politbueros des ZK, Herr Ott, Abteilung Internationale Verbindungen, betr "Zur Wiederaufnahme der chinesich-amerikanischen 'Botschaftergespraeche amd 20. Januar 1970 in Warschau (Information der Botschaft der DDR in der Volksrepublik China),'" 19 March 1970, BAL-SAMPO DY/30/J IV 2/2J-2886, 6.

109. CIA Directorate of Intelligence, Intelligence Report "Soviet Thinking About the Danger of a Sino-US Rapprochement," February 1971, <http://www.foia.cia.gov/cpe.asp>, ESAU Document #50, 51.

110. Ibid., 52–54.

111. Letter, Minister for Agriculture to Minister for Economics, "Reexportklausel bei der UdSSR," 29 July 1966, B102/99987.

112. Memo, Dr. Becker, "Deutsch-sowjetischer Handelsvertrag," 28 September 1970, BAK 102/99988.

113. Telegram, Herr Massion to German Foreign Office, "Handel der Sowjetunion mit Berlin," 15 April 1970, BAK 102/100001.

114. Memo, Dr. Neundörfer, "Bisherige Haltung der Sowjetunion gegenüber Berlin im deutsch-sowjetischen Warenverkehr," 7 October 1970, BAK 102/100001.

115. Letter, Foreign Minister, Scheel, to Economics Minister, Schiller, "Deutsch-sowjetische Wirtschaftskommission," 24 January 1972, BAK 102/100002, 1.

116. Letter, Chancellor Brandt to Egon Bahr, 3 August 1970, Bundeskanzler, Mappe 2, WBA, 1–2.

117. Letter, Chancellor Brandt to John J. McCloy, 24 March 1971, Bundeskanzler, Mappe 43, WBA, 3–4.

118. Letter, Economics Ministry, Schulte-Steinberg, to Economics Minister Schiller, "Interview von Herrn Minister für die Pariser Zeitung Les Echos," 12 October 1970, BAK 102/10001, 2.

119. German Foreign Office, Dr. Bräutigam, to Economics Ministry, Lukas, "Vortrag von Jurij A. Shukow," 4 December 1970, BAK 102/99988.

120. MemCon, Visit of Minister Schiller with Prime Minister Kosygin, 26 September 1970, BAK 102/100023, 7–8.
121. Memo, Dr. Becker, "Deutsch-sowjetisches Handelsabkommen," 30 September 1970, BAK 102/99988.
122. Letter, Economics Ministry, Dr. Thieme, to Economics Minister Schiller, "Aufnahme der deutsch-sowjetischen Verhandlungen über ein Handelsabkommen," 15 December 1970, BAK 102/99988.
123. Stent, *From Embargo to Ostpolitik,* 182.
124. Ibid., 182–183.
125. Memo, Dr. Becker, "Deutsch-sowjetische Wirtschaftsverhandlungen," 2 March 1971, BAK 102/99988.
126. Letter, Economics Ministry, Dr. Hanemann, to Economics Minister Schiller, "Deutsch-sowjetische Wirtschaftsverhandlungen," 5 March 1971, BAK 102/10001.
127. "24. Parteikongress der KpdSU," n.d., PAAA, II A 4 82.00, 1. See also Garthoff, *Détente and Confrontation,* 46.
128. Memo, Staatssekretaer Dr. Beil, Ministerium fuer Wissenschaft und Technik, Vorlage "Oekonomische, wissenschaftlich-technische Zusammenarbeit mit den kapitalistischen Industrielaendern," 27 August 1973, BAL-SAMPO DL/2/VA1502, 2.
129. Zentralkomittee der SED, Politbuero, BAL-SAMPO DY/30/ J IV 2/2 J-5045, "Reisebericht ueber Erfahrungsaustausch mit der Sowjetunion ueber die Vorbereitung und Durchfuehrung von Investitionen, and denen auslaendische Unternehmen beteiligt sind.," Berlin 19 October 1973 by K. Fichtner., 6–7.
130. Ibid., 9
131. Ibid., 10.
132. Letter, Rainer Barzel to Willy Brandt, RWWA 72-1018-1, 1–3.
133. Kissinger, *The White House Years,* 534.
134. Marilyn Berger, "Bonn Official, Kissinger Confer," *Washington Post,* 22 December 1970, A18.
135. This is in sharp contrast to Stephen Ambrose, who depicted Kissinger as suspicious of *Ostpolitik* while Nixon embraced it. Ambrose, vol. 2, 464.
136. Recording of Conversation between Nixon and Kissinger, 29 May 1971 [NARA NPMP], White House Tapes, Conversation 507-4.
137. Letter, U.S. Ambassador in Bonn, Rush, to Henry A. Kissinger, 28 March 1971, folder "Ambassador Rush - Berlin Vol. I [1 of 2]," Box 59, Henry A. Kissinger Office Files, Country Files-Europe, NSCF, NPMS, NA.
138. MemCon between Henry A. Kissinger and Soviet Ambassador in Washington, Dobrynin, on 27 April 1971, Tab 1 of Memo, Henry A. Kissinger, "Meeting with Ambassador Dobrynin, April 27, 1971," folder "Berlin - Vol. 3 [1 of 2]," Box 59, NSCF Henry A. Kissinger Office Files Country Files-Europe, NPMS, NA.
139. Letter, U.S. Ambassador in Bonn, Rush, to Henry A. Kissinger, 5 May 1971, folder "Ambassador Rush - Berlin Vol. I [1 of 2]," Box 59, Henry A. Kissinger Office Files, Country Files-Europe, NSCF, NPMS, NA. For Falin's role, see Letter, U.S. Ambassador in Bonn, Rush, to Henry A. Kissinger, 28

May 1971, folder "Ambassador Rush - Berlin Vol. I [1 of 2]," Box 59, Henry A. Kissinger Office Files, Country Files-Europe, NSCF, NPMS, NA.

140. Recording of Conversation with President Nixon in the Oval Office, 14 June 1971, White House Tapes, OVAL 519-15, NPMP, NA.

141. David C. Geyer, "The Missing Link: Henry Kissinger and the Back-Channel Negotiations on Berlin," in David C. Geyer and Bernd Schaefer, eds., *American Détente and German Ostpolitik, 1969–1972* (Washington, D.C.: Supplement 1 to the Bulletin of the German Historical Institute, 2004), 80–92, 91–92.

142. Ibid.

143. Talking Points Memo, Visit Chancellor Brandt to the U.S. on April 10/11, 1970, "Verhältnis Europa-USA // Handelspolitik," 13 March 1970, BAK 102/111903, 1.

144. Letter, Günter Grass to Chancellor Brandt, 25 March 1970, Mappe 6, Bundeskanzler, WBA, 1–3.

145. Matusow, *Nixon's Economy,* 132–137.

146. Letter, Parlamentarischer Staatssekretär, Dr. Katharina Focke, to Defense Minister Helmut Schmidt, 28 July 1971, BAK 136/6220.

147. Letter, MdB, Dr. Kurt Birrenbach, to Chancellor Brandt, "Devisenausgleich mit den Vereinigten Staaten," 2 July 1971, BAK 136/6220, 2.

148. Letter, Chancellor Brandt to Dr. Kurt Birrenbach, 22 July 1971, BAK 136/6220, 1–2.

149. Ibid.

150. Draft Letter, Chancellor Brandt to President Nixon, n.d., BAK 136/6921.

151. Letter, Chancellor Brandt to President Nixon, 15 May 1972, BAK 136/6921.

152. Memo, Minister Bahr to Chancellor Brandt, "Europäische Reaktion auf amerikanische Vietnam-Politik," 4 January 1973, Mappe 190, Bundeskanzler, WBA.

153. Letter, Minister Ehmke to North Atlantic Assembly, Erik Blumenfeld, 21 July 1972, BAK 136/6921; North Atlantic Assembly, Eric Blumenfeld, to Chancellor's Office, Minister Ehmke, 2 August 1972, BAK 136/6921.

154. Letter, Economics Ministry, Fischer, to Chancellor's Office, Minister Ehmke, "Schreiben des Vorsitzenden des Politischen Ausschusses der Nordatlantischen Versammlung," 18 July 1972, BAK 136/6921.

155. FRUS, Germany and Berlin 1969–1972, vol. XL, 944, 946.

156. Ibid., 937.

157. MemCon, Meeting Chancellor Brandt and General Secretary Brezhnev in Oreanda, 17 September 1971, Mappe 1, Ordner 430, DEB, 3.

158. Ibid., 8.

159. Ibid., 12.

160. Memo, Chancellor Brandt, "Gespräch mit Breschnew," 12 August 1970, Mappe 1, Ordner 429A, DEB, 3.

161. Ibid.

162. Translator's Protocol, Conversation of Chancellor Brandt with General Secretary Brezhnev on 12 August 1970, Mappe 1,Ordner 429A, DEB, 7.

163. Ibid.

164. Ibid., 10–11.
165. Memo, Heinz Kühn, "Bericht über meine Moskau-Reise vom 3.-12. April 1972," n.d., BAK 102/100023, 4.
166. Ibid., 5.
167. Ibid., 6.
168. Sarotte, *Dealing with the Devil*, 24.
169. Keworkow, *Der geheime Kanal*, 109.
170. Ibid., 110–119.
171. Ibid., 104.
172. Ibid., 105–106.
173. Gottfried Niedhardt, "*Ostpolitik*: Phases, Short-term Objectives, and Grand Design," in Geyer and Schaefer, *American Détente and German Ostpolitik*, 80–92, 92.
174. Jeremi Suri, *Henry Kissinger and the American Century* (Cambridge, MA: Belknap Press, 2007), 246–247.

Chapter 4

1. On this point and the importance of viewing the Eastern Treaties as a recognition of reality, not as a quasi peace treaty, see Gottfried Niedhardt in Bange and Niedhart, eds., *Helsinki 1975 and the Transformation of Europe*, 40–44.
2. Nixon, *Memoirs*, 390.
3. "Doing Business with Brezhnev," *New York Times*, 17 October 1971, E10.
4. David Geyer sees the Soviet-American summit in 1972 as the price the Soviets had to pay for the Four Power Agreement on Berlin. Geyer, "The Missing Link," 92.
5. For details on the last point, see Garthoff, *Détente and Confrontation*, 334–338.
6. "The New Equilibrium," *New York Times*, 3 June 1972, 28.
7. Flora Lewis, "Nixon Accord With Soviet Union Embitters NATO Officials," *New York Times*, 26 July 1972, 1.
8. Robert J. Pranger, ed., *Détente and Defence: A Reader* (Washington, D.C.: American Enterprise Institute, 1976), 114.
9. For a more detailed account of the political and economic factors, see Bruce W. Jentleson, "From Consensus to Conflict: the Domestic Political Economy of East-West Energy Trade Policy," *International Organization* 38, no. 4 (Autumn, 1984): 625–660, 646–660.
10. Testimony by Henry A. Kissinger to the Senate Foreign Relations Committee, 19 September 1974, as cited in Henry A. Kissinger, *American Foreign Policy* (New York: Norton, 1977), 158–159.
11. Report, Senate Foreign Relations Committee, "Multinational Corporations and U.S. Foreign Policy," pt. 10, p. 109, as cited in Jentleson, "From Consensus to Conflict," 646.
12. Zubok, *A Failed Empire*, 220.
13. Ibid., 221–222.

14. Wolfgang Leonhard, *Dämmerung im Kreml: Wie eine neue Ostpolitik aussehen müßte* (Stuttgart: Deutsche Verlags Anstalt, 1984), 206.

15. Ministerstvo inostrannykh del SSSR, *Za mir i bezopasnost' narodov : dokumenty vneshnei politiki SSSR .. god.* [For the People's Peace and Security: Foreign Policy Documents, 1972] (Moscow : Izd-vo Politicheskoi literatury, 1989), 120–121.

16. Harry Gelman, *The Brezhnev Politburo and the Decline of Détente* (Ithaca: Cornell University Press, 1984), 159. In a footnote, Gelman cites a Soviet samizdat as the source for Brezhnev's comments. Though the accuracy of this source may be questioned, it is certain that the tone of Brezhnev's speeches during the period became more strident.

17. For statements about Brezhnev's ambivalence at the time, see Garthoff, *Détente and Confrontation*, 483. For more of Brezhnev's motives, see Roy Laird, *The Politburo: Demographic Trends, Gorbachev, and the Future* (Boulder, CO: Westview Press, 1986.).

18. For a good example, see Suslov's comments in Ministerstvo inostrannykh del SSSR, *Za mir i bezopasnost' narodov : dokumenty vneshnei politiki SSSR .. god.* [For the People's Peace and Security: Foreign Policy Documents, 1972] (Moscow : Izd-vo Politicheskoi literatury, 1989), "Ministerstvo inostrannykh del SSSR, *Za mir i bezopasnost' narodov,*" 67–68.

19. Letter, Minister Egon Bahr to German Embassy in Moscow, Mr. Golowin, 28 April 1973, Mappe 2, Ordner 432, DEB.

20. Memo, Egon Bahr, "Nachricht von V. Lednew," 22 March 1973, Mappe 2, Ordner 432, DEB.

21. Memo, Egon Bahr to Chancellor Brandt, "Gang des Plenums des ZK," 7 May 1973, Mappe 2, Ordner 432, DEB.

22. Letter, German Ambassador to the Soviet Union, Sahm, to German Foreign Office "Sowjetisch-Amerikanische Beziehungen," 10 February 1972, PAAA 112699.1742, Folder "Sowjetische Beziehungen Us-Z," 1.

23. Edemskiy highlights the worries even liberal Politburo members held when it came to a strengthening of West German–East German contacts. Edemskiy, "Dealing with Bonn," 30f.

24. Most notable of these, of course, would be China. China postulated that the Soviet Union, in reaching an agreement with the United States, had "sold the sovereignty of the German Democratic Republic" with the signing of the Four Power Agreement. Information 3/72 fuer die Mitglieder und Kandidaten des Politbueros, Herr Markowski, Abteilung Internationale Verbindungen, Berlin 6.1. 1972, „betr: Leitartikel der Pekinger ‚Volkszeitung', der ‚roten Fahne' und ‚Armeezeitung' vom 1.1.1972, BAL-SAMPO DY/30/J IV 2/2J-3893, 2.

25. Excerpts from questions asked by CDU/CSU delegate Dr. Evers during a Q&A session of the German Parliament, 8 June 1973, 2268, Drucksache 7/653 Frage A 117, cited in: BAK 136/18091.

26. Telegram, German Embassy Prague, Finckenstein, to German Foreign Office, "Beteiligung West-Berlins an Brünner Maschinenbaumesse," 7 September 1972, BAK 102/241886.

27. News clip, "Interview mit Staatssekretär Egon Bahr für die Sendung 'Echo des Tages' im WDR/NDR am 18. April 1972," BAK 136/16566.

28. Memo, Chancellor's Office, Minister Ehmke, "Aus den Protokollen zum Moskauer Vertrag," n.d., BAK 136/16566. This is a copy of the six pages that opposition leader Barzel handed to Brandt with the request to verify if this was the actual protocol.

29. Telegram, Governing Major of Berlin to Senator for Federal Affairs, "Sowjetische Handels- und Industrieausstellung 1973," 7 May 1973, BAK 136/18091. See also attachment I.

30. Telegram, German Embassy in Moscow, Lüders, to German Foreign Office, "Sowjetische Publikation zum Berlin-Abkommen," 17 May 1973, Mappe 1, Ordner 432, DEB, 4.

31. Ibid., 1-4.

32. MemCon, Henry A. Kissinger to President Nixon, 11 May 1973, folder: "Kissinger's Conversations at Zavidovo, May 5–8, 1973," Box 75, NSCF, NPMS, NA.

33. Jussi Hanhimäki, *The Flawed Architect* (New York: Oxford University Press, 2004), 340–344.

34. James M. Goldgeier, "The United States and the Soviet Union: Lessons of Détente," in: Richard N. Haass and Meghan L. O'Sullivan, eds., *Honey and Vinegar: Incentives, Sanctions, and Foreign Policy* (Washington, D.C.: The Brookings Institution, 2000), 120–136, 125.

35. "Observations on East-West Economic Relations: U.S.S.R. and Poland: A Congressional Trip Report," November-December 1972, Records of the United States Senate, Record Group 46; National Archives, Washington, DC, 2.

36. Ibid., 8.

37. Hanhimäki, *Flawed Architect,* 341. For a strongly anti-Jackson account, see Henry Kissinger, *Years of Renewal* (New York: Simon & Schuster, 1999), 128–135.

38. MemCon, Henry A. Kissinger to President Nixon, 11 May 1973, folder: "Kissinger's Conversations at Zavidovo, May 5–8, 1973," Box 75, NSCF, NPMS, NA.

39. Memo, Egon Bahr, "Nachricht von V. Lednew," 22 March 1973, Mappe 2, Ordner 432, DEB.

40. Letter, Egon Bahr to Henry A. Kissinger, 17 January 1973, Mappe 1, Ordner 439,DEB, and Letter, Henry A. Kissinger to Egon Bahr, 18 January 1973, Mappe 1, Ordner 439, DEB.

41. Letter, President Nixon to Chancellor Brandt via Henry A. Kissinger and Egon Bahr, 3 March 1973, Mappe 1, Ordner 439, DEB.

42. Ibid.

43. MemCon, Conversation Chancellor Brandt with President Nixon at US Embassy in Paris, 6 April 1974, Mappe 2, Ordner 440, DEB, 3.

44. MemCon, Conversation Chancellor Brandt with General Secretary Brezhnev, 20 May 1973, Mappe 1, Ordner 435, DEB, 8–9.

45. MemCon, Conversation Chancellor Brandt with President Nixon at U.S. Embassy in Paris, 6 April 1974, Mappe 2, Ordner 440, DEB, 4–5.

46. Ash, *In Europe's Name,* 68.

47. Letter, Egon Bahr to Chancellor Brandt, 15 April 1973, Mappe 1, Ordner 436, DEB, 1–2.

48. MemCon, Conversation Chancellor Brandt with General Secretary Brezhnev, 20 May 1973, Mappe 1, Ordner 435, DEB, 10–11.
49. MemCon, Conversation Chancellor Brandt with U.S. Ambassador Martin J. Hillenbrand, 22 May 1973, Mappe 1, Ordner 440, DEB, 4.
50. Memo, Economics Ministry, Sanne, "Beteiligung Berliner Firmen an deutsch-sowjetischer Zusammenarbeit," 22 May 1973, BAK 136/18091, 1–2.
51. Talking Points for Brezhnev Visit, "421 – Allgemeine Entwicklung der Wirtschaftsbeziehungen; industrielle Kooperation; Wirtschaftskommission; Großprojekte," 2 May 1973, BAK 102/100026, 1.
52. MemCon, Conversation General Secretary Brezhnev with representatives of German industry on 20 May 1973 in Bonn, BAK 102/100026, 5.
53. Ibid., 4.
54. Ibid., 3.
55. Ibid., 4.
56. Ibid., 5.
57. Talking Points for the German-Soviet Conference, "Mögliche Gesprächsthemen im Bereich der deutsch-sowjetischen Wirtschaftsbeziehungen," 12 July 1973, BAK 102/100002, 2–3.
58. Memo, "Sprechzettel für Messen und Ausstellungen 1974," 19 October 1973, BAK 102/100002, 2–3.
59. For a detailed account of these negotiations see Hanhimäki, *Flawed Architect*, 277–280.
60. Ibid., 277–278.
61. Hedrick Smith, "In Brezhnev's Baggage, A Supply of Ebullience," *New York Times*, 21 June 1973, 1, 17.
62. James Reston, "The Nixon-Brezhnev Promises," *New York Times*, 22 June 1973, 35.
63. Hanhimäki, *Flawed Architect*, 281.
64. Hedrick Smith, "Building of Soviet Pipeline is Falling Behind Schedule," *New York Times*, 24 March 1973, 43.
65. See Hanhimäki, *Flawed Architect*, 276.
66. Flora Lewis, "Europe Reacts Warily to U.S.-Soviet Accords," *New York Times*, 25 June 1973, 17.
67. Attachment to Letter, Egon Bahr to Chancellor Brandt, 30 July 1973, Mappe 2, Ordner 432, DEB.
68. Ibid.
69. Letter, Direktor Osteuropa Institut, Dr. Heinrich Vogel, to Egon Bahr, 26 July 1973, Mappe 2, Ordner 432, DEB.
70. Uwe Engelbrecht, "Breschnew tadelt Bundesrepublik," *Cologneer Stadt-Anzeiger*, 16 August 1973, Mappe 2, Ordner 432, DEB.
71. Draft Letter, Chancellor Brandt to Brezhnev, n.d. [after 16 August 1973], Mappe 2, Ordner 432, DEB.
72. Telegram, German Embassy at the United Nations, Gehlhoff, to the German Foreign Office, "DDR-Erklärung zu Berlin anläßlich IMCO- Beitritts," 1 November 1973, BAK 136/18091.
73. Memo, Economics Ministry, Germelman, to Economics Minister, "Beitritt der DDR zur IMCO," 8 November 1973, BAK 136/18091.

74. Memo, Vermerk 210-505.35, Lücking, Bonn, 9 November 1973, betr: Beitritt der DDR zur IMCO, BAK 136/18091, 3.
75. Ibid.
76. Talking Points for the German-Soviet Conference, "Mögliche Gesprächsthemen im Bereich der deutsch-sowjetischen Wirtschaftsbeziehungen," 12 July 1973, BAK 102/100002, 2–3.
77. Ibid., 6.
78. Memo, "Sprechzettel für Messen und Ausstellungen 1974," October 19, 1973. BAK 102/100002, 2–3. Includes Chart: Soviet Debt to Germany in Million DM

1967	1968	1969	1970	1971	1972	1973 (est.)
230	570	550	1,290	1,250	1,890	3,600

79. Draft Memo, Dr. Barth, "Kursk-Projekt," 18 September 1973, BAK 102/135253, 2.
80. Memo, Dr. Gebert,"Hüttenwerksprojekt Kursk," 26 July 1973, BAK 102/135253, 2.
81. Sodaro argues that it was clear to the Soviet leadership by 1970 that foreign trade would only happen without domestic reform.
82. Michael J. Sodaro, *Moscow, Germany, and the West from Khrushchev to Gorbachev* (Ithaca: Cornell University Press, 1990), 201.
83. Stent, *From Embargo to Ostpolitik,* 178. See also Jochen Bethkenhagen, "Soviet-West German Economic Relations: The West German Perspective" in Angela Stent, ed., *Economic Relations with the Soviet Union: American and West German Perspectives* (Boulder, CO: Westview Press, 1985), 69–89, 87.
84. Memo, "Deutsch-Sowjetische Wirtschaftsbeziehungen," 10 December 1973, BAK 102/100002.
85. Otto Wolff von Amerongen, "Wirtschaftsbeziehungen mit der Sowjetunion," *Osteuropa* 1 (1974): 3–12, 4.
86. Ibid., 5.
87. Ibid., 6–7.
88. Ibid., 8.
89. Memo, "Analyse der Volkswirtschaftlichen Abteilung der Bundesbank," April 1976, Nachlaß Otto Wolff von Amerongen, 72-413-1, RWWA. Also contains the CIA report. For a more detailed illustration of the "difficult year 1975," see Rudolph, *Wirtschaftsdiplomatie im Kalten Krieg,* 325.
90. For a detailed account, see Henry Kissinger, *Years of Upheaval* (Boston: Little, Brown, 1982), 450–467.
91. Letter, Brezhnev to Nixon, 24 October 1973, folder: "Dobrynin/Kissinger Vol. 20 (October 12–November 27)," Box 69, HAK Office Files, NPMP, NA, 1–2.
92. Coit D. Blacker, "The Kremlin and Détente: Soviet Conceptions, Hopes, and Expectations," in Alexander L. George, ed., *Managing U.S.-Soviet Rivalry* (Boulder, CO: Westview Press, 1983), 119–137.
93. Kissinger, *Years of Upheaval,* 708.
94. Ibid., 710.
95. "Bonn Bids U.S. Halt Arms to Israel Via Germany," *New York Times,* 26 October 1973, 20.

96. Kissinger, *Years of Upheaval,* 714.

97. David Binder, "Bonn Is Singled Out," *Special to The New York Times,* 27 October 1973, 65.

98. Cable, U.S. Embassy in Bonn to State Department, "Secretary's Meeting with FRG Ambassador von Staden, October 26," 27 October 1973, RG 59, SN 70–73, POL 7 US/Kissinger, NA.

99. John W. Finney, "U.S. Reports Accord With Bonn on Shipments to Israel," *Special to The New York Times,* 13 November 1973, 13.

100. Letter, Egon Bahr to Chancellor Brandt, 31 October 1973, Mappe 2, Bundeskanzler, WBA, 1.

101. Letter, Minister Bahr to Chancellor Brandt, November 9, 1973, Mappe 190, Bundeskanzler, WBA, 1.

102. Letter, Egon Bahr to Chancellor Brandt, Bonn, 14 December 1973, Mappe 1, Ordner 436, DEB.

103. Letter, Minister Bahr to Chancellor Brandt, 9 November 1973, Mappe 190, Bundeskanzler, WBA, 1.

104. Letter, Minister Bahr to Chancellor Brandt, 5 November 1973, Mappe 190, Bundeskanzler, WBA, 1.

105. Ibid., 2–3.

106. Letter, Chancellor Brandt to Prime Minister Brezhnev, 7 November 1973, Mappe 1, Ordner 432, DEB.

107. Letter, Henry A. Kissinger to Finance Minister, Helmut Schmidt, n.d. [after 5 November 1973], Mappe 1, Ordner 436, DEB.

108. Letter, President Nixon to Chancellor Brandt, 15 March 1974, Mappe 2, Ordner 440, DEB, 3.

109. Telegram, German Ambassador in Moscow, Sahm, to German Foreign Office, "Gespräch O. A. Friderichs mit Kossygin," 5 October 1973, BAK 102/135258.

110. Ibid.

111. Telegram, German Ambassador in Moscow, Sahm, to German Foreign Office, "Besuch Bundesbankpräsident Klasen in der SU," 12 October 1973, BAK 102/135258, 2.

112. Letter, Otto A. Friedrich to Economics Minister Friderichs, "Zusammenfassende Notiz über einen Besuch in Moskau vom 1. bis 5. Oktober 1973," 17 October 1973, BAK 102/135258, 2–3.

113. Ibid., 4.

114. MemCon, "Conversation between Todor Zhivkov –Leonid I. Brezhnev, Voden Residence [Bulgaria]," 20 September 1973, Central State Archive, Sofia, Fond 378-B, File 360, quoted from CWIHP.

115. Memo, "Sprechzettel für Messen und Ausstellungen 1974," 19 October 1973, BAK 102/100002, 1–3.

116. Letter, Chief Editor, *Industriemagazin,* Peter K. Pernutz, to Berthold Beitz, 29 November 1973, Mappe „Ernst Wolf Mommsen," Ordner 108, DEB.

117. Letter, Economics Minister Friderichs to Chancellor Brandt, 6 December 1973, BAK 102/135253, 1–2.

118. Letter, Chancellor Brandt to Economics Minister Friderichs, n.d. [before 10 December 1973], BAK 102/135253.

119. Letter, Chairs of Salzgitter, Krupp, Korf Konsortium, Hans Birnbaum, Willy Korf, and Ernst Mommsen to Economics Minister Friderichs, 17 December 1973, BAK 102/135253, 3–4.

120. Letter, Minister Heinz-Herbert Karry to Economics Minister Friderichs, "Tagung der deutsch-sowjetischen Kommission für wissenschaftlich-technische Zusammenarbeit," 18 January 1974, BAK 102/99998, 2.

121. Memo, "Resumé der Ansprache des stellv. Vorsitzenden des Ministerrats der UdSSR Nowikow am 15.1.1974 anläßlich einer Weinprobe im Kloster Eberbach," 15 January 1974, BAK 102/99998, 3.

122. MemCon, Chancellor Brandt with Deputy Chair of the Ministerial Council of the Soviet Union, Novikov, on 18 January 1974, BAK 102/99998, 9.

123. Rudolph, *Wirtschaftsdiplomatie im Kalten Krieg*, 318.

124. Telegram, German Embassy in Moscow to German Foreign Office, "dritte Tagung Wirtschaftskommission," 21 January 1974, BAK 102/99998; Telegram, German Embassy in Moscow to German Foreign Office, "Gespräche von Bundesminister Bahr in Moskau," 3 February 1974, BAK 102/99998.

125. Letter, Chair, Salzgitter Corp, Hans Birnbaum, to Finance Ministry Undersecretary Hans Hermsdorf, "Projekt Kursk," 5 February 1974, Mappe 1, Ordner 432, DEB.

126. Letter, Economics Minister Friderichs to Chancellor Brandt, 27 February 1974, Mappe 1, Ordner 433, DEB.

127. Letter, Chair, Krupp GmbH, Ernst Wolf Mommsen, to Chancellor Brandt, 2 April 1974, BAK 102/135253.

128. Letter, Chancellor Brandt to General Secretary Brezhnev, 14 March 1974, Mappe 1, Ordner, 433, DEB.

129. Memo, Economics Ministry, Gayman, "Ausfuhr eines Hüttenwerks in die UdSSR (Kursk)," 25 October 1974, BAK 102/135253, 1–2; Telegram, German Ambassador to Moscow, Sahm, to German Foreign Office, "Hüttenwerk Kursk," 13 December 1974, BAK 102/ 135253.

130. MemCon, General Secretary Brezhnev with Representatives of German Industry, 20 May 1973, Bonn, BAK 102/100026, 2–5.

131. Talking Points for the Brezhnev Visit, "413 – Bezug von angereichertem Uran aus der Sowjetunion," 2 May 1973, BAK 102/100026, 1.

132. Memo, RD Kreuzberg to MinDir Kleindienst, "Sprechzettel für den Breschnew-Besuch," 3 May 1973, BAK 102/100026.

133. MemCon, Conversation Chancellor Brandt with Deputy Chair of the Ministerial Council of the Soviet Union, Novikov, 18 January 1974, BAK 102/99998, 4.

134. Memo, Ministerialrat Bernhard Kahl, "Bericht über die am 16. und 17. Januar 1974 durchgeführten Dienstreisen Nr. 131/74 und Nr. 137/74 nach Erlangen und Mülheim/Ruhr," 5 February 1974, BAK 102/99998, 2–3.

135. Telegram, German Embassy in Moscow to German Foreign Office, "Gespräche von Bundesminister Bahr in Moskau," 2 March 1974, BAK 102/99998.

136. COCOM Record of Discussion, COCOM Doc (74) 2018, 15 October 1974, BAK 102/135253, 2; Telegram, Dr. Rupprecht to Diplogerma, Dr. Schroembgens, "Ausfuhr eines 1300 MW Kernkraftwerks in die UdSSR," 21 October 1974, BAK 102/135253.

137. Letter, Diplogerma, Dr. Schroembgens, to Economics Ministry, "COCOM," 18 October 1974, BAK 102/135253, 2.
138. Telegram, German Embassy in Moscow to German Foreign Office, "dritte Tagung Wirtschaftskommission," 21 January 1974, BAK 102/99998; Telegram, German Embassy in Moscow to German Foreign Office, "Gespräche von Bundesminister Bahr in Moskau," 3 February 1974, BAK 102/99998.
139. Rudolph, *Wirtschaftsdiplomatie im Kalten Krieg,* 318.
140. Memo, Dr. Jahnke, "Deutsch-sowjetische Wirtschaftsbeziehungen," 25 April 1974, BAK 102/100002.

Chapter 5

1. Cabinet Meeting Minutes, 8 January 1975, Box 3, James E. Connor Files, Gerald R. Ford Presidential Library [FPL], 16.
2. Ibid., 15.
3. Dobrynin, *In Confidence,* 268.
4. For more details on the Stevenson amendment, see Funigiello, *American-Soviet Trade in the Cold War,* 188–189.
5. Peter Osnos, "Soviets Renew Criticism of U.S. But Continue to Endorse Détente," *Washington Post,* 15 January 1975, A1.
6. As quoted in Marilyn Berger, "Soviets Nullify '72 Pact; Call Terms Of Trade Law Discriminatory Soviets Refuse Trade Terms," *Washington Post,* 15 January 1975, A1. See also Victor Zorza, "Trade, Emigration and Detente," *Washington Post,* 16 January 1975, A23.
7. President Ford's State of the Union Address, 15 January 1975, as quoted in <http://www.janda.org/politxts/State%20of%20Union%20Addresses/1975-1977%20Ford%20T/GRF75.html>.
8. John Lewis Gaddis argues that because of Watergate, Ford had to strictly abide by the law and had no choice but to go through Congress in order to fund the pro-American Angolan National Front. Congress promptly opposed any kind of U.S. support, leaving Angola in Moscow's hands. *The Cold War,* 176–179.
9. Gallup polls on 9 July 1974, 25 February 75, and 18 November 1975.
10. Michael Kreile, "West Germany: The Dynamics of Expansion," in *International Organization* 31, no. 4, *Between Power and Plenty: Foreign Economic Policies of Advanced Industrial States,* (Autumn 1977): 775–808, 792.
11. Juergen Kellermeier, ed., *Deutschland 1976: Zwei Sozialdemokraten im Gespraech* (Hamburg: Rowohlt Taschenbuch Verlag, 1976), 138–139.
12. MemCon between Comrade Honecker and L.I. Brezhnev at the meeting of the Soviet party and government delegation with the politburo of the central committee of the SED, 8 October 1974, BAL-SAMPO DY/30/IV 2/201, 1581, 6.
13. Ibid., 7.
14. Helmut Schmidt, *Menschen und Maechte* (Berlin: Siedler Verlag, 1987), 58.
15. Ibid., 59.

16. Kreile, "West Germany," 791.
17. Theodore Shabad, "Soviet Opens Big Natural-Gas Field Relatively Near to Markets in Europe," *New York Times*, 20 February 1974, 51.
18. MemCon, "Comrade L.I. Brezhnev with Leaders of Fraternal Parties of Socialist Countries in Budapest," 18 March 1975, National Security Archives [NSArch], 3.
19. Ibid., 3.
20. Heinrich Machowski, "Soviet-West German Economic Relations: The Soviet Perspective," in Stent, *Economic Relations with the Soviet Union*, 49–67, 49.
21. See also Hanson, 156. He sees much of this redirection of resources based on the lucrative price of oil and gas in the wake of the 1973 energy crisis.
22. Memo, 19 February 1974, BAL-SAMPO DL/2/ KOKO/1394, 548.
23. Vorlage fuer das Politbuero des ZK der SED, Horst Sindermann, betr "Errichtung einer Raffinerie mit einem Jahresdurchsatz von 3 Mio t Erdoel," Berlin, 10 April 1972, BAL-SAMPO DY/30-2825.
24. Letter, Wambutt to Dr. Mittag, Abt Grundstoffindustrie, Berlin, 5 December 1972, BAL-SAMPO DY/30-2825,1–2.
25. Memo, Deputy Minister Behrendt, SV, "Information: Verhandlungen mit Kleindienst ueber den wetiteren Export von Mineraloelerzeugnisen der DDR nach Berlin (West) und in die BRD," Berlin, 22 December 1975, DY/30-2825,1-21-2.
26. MemCon of conversation between Gerhard Schuerer and Tichonov on July 31, 1974 in Moscow. Secret. BAL-SAMPO DL/2/ KOKO/1394, 2.
27. "East Germany Growing Economic Problems," *The National Intelligence Daily*, 29 August 1977, Remote Archives Capture Project [RAC] NLC-12-57-2-8-6 1-3, 2–3.
28. Memo, Lücking, "Einbeziehung Berlins in multilaterale Verträge," 19 March 1974, BAK 136/18091.
29. Memo, Lücking, "Protest der DDR gegen die Einbeziehung von Berlin (West) in das IAEO-Statut," 19 March 1974, BAK 136/18091; Telegram, Genf and Herbst, to German Foreign Office, "Proteste der DDR gegen die Einbeziehung Berlins (West) in multilaterale Verträge," 2 April 1974, BAK 136/18091.
30. MemCon, Minister Bahr and Deputy Foreign Secretary Rush, 31 January 1974, Mappe 2, Ordner 302, DEB, 1.
31. Letter, General Secretary Brezhnev to Chancellor Brandt, 9 February 1974, Mappe 1, Ordner 432, DEB.
32. Memo, Lueders, "Konsultation mit den vier aliierten Botschaftern," 28 February 1974, Mappe 1, Ordner, 433, DEB.
33. MemCon, Egon Bahr with Brezhnev in Moscow, 27 February 1974, Mappe 2, Ordner 433, DEB, 9–10.
34. Telegram, German Embassy in Vienna, Dungern, to German Foreign Office, "Berlin-Klausel in deutsch-österreichischen Verträgen," 17 April 1974, BAK 136/18091, 1.
35. Ibid.
36. MemCon, "Gespräche zwischen Herrn D2 und Botschafter Steiner," 22 December 1975, BAK 136/18091.

37. Harry Schleicher, "Formel 'Land Berlin' bleibt: Österreicher wollen Moskau und Bonn zufrieden stellen," *Frankfurter Rundschau,* 22 December 1976, 2.
38. MemCon, "Comrade L.I. Brezhnev with Leaders of Fraternal Parties of Socialist Countries in Budapest," 18 March 1975. NSArch, 5.
39. Ibid., 6.
40 CIA Directorate of Intelligence, Intelligence Report "Soviet Thinking About the Danger of a Sino-US Rapprochement," February 1971, <http://www.foia.cia.gov/cpe.asp>, ESAU Document #56, ii.
41. Kissinger, *Years of Renewal,* 636.
42. Cabinet Meeting, 8 August 1975, Memorandum of Conversation, 8/8/75, Box 14, National Security Adviser, Memoranda of Conversations, FPL.
43. Dobrynin, *In Confidence,* 346. Also see William G. Hyland, *Mortal Rivals* (New York: Simon & Schuster, 1987), 114–119.
44. "East Germany Growing Economic Problems," *National Intelligence Daily,* 29 August 1977, RAC NLC-12-57-2-8-6 1-3, 1–2. Also see Figure 1.
45. "USSR: Improving Hard Currency Trade and Payments Position," CIA National Foreign Assessment Center, April 1978, RAC NLC-12-57-1-14-0, 1.
46. MemCon, "Comrade L.I. Brezhnev with Leaders of Fraternal Parties of Socialist Countries in Budapest," 18 March 1975. NSArch, 6.
47. Telegram, German Foreign Office to German Embassy in Washington, "Östliche Proteste gegen die Erstreckung des V-Vertrages auf Berlin," 9 October 1975, BAK 136/18091.
48. Telegram, German Embassy in Bucharest, Mehr, to German Foreign Office, "Rumänien verweigert Einbeziehung Berlins, betr: Abschluß wissenschaftlich-technischen Teilabkommens," 6 March 1975, BAK 136/18091.
49. Memo, Economics Ministry, Sanne, to Chancellor Schmidt, "Artikel von MD van Well im Europa-Archiv," 27 October 1976, B 136/19209, 1–2.
50. Ibid.
51. Ibid., 2–3.
52. Telegram, German Ambassador in Belgrade, von Puttkamer, to German Foreign Office, "Jugoslawische Haltung zu Berlin," 12 June 1978, BAK 136/19209, 2–6.
53. Cabinet Meeting, 29 June 1976, Memorandum of Conversation, 6/29/76, Box 20, National Security Adviser. Memoranda of Conversations, FPL, 2.
54. NSC NSSM #237, subject: U.S. International Energy Policy, 5 February 1976, Box 2, National Security Decision Memoranda and Study Memoranda, FPL, 1–2.
55. NSC NSSM #247, subject: U.S. Policy Toward East-West Economic Relations, 18 October 1976, Box 2, National Security Decision Memoranda and Study Memoranda, FPL, 1–2.
56. President Ford's State of the Union Address 1977, as quoted in <http://www.janda.org/politxts/State%20of%20Union%20Addresses/1975-1977%20Ford%20T/GRF77.html>.
57. "Carter," *Der Spiegel* (45/1976), 1 November 1976, 148.
58. Dan Caldwell, "US Domestic Politics and the Demise of Détente," in Odd Arne Westad, ed., *The Fall of Détente: Soviet-American Relations during the*

Carter Years, Nobel Symposium 95 (Oslo: Scandinavian University Press, 1997), 99–107.

59. "Transcript of Foreign Affairs Debate Between Ford and Carter," *New York Times,* 7 October 1976, 36–38, 38.
60. "Carter Suggests That U.S. Foster Rights Overseas," *New York Times,* 9 September 1976, 32.
61. Inaugural Address by President Jimmy Carter, 20 January 1977. Source: <http://www.re-quest.net/history/inaugurals/carter/index.htm>.
62. "Western Europe's Reaction," *New York Times,* 22 January 1977, 11.
63. While U.S. exports to the Soviet Union had continued to rise after a dip in 1974, this was partially due to Soviet grain purchases and partially due to residual deals negotiated in earlier years. For this, see Funigiello, *American-Soviet Trade in the Cold War,* 189.
64. Bernard Gwerzman, "U.S. Again Comments on Soviet Dissident," *New York Times,* 8 February 1977, 65.
65. Letter, President Carter to General Secretary Leonid I. Brezhnev, 15 February 1977, CWIHP.
66. "Carter Spins the World," *Time,* 8 August 1977, 7.
67. Letter, Brezhnev to Carter, 4 February 1977, CWIHP.
68. CPSU Central Committee Politburo Decision "About the Instruction to the Soviet Ambassador," 18 February 1977, CWIHP, 1. Ginzburg and other high profile Soviet dissidents were part of the "Helsinki Group," a self-proclaimed watchdog organization monitoring the Soviet Union's compliance with the Helsinki Accords.
69. "Gerechtigkeit in einer sündigen Welt," *Der Spiegel* (16/1977), 11 April 1977, 106–107.
70. Ibid., 117–118.
71. Ibid., 117.
72. Ibid., 120.
73. Ibid., 122.
74. For a detailed treatment of these issues, see Klaus Wiegrefe, *Das Zerwuerfnis: Helmut Schmidt, Jimmy Carter und die Kriese der deutsch-amerikanischen Beziehungen* (Berlin: Propylaen, 2005), 71–122.
75. Ibid., 126–127.
76. Schmidt, *Menschen und Maechte,* 222.
77. Letter, President Carter to Chancellor Schmidt, 29 April 1977, NSArch, Brzezinski Material, President's Correspondence With Foreign Leaders File, Fiji through Germany, Federal Republic of, Folder: "Germany, Federal Republic of: Chancellor Helmut Schmidt," Box 6, Carter Presidential Library [CPL], 2–4.
78. "SCHMIDT-REISE: Missionarischer Eifer," *Der Spiegel* (29/1977), 11 July 1977, 28.
79. "Carter Policy Attacked by President Giscard," *The London Times,* 19 July 1977, 1.
80. "SCHMIDT-REISE: Kleines Mirakel," *Der Spiegel* (30/1977), 18 July 1977, 28. On "Enemy of Détente," see "Russia Sees Mr. Carter as 'Enemy of Détente,'" *The London Times,* 8 June 1977, 9.

81. "Bonn Indicates Moscow Is Displeased With Carter," *New York Times*, 7 July 1977, 2.
82. "Carter Surprised at Russian Anger," *The London Times*, 27 June 1977, 6.
83. "Summit 'Discussed' in Carter-Brezhnev Exchange of Messages," *The London Times*, 5 July 1977, 8.
84. "SCHMIDT-REISE: Kleines Mirakel," *Der Spiegel* (30/1977), 18 July 1977, 28.
85. Ibid.
86. David Cross, "Mr. Carter Admits Russia Unlikely to Move on Human Rights," *The London Times*, 22 July 1977, 1.
87. Letter, Carter to Brezhnev, 14 February 1977, CWIHP; Record of Conversation between Soviet Foreign Minister Gromyko and President Carter, 23 September 1977, CWIHP 1–6.
88. Ibid., 4.
89. "Is President Carter Wising Up to the Ways of Washington?" *The London Times*, 3 November 1977, 14.
90. David Cross, "Mr. Carter Accuses Russia of Continued Human Rights Abuses," *The London Times*, 7 December 1977, 6.
91. "BONN/WASHINGTON: Nichts als Verachtung," *Der Spiegel* (8/1978), 20 February 1978, 30.
92. Ibid., 31.
93. Svetlana Savranskaya, "Unintended Consequences: Soviet Interests, Expectations and Reactions to the Helsinki Conference," in Bange and Niedhart, *Helsinki 1975*, 186f.
94. Juergen Leinemann, "Der Genuß, Carter selbst zu erleben," *Der Spiegel*, 5 June 1978, 118–120, 118.
95. "Carter und Schmidt: Neue Sachlichkeit," *Der Spiegel*, 17 July 1978, 19.
96. "Speech of the President on Soviet-American Relations at the U.S. Naval Academy," *New York Times*, 8 June 1978, A22.
97. David Cross, "Mr. Carter Risks Anger of 'Hawks' over More Talks with Russia," *The London Times*, 18 July 1978, 5.
98. "'Vendetta' on Russia Denied by Mr. Carter," *New York Times*, 21 July 1978, 1.
99. David Cross, "Mr. Carter Plans No More Reprisals over Soviet Dissident Trials," *The London Times*, 22 July 1978, 6.
100. Political Letter of Soviet Ambassador to the United States Anatoly F. Dobrynin, 11 July 1978, CWIHP, 2.
101. Ibid.
102. Speech by L. I. Brezhnev to CPSU CC Politburo, 8 June 1978, CWIHP, 1–2.
103. Ibid., 2.
104. "Sowjet-Union kürzt Öl- und Gas-Ausfuhr," *Der Spiegel* (11/1979), 12 March 1979, 129.
105. Memorandum from William E. Odom to Zbigniew Brzezinski, Subject: "Weekly Report on Soviet Affairs," 16 July 1979, RAC NLC-6-81-4-20-0, 2.
106. Ibid., 1.

107. The SPD functionary and Bundestag member Herbert Wehner started a nationwide debate when he claimed that the Soviet military might was defensive in nature. See "Die Sowjets sind keine Teufel," *Der Spiegel* (13/1979), 26 March 1979, 31.

108. John Vinocur, "Target Europe," *New York Times,* 21 October 1979, E1.

109. The United States Information Agency was renamed United States International Communication Agency during the Carter Administration and reverted to its original name in 1982. The USICA survey is found in "Western European Views on Key Issues: Troubled US-European Economic Relations," 15 June 1979, RAC NLC-4-23-3-11-7, 1.

110. Ibid., 3.

111. Memorandum, Central Intelligence Agency, National Foreign Assessment Center, Subject: "Changing Power Relations among OECD States," 22 October 1979, RAC NLC-7-16-10-14-1, 1.

112. Ibid., 11.

113. Ibid., 14.

114. Odd Arne Westad, "The Road to Kabul: Soviet Policy on Afghanistan, 1978–1979," in Westad, *The Fall of Détente: Soviet-American Relations during the Carter Years* (Oslo: Scandinavian University Press: 1997), 141.

115. David Cross, "Soviet Role in Kabul Threat to Peace, Mr. Carter Declares," *The London Times,* 29 December 1979, 1.

116. Memo from Stuart Eizenstat to President Carter, "Proposed Grain Embargo," 3 January 1980, CF O/A #743, "Soviet Grain Embargo, 10/75-1/15/1980," Box 2 of 3, CPL.

117. Memo from Alonzo McDonald to Carter, "Commercial Sanctions," 4 January 1980, CF O/A #743, "Soviet Grain Embargo, 10/75- 1/15/1980," Box 2 of 3, 1, CPL.

118. Ibid., 2.

119. Funigiello, *American-Soviet Trade in the Cold War,* 191.

120. "France against Any Steps in Retaliation," *The London Times,* 7 January 1980, 4.

121. CIA National Foreign Assessment Center, 15 January 1980, "Review of Soviet Internal Affairs," RAC NLC-12-59-5-10-8, 4–5.

122. Telegram, 11 January 1980, Sec. State to Ambassador FRG, Subject: "Presidential Message to Chancellor Schmidt," NSA Brzezinski Material, Presidents Correspondence with Foreign Leaders, Germany, Federal Republic through Guatemala, Germany, Folder: "Federal Republic of: Chancellor Schmidt, 1-2/80," CPL, 2.

123. Ibid., 4.

124. CPSU CC Politburo Decision, with Report by Gromyko-Andropov-Ustinov-Ponomarev, 27 January 1980, CWIHP, 2.

125. Letter, Chancellor Schmidt to President Carter, 21 January 1980, NSA Brzezinski Material, Presidents Correspondence with Foreign Leaders, Germany, Federal Republic through Guatemala, Germany, Folder: "Federal Republic of: Chancellor Schmidt, 1-2/80," CPL.

126. Schmidt, *Menschen und Maechte,* 252–253.

127. Michael Binjon, "Soviets Move to Liquidate Dissent," *The London Times*, 25 January 1980, 6.

128. Memo, Secretary of Agriculture Robert Bergland to President Carter, 14 March 1980, "Suspension of Grain Exports to the USSR," Folder: "Soviet Grain Embargo, 2/25/1980 to 9/80," CF O/A #743, Box 2 of 3, CPL, 2.

129. Ibid., 1.

130. Ibid., 4.

131. Letter, Carter to Schmidt, 27 March 1980, NSA Brzezinski Material, Presidents Correspondence with Foreign Leaders, Germany, Federal Republic through Guatemala, Germany, Folder: "Federal Republic of: Chancellor Schmidt, 3-8/80," CPL.

132. "USA: Gilt nicht mehr," *Der Spiegel* (13/1980), 24 March 1980, 129.

133. "USA:/Europa:Wir haben die Schnauze voll," *Der Spiegel* (27/1980), 30 June 1980, 100.

134. "Nach der Moskau-Reise von Helmut Schmidt: Das lief in Moskau – Zukker," *Der Spiegel* (28/1980), 7 July 1980, 2–3.

135. Letter, Dana I. Robinson, General Manager Exclusitrade to NSC Member Brigadier General William Odom, Subject: Export Control over U.S. Technology to USSR, 19 October 1980, RAC NLC-12-49-10-7-7, 3.

136. Ibid., 5–6.

137. Funigiello, *American-Soviet Trade in the Cold War*, 194.

138. "Soviet Energy Exports and Western European Energy Security," Hearing before the Subcommittee on Energy, Nuclear Proliferation, and Government Processes of the Committee on Governmental Affairs, United States Senate, 14 October 1981, Records of the United States Senate, Record Group 46; National Archives, Washington, DC., 2.

139. Ibid., 3–4.

140. Helmut Schmidt, *Die Deutschen und ihre Nachbarn: Menschen und Maechte II* (Berlin: Siedler Verlag, 1990), 260.

141. Bernard Gwertzman, "U.S. and Bonn Said to Agree to Avoid 'Crisis' in West," *New York Times*, 5 January 1982, A6.

142. William Safire, "The Kremlin Pipeline," *New York Times*, 3 January 1982, E19.

143. John Maclean, "No Soviet Grain Embargo – Haig," *New York Times*, 7 January 1982, 4.

144. "France, W. Germany Take Stand on Poland," *Chicago Tribune*, 14 January 1982, A6.

145. William Safire, "Helmut's Pipeline," *New York Times*, 19 February 1982, A31.

146. Dan Morgan and Bradley Graham, "Anti-Soviet Sanctions Trouble W. Germans," *Washington Post*, 23 March 1982, A1.

147. Helmut Schmidt's speech before the Bundestag on 25 June 1982, as quoted in Clyde H. Farnsworth, "Soviet-Europe Gas Pact Split U.S. Aides," *New York Times*, 26 June 1982, 6.

148. John Vinocur, "Many are the Ways to Measure Allied Trade With Eastern Bloc," *New York Times*, 17 January 1982, E3.

149. William Safire, "The Sakhalin Deal," *New York Times*, 28 May 1982, A27.

150. Dusko Doder, "West Germans Grant Soviets Pipeline Loan," *Washington Post*, 14 July 1982, A1.
151. Josef Joffe, "Europe and America: The Politics of Resentment (Cont'd)," in *Foreign Affairs* vol. 61,3 (Spring 1983): 569–590, 571f. The figures cited in this article rely on a study by Wharton Econometric Forecasting Associates, "Comparative Advantage in Soviet Grain and Energy Trade," Washington, D.C., 10 September 1982.
152. Heller and Nekrich, *Utopia in Power*, 647–648.
153. Bruce Jentleson, *Pipeline Politics: The Complex Political Economy of East-West Energy Trade* (Ithaca, NY: Cornell University Press, 1986).

Chapter 6

1. See Bruce Jentleson, *Pipeline Politics: The Complex Political Economy of East-West Energy Trade* (Ithaca, NY: Cornell University Press, 1986).
2. Rudolph, *Wirtschaftsdiplomatie im Kalten Krieg*, 322.

 # BIBLIOGRAPHY

Unpublished Primary Sources

Amerongen, Otto Wolff von (Nachlass). Rheinisch-Westfälisches Wirtschafts-archiv, Cologne.

Auswärtiges Amt (Correspondence 1966–1974). Politisches Archiv des Auswärtigen Amts, Berlin.

Bahr, Egon (Depositorium). Archiv der sozialen Demokratie der Friedrich-Ebert-Stiftung, Bonn.

Brandt, Willy (Nachlass). Willy Brandt Archiv, Archiv der sozialen Demokratie der Friedrich-Ebert-Stiftung, Bonn.

Bundeskanzleramt (Correspondence 1969–1975). Bundesarchiv Koblenz.

Bundeswirtschaftsministerium (Correspondence 1966–1975). Bundesarchiv Koblenz.

CIA Directorate of Intelligence. The CAESAR, POLO, ESAU Papers, online at <http://www.foia.cia.gov/cpe.asp>.

Gerald L. Ford Presidential Library, Ann Arbor, MI.

Jimmy Carter Presidential Library, Atlanta, GA.

Kissinger, Henry A. TELCONS, National Archives II, College Park, MD.

Mannesmann Röhrenwerke (Business Correspondence and Board Meetings). Mannesmann Archiv, Mülheim an der Ruhr.

Nixon Project (White House Documents). National Archives II, College Park, MD.

Remote Archives Capture Project (RAC). National Archives. College Park, MD.

Records of the United States Senate, National Archives, Washington, DC.

Richard Nixon Library and Birthplace Foundation. "Transcripts of Newly Released White House Tapes." 24 May 2005.

Stiftung Archiv Massenorganisationen und Parteien der DDR. SAMPO, Bundesarchiv Licherfelde.

U.S. Department of State. RG 59, National Archives II, College Park, MD.

Published Primary Sources

Auswärtiges Amt, ed. *Aussenpolitik der Bundesrepublik Deutschland: Dokumente von 1949–1994.* Cologne: Verlag Wissenschaft & Politik, 1995.

Böhme, Erich, and Klaus Wirtgen, eds. *Willy Brandt: Die Spiegel-Gespräche 1959–1992.* Stuttgart: Deutsche Verlags-Anstalt, 1993.

Cold War International History Project. Virtual Archive. Woodrow Wilson Center, Washington, D.C.

Drescher, S. H., ed. *EMNID-Informatonen*, vols. 21–23. Bielefeld, Emnid-Institut GmbH &Co, 1969–1971.

For the People's Peace and Security: Foreign Policy Documents, 1972]. Moscow : Izd-vo Politicheskoi literatury, 1989.

Gallup Organization, ed. *The Gallup Poll*. CD-ROM. Wilmington, DE: Scholarly Resources, 1997.

Jacobsen, Hans-Adolf, and Tomala Mieczyslaw, eds.. *Bonn und Warschau 1945– 1991: Die deutsch-polnischen Beziehungen—Analyse und Dokumentation*. Cologne: Verlag Wissenschaft & Politik, 1992.

Kellermeier, Juergen, ed., *Deutschland 1976: Zwei Sozialdemokraten im Gespraech*. Hamburg: Rowohlt Taschenbuch Verlag, 1976.

Link, Horst Günther, ed. *Quellen zu den deutsch-sowjetischen Beziehungen: 1945– 1991*. Darmstadt: Wissenschaftliche Buchgesellschaft, 1999.

Maerz, Peter, ed. *Dokumente zu Deutschland: 1944–1994*. Munich: Olzog Verlag, 1996.

Meissner, Boris, ed. *Moskau Bonn: Die Beziehungen zwischen der Sowjetunion und der Bundesrepublik Deutschland. 1955–1973. Dokumentation*, vol. 2. Cologne: Verlag Wissenschaft & Politik, 1975.

The National Security Archives. George Washington University, Washington, D.C.

Noelle-Neumann, Elisabeth, ed. *Jahrbuch der öffentlichen Meinung: 1968–1973*. Allensbach: Verlag für Demoskopie, 1974.

Public Papers of the President of the United States: John F. Kennedy, 1963. Washington, D.C.: United States Government Printing Office, 1964.

Public Papers of the President of the United States: Richard Nixon, 1969–1973. 5 vols. Washington, D.C.: United States Government Printing Office, 1971–1975.

Statistical Yearbook, Department of International Economic and Social Affairs. Statistical Office, United Nations, New York, 1969–1987.

U.S. Department of State. *Foreign Relations Series (FRUS)*. Washington, D.C.

Memoirs, Diaries, Interviews

Adenauer, Konrad. *Erinnerungen*. Frankfurt a. M.: Fischer Bücherei, 1967.

Bahr, Egon. *Zu meiner Zeit*. Munich: Karl Blessing Verlag, 1996.

Barzel, Rainer. *Im Streit und umstritten: Anmerkungen zu Konrad Adenauer, Ludwig Erhard und den Ostverträgen*. Frankfurt a. M.: Ullstein, 1986.

Birrenbach, Kurt. *Meine Sondermissionen: Rückblick auf zwei Jahrzehnte bundesdeutscher Aussenpolitik*. Dusseldorf: Econ Verlag, 1984.

Brandt, Willy. *Ordeal of Coexistence*. Cambridge, MA: Harvard University Press, 1963.

———. *A Peace Policy for Europe*. New York: Holt, Rinehart and Winston, 1969.

———. *Bundeskanzler Brandt: Reden und Interviews*. Hamburg: Hoffmann und Campe Verlag, 1971.

———. *People and Politics: The Years 1960–1975*. Boston: Little, Brown, 1978.

———. *Erinnerungen*. Zürich: Propyläen, 1989.

Christians, F. Wilhelm. *Wege nach Russland: Bankier im Spannungsfeld zwischen Ost und West*. Hamburg, Germany: Hoffmann und Campe, 1989.

Dobrynin, Anatoly. *In Confidence: Moscow's Ambassador to America's Six Cold War Presidents (1962–1986)*. New York: Random House, 1995.

Falin, Valentin. *Politische Erinnerungen*. Munich: Knaur, 1995.

Gromyko, Andrei. *Memoirs*. London: Hutchinson, 1989.

Hillenbrand, Martin J. *Fragments of Our Time: Memoirs of a Diplomat*. Athens: The University of Georgia Press, 1998.

Keworkow, Wjatscheslaw. *Der geheime Kanal: Moskau, der KGB und die Bonner Ostpolitik*. Berlin: Rowohlt, 1995.

Kissinger, Henry. *American Foreign Policy*. New York: Norton, 1977.

———. *The White House Years*. Boston: Little, Brown, 1979.

———. *Years of Upheaval*. Boston: Little, Brown, 1982.

———. *Diplomacy*. New York: Simon & Schuster, 1994.

———. *Years of Renewal*. New York: Simon & Schuster, 1999.

Nixon, Richard. *The Memoirs of Richard Nixon*. New York: Grosset & Dunlap, 1978.

Schmidt, Helmut. *Menschen und Maechte*. Berlin: Siedler Verlag, 1987.

———. *Die Deutschen und ihre Nachbarn: Menschen und Maechte II*. Berlin: Siedler Verlag, 1990.

Secondary Literature

Adler-Karlsson, Gunnar. *Western Economic Warfare 1947–1967: A Case Study in Foreign Economic Policy*. Stockholm: Almquist & Wiksell, 1968.

Ambrose, Stephen E. *Nixon, vol 1: The Education of a Politician, 1913–1962*. New York: Simon & Schuster, 1987.

———. *Nixon, vol 2: The Triumph of a Politician, 1962–1972*. New York: Simon & Schuster, 1989.

Ash, Timothy Garton. *In Europe's Name: Germany and the Divided Continent*. New York: Random House, 1993.

Bange, Oliver and Gottfried Niedhart, eds., *Helsinki 1975 and the Transformation of Europe*. New York: Berghahn Books, 2008.

Bender, Peter. *Neue Ostpolitik: Vom Mauerbau bis zum Moskauer Vertrag*. Munich: Deutscher Taschenbuch Verlag, 1986.

Berghahn, Volker R., ed. *Quest for Economic Empire: European Strategies of German Big Business in the Twentieth Century*. Providence, RI: Berghahn Books, 1996.

Bertsch, Gary K. *East-West Strategic Trade, COCOM and the Atlantic Alliance*. Totowa, NJ: Allenheld, Osmun, 1983.

———. *Controlling East-West Trade and Technology Transfer: Power, Politics, and Policies*. Durham, NC: Duke University Press, 1988.

Birnbaum, Karl E. *Peace in Europe: East-West Relations 1966–1968 and the Prospects for a European Settlement*. Oxford: Oxford University Press, 1970.

―――. *East and West Germany: A Modus Vivendi*. Lexington, MA: Lexington Books, 1973.

Blacker, Coit D. "The Kremlin and Détente: Soviet Conceptions, Hopes, and Expectations," in Alexander L. George, ed., *Managing U.S.-Soviet Rivalry*. Boulder, CO: Westview Press, 1983, 119–137.

Bundy, William. *A Tangled Web: The Making of Foreign Policy in the Nixon Presidency*. New York: Hill and Wang, 1998.

Costigliola, Frank. "Kennedy, the European Allies, and the Failure to Consult." In *Political Science Quarterly* 110, no. 1 (Spring 1995): 105–123.

Clemens, Clay. *Reluctant Realists: The Christian Democrats and West German Ostpolitik*. Durham, NC: Duke University Press, 1989.

―――. "Amerikanische Entspannungs- und deutsche *Ostpolitik*: 1969–1975." In *Die USA und die Deutsche Frage: 1945–1990,* ed. Wolfgang-Uwe Friedrich. Frankfurt a. M.: Campus Verlag, 1991.

Czempiel, Ernst-Otto. "Auf der Suche nach neuen Wegen: Die deutsch-amerikanischen Beziehungen 1961–1969." In *Die USA und die Deutsche Frage: 1945–1990,* ed. Wolfgang-Uwe Friedrich. Frankfurt a. M.: Campus Verlag, 1991.

Dallek, Robert. *Nixon and Kissinger: Partners in Power*. New York: Harper Perennial, 2007.

Destler, I. M. *Making Foreign Economic Policy*. Washington, D.C.: Brookings, 1980.

Dobson, Alan P. *US Economic Statecraft for Survival, 1933–1991: Of Sanctions, Embargoes, and Economic Warfare*. New York: Routledge, 2002.

Dyson, Kenneth H. F. *European Détente: Case Studies of the Politics of East-West Relations*. New York: St. Martin's Press, 1986.

Edmonds, Robin. *Soviet Foreign Policy: The Brezhnev Years*. New York: Oxford University Press, 1983.

Edemskiy, Andrey. "Dealing with Bonn: Leonid Brezhnev and the Soviet Response to West German Ostpolitik," in Fink and Schaefer, *Ostpolitik 1969–1974,* 15–38.

Feldman, Gerald D. Book Review on *"Quest for Economic Empire: European Strategies of German Big Business in the Twentieth Century,"* edited by Volker R. Berghahn *in Central European History* 29, no. 4 (1996): 599–601.

Fink, Carole and Bernd Schaefer, eds., *Ostpolitik 1969–1974: European and Global Responses*. Cambridge: German Historical Institute and Cambridge University Press, 2009.

Fletcher, Willard Allen, Stephen F. Szabo, and Stanley R. Sloan. *United States-German Relations, Past and Present*. Washington, D.C.: Library of Congress, European Division, 1984.

Funigiello, Philip J. *American-Soviet Trade in the Cold War*. Chapel Hill: University of North Carolina Press, 1988.

Gaddis, John Lewis. *Strategies of Containment: A Critical Appraisal of Postwar American National Security Policy*. Oxford: Oxford University Press, 1982.

―――. *We Now Know: Rethinking Cold War History*. Oxford: Clarendon, 1997.

―――. *The Cold War: A New History*. New York: Penguin Press, 2005.

Garthoff, Raymond L. *Détente and Confrontation: American-Soviet Relations from Nixon to Reagan*. Washington, D.C.: Brookings Institution, 1985.

Gelman, Harry. *The Brezhnev Politburo and the Decline of Détente.* Ithaca: Cornell University Press, 1984.

Geyer, David C., and Bernd Schaefer, eds. *American Détente and German Ostpolitik, 1969–1972.* Washington, DC: Supplement 1 to the Bulletin of the German Historical Institute, 2004.

Gortemaker, Manfred. *Geschichte der Bundesrepublik Deutschland von der Gründung bis zur Gegenwart.* Munich: Beck, 1999.

Goldgeier, James M. "The United States and the Soviet Union: Lessons of Détente." In *Honey and Vinegar: Incentives, Sanctions, and Foreign Policy,* ed. Richard N. Haass and Meghan L. O'Sullivan. Washington, D.C.: Brookings Institution, 2000.

Goldman, Marshall I. *Petrostate: Putin, Power, and the New Russia.* New York: Oxford University Press, 2008.

Granieri, Ronald. *The Ambivalent Alliance: Konrad Adenauer, The CDU/CSU, and the West, 1949–1966.* Providence, RI: Berghahn Books, 2004.

Gray, William Glenn. *Germany's Cold War: The Global Campaign to Isolate East Germany, 1949–1969.* Raleigh: University of North Carolina Press, 2003.

Griffith, William E. *The Ostpolitik of the Federal Republic of Germany.* Cambridge: MIT Press, 1978.

Hanhimäki, Jussi. *The Flawed Architect.* New York: Oxford University Press, 2004.

Hanson, Philip. *The Rise and Fall of the Soviet Economy: An Economic History of the USSR from 1945.* London: Longman, 2003.

Heller, Mikhail, and Aleksandr Nekrich. *Utopia in Power: The History of the Soviet Union from 1917 to the Present.* New York: Summit Books, 1982.

Herring, George C. *America's Longest War: The United States and Vietnam, 1950–1975.* New York: Alfred A Knopf, 1979.

Hyland, William G. *Mortal Rivals.* New York: Simon & Schuster, 1987.

Jacobsen, Hans-Adolf, and Tomala Mieczyslaw. *Bonn und Warschau 1945–1991: Die deutsch-polnischen Beziehungen — Analyse und Dokumentation.* Cologne: Verlag Wissenschaft & Politik, 1992.

Jacobsen, Hans-Dieter. *Die Ost-West-Wirtschaftsbeziehungen als deutsch-amerikanisches Problem.* Baden-Baden: Nomos Verlag, 1986.

Jentleson, Bruce W. "From Consensus to Conflict: The Domestic Political Economy of East-West Energy Trade Policy." *International Organization* 38, no. 4 (Autumn, 1984): 625–660.

———. *Pipeline Politics: The Complex Political Economy of East-West Energy Trade.* Ithaca, NY: Cornell University Press, 1986.

Kotkin, Stephen. *Armageddon Averted: The Soviet Collapse 1970–2000.* New York: Oxford University Press, 2001.

Kreile, Michael. "West Germany: The Dynamics of Expansion," in *International Organization* 31, no. 4, (Autumn 1977): 775–808.

———. *Osthandel und Ostpolitik.* Baden-Baden: Nomos Verlagsgesellschaft, 1978.

Kunz, Diane B. *Butter and Guns: America's Cold War Economic Diplomacy.* New York: The Free Press, 1997.

Laird, Roy. *The Politburo: Demographic Trends, Gorbachev, and the Future.* Boulder, CO: Westview Press, 1986.

Leonhard, Wolfgang. *Dämmerung im Kreml: Wie eine neue Ostpolitik aussehen müßte.* Stuttgart: Deutsche Verlags Anstalt, 1984.

Marcowitz, Reiner. *Option für Paris? Unionsparteien, SPD und Charles de Gaulle 1958 bis 1969.* Munich: Oldenbourg Verlag, 1996.

Mastanduno, Michael. *Economic Containment: COCOM and the Politics of East-West Trade.* Ithaca, NY: Cornell University Press, 1992.

Matusow, Allen J. *Nixon's Economy: Booms, Busts, Dollars, and Votes.* Lawrence: University Press of Kansas, 1998.

Merseburger, Peter. *Willy Brandt 1913–1992: Visionär und Realist.* Stuttgart and Munich: Deutsche Verlags-Anstalt, 2002.

Nelson, Keith L. *The Making of Détente: Soviet-American Relations in the Shadow of Vietnam.* Baltimore: Johns Hopkins University Press, 1995.

Newnham, Randall. *Deutsche Mark Diplomacy: Positive Economic Sanctions in German-Russian Relations.* University Park: Pennsylvania State University Press, 2002.

Powaski, Ronald E. *The Entangling Alliance: The United States and European Security 1950–1993.* Westport, CT: Greenwood Press, 1994.

Pranger, Robert J. ed. *Détente and Defence: A Reader.* Washington, D.C.: American Enterprise Institute, 1976.

Prowe, Diethelm. "Der Brief Kennedys an Brandt vom 18. August 1961: Eine zentrale Quelle zur Berliner Mauer und der Entstehung der Brandtschen Ostpolitik." *Vierteljahrshefte für Zeitgeschichte* 33, no. 2 (1985): 373–383.

Rudolph, Karsten. *Wirtschaftsdiplomatie im Kalten Krieg: Die Ostpolitik der westdeutschen Großindustrie 1945–1991.* Campus Verlag: Frankfurt, 2004.

Rueckert, Axel. "Ostpolitik und Ostgeschaeft." *Dokumente: Zeitschrift für übernationale Zusammenarbeit* 27 (April 1971): 70–76.

Sarotte, Mary E. *Dealing with the Devil: East Germany, Détente, and Ostpolitik, 1969–1973.* Chapel Hill: University of North Carolina Press, 2001.

———. "A Small Town in (East) Germany: The Erfurt Meeting of 1970 and the Dynamics of Cold War Détente," *Diplomatic History* 25, no. 1 (2001): 85-104.

Schmidt, Wolfgang. *Kalter Krieg, Koexistenz und kleine Schritte: Willy Brandt und die Deutschlandpolitik 1948–1963.* Wiesbaden: Westdeutscher Verlag, 2001.

Schulzinger, Robert D. *American Diplomacy in the Twentieth Century.* New York: Oxford, 1984.

Schwartz, Thomas A. "The United States and Germany after 1945: Alliances, Transnational Relations, and the Legacy of the Cold War." *Diplomatic History* 19, no. 4 (1995): 549–568.

———. *Lyndon Johnson and Europe: In the Shadow of Vietnam.* Cambridge, MA: Harvard University Press, 2003.

Seppain, Helene. *Contrasting US and German Attitudes to Soviet Trade, 1917–91: Politics by Economic Means.* New York: St. Martin's Press, 1992.

Shevchenko, Arkady N. *Breaking With Moscow.* New York: Ballantine Books, 1985.

Sodaro, Michael J. *Moscow, Germany, and the West from Khrushchev to Gorbachev.* Ithaca, NY: Cornell University Press, 1990.

Spaulding, Robert Mark. *Osthandel and Ostpolitik: German Foreign Trade Policies in Eastern Europe from Bismarck to Adenauer.* Providence, RI: Berghahn Books, 1997.

Stent, Angela E. *From Embargo to Ostpolitik: The Political Economy of West German-Soviet Relations, 1955–1980.* London: Cambridge University Press, 1981.
———. *Economic Relations with the Soviet Union: American and West German Perspectives.* Boulder, CO: Westview Press, 1985.
Stulberg, Adam N. *Well-Oiled Diplomacy: Strategic Manipulation and Russia's Energy Statecraft in Eurasia.* New York: State University of New York Press, 2008.
Suri, Jeremi. *Power and Protest: Global Revolution and the Rise of Détente.* Cambridge, MA: Harvard University Press, 2003.
———. *Henry Kissinger and the American Century.* Cambridge, MA: Belknap Press, 2007.
Szabo, Stephen F. *Parting Ways: The Crisis in German-American Relations.* Washington, D.C.: Brookings Institution Press, 2004.
Vogtmeier, Andreas. *Egon Bahr und die Deutsche Frage: Zur Entwicklung der sozialdemokratischen Ost- und Deutschlandpolitik vom Kriegsende bis zur Vereinigung.* Bonn: Dietz, 1996.
Von Amerongen, Otto Wolff. "Wirtschaftsbeziehungen mit der Sowjetunion," In *Osteuropa* 1 (1974): 3–12.
Von Dannenberg, Julia. *The Foundations of Ostpolitik: The Making of the Moscow Treaty between West Germany and the USSR.* Oxford: Oxford University Press: Oxford, 2008.
Westad, Odd Arne, ed. *The Fall of Détente: Soviet-American Relations during the Carter Years.* Nobel Symposium 95. Oslo: Scandinavian University Press, 1997.
Wiegrefe, Klaus. *Das Zerwuerfnis: Helmut Schmidt, Jimmy Carter und die Kriese der deutsch-amerikanischen Beziehungen.* Berlin: Propylaen, 2005.
Zubok, Vladislav M. *A Failed Empire: The Soviet Union in the Cold War from Stalin to Gorbachev.* Chapel Hill: The University of North Carolina Press, 2007.

INDEX